Searching in Shadow
Victorian Prose and Thought

James Haydock

authorHOUSE®

AuthorHouse™
1663 Liberty Drive
Bloomington, IN 47403
www.authorhouse.com
Phone: 1-800-839-8640

Published by AuthorHouse 3/12/2013

ISBN: 978-1-4817-1960-5 (sc)
ISBN: 978-1-4817-1961-2 (e)

Library of Congress Control Number: 2013903575

Any people depicted in stock imagery provided by Thinkstock are models,
and such images are being used for illustrative purposes only.
Certain stock imagery © Thinkstock.

This book is printed on acid-free paper.

The views expressed in this work are solely those of the author and do not necessarily reflect
the views of the publisher, and the publisher hereby disclaims any responsibility for them.

Man has walked by the light of
conflagrations and amid the sound of
falling cities, and now there is darkness
and long watching till it be morning.

-- Thomas Carlyle, 1831

Roam on! The light we
sought is shining still.

-- Matthew Arnold, 1865

They searched in shadows, seeking light.

-- *The Times*, 1904

By James Haydock

Victorian Sages
Stormbirds
Beacon's River
Against the Grain
Portraits in Charcoal: George Gissing's Women
On a Darkling Plain: Victorian Poetry and Thought
Searching in Shadow: Victorian Prose and Thought

CONTENTS

Elements of Victorian Prose...1

Thomas Babington Macaulay 9

Thomas Carlyle 23

John Henry Newman..54

John Stuart Mill...73

John Ruskin 95

Matthew Arnold...136

Three Opponents of Democracy..170

Charles Darwin..180

Thomas Henry Huxley...192

Science and the Higher Criticism 211

Three Voices Heard 220

William Morris 233

Walter Horatio Pater 247

Robert Louis Stevenson 258

Reading Victorian Literature 269

A List of Authors and Titles 287

Elements of Victorian Prose

The extraordinary prose of the Victorian Era, composed by distinguished thinkers and problem solvers, reflects with little distortion the complexity of a very eventful period. It mirrors faithfully social and political change in England from 1832 to 1848, full-fledged Victorianism from 1848 to 1867, and eventual decline from 1867 to 1901. It presents in dynamic detail the main issues and events of the day as it proposes solutions to a glut of problems. In no other time, except perhaps our own, have gifted human beings attempted to juggle so many explosive issues and so many significant events in the midst of contentious and often bitter opposition. In the pages of Carlyle, Ruskin, Arnold and others you will hear the clamor of conflicting ideas and opinions. In their work vigorous minds probe the implications of the new science, the growth of democracy, the proliferation of industrialism, a developing faith in pragmatic progress, and a decline of unswerving faith in the religious arena. Some of these men marched in step with their age (Macaulay, Mill, Huxley), but others (Carlyle, Ruskin, Newman) opposed many of the main tendencies of the day. Walter Pater and his followers attempted to ignore altogether the biting problems of turbulent times and urged retreat into feeling as the best course any sane person could take.

In general Victorian readers were eager to receive and test new ideas and theories from any source. That accounts in part for the many books of expository prose that were published each year. Some of these books not only attained wide influence, but also displayed qualities of

1

originality that validated them as genuine literature. The authors were social critics in a number of fields, and they viewed themselves as self-appointed teachers and leaders. They were learned men in philosophy, religion, science, political and economic theory, history and the arts. They were skilled in the art of writing, often producing prose as graceful and eloquent as any Ciceronian text. Each in his own way tried with all his strength and talent to rescue the nation from a labyrinth of formidable contemporary problems.

Five of them – to name a selective few – had distinctive answers to the questions of the day, clear solutions (or so they thought) to troublesome problems. Carlyle's solution was to reclothe the old puritan religion with a mystical transcendentalism cut from the fabric of German philosophy and literature. Newman argued for a return to the dogmas of the Roman Catholic Church. Ruskin followed at first the beacon of art and later placed his hope in Carlylean social and economic doctrines. Arnold's mission was to spread sweetness and light in the attempt to inculcate culture, or the development of one's best self, in the multiple individuals that make up society. One person improving himself improved all of society. All four earnestly sought to improve the future by changing the present. At the end of the century, however, Pater tended to question the worth of intellectual and moral struggle. In place of a determined and resolute march of mind, he advised retreat into sensibility. In one way or another, often with lectures and always with incessant publication of books and articles, each made his voice heard. The usual procedure was to give a lecture to a select audience, publish it later as an article in a magazine or journal, and then publish it again as part of a book. That helps explain why the books, written mainly for the middle class with its power to shake and move, were often quite long.

Other reasons for the infamous length of Victorian prose works, as well as the novels of the day, would be the slower pace of Victorian life, the lure and power of the printed word among readers, and fewer competing interests to distract them. The writers of prose in any form were as a rule not required by publishers to keep a book to a certain length. They assumed, therefore, that whatever they wrote was important enough for full development, and they never hesitated to use a hundred words when ten could have said the same thing, though perhaps not better. They were to a person concerned with style, the presentation of a unique style, and that required room. The oldest of the group, though not the first in our discussion, was Thomas Carlyle. Because he got off to a slow start, he wrote and published his books simultaneously with authors more than ten years younger. During his long career he applied his thought and talent to many subjects and developed a memorable style. Even though he came to be known as a philosopher, it is difficult to separate his philosophical writings from those on other subjects. His doctrine of work, for example, is not to be found under any one title; it runs through many titles. He fiercely attacked the rationalism and empiricism of his time, and he pioneered German idealism with its emphasis on mind and spirit as controlling force. Though presented in a style sometimes difficult to read, Carlyle's strong opinions widely influenced the work of younger writers.

A master idea among most of these writers was the belief that struggle is a necessary ingredient for growth. An evolutionist pushed the idea into fantasy when his theory postulated the long neck of the giraffe grew longer because the animal struggled over many years to reach higher leaves. Struggle and consequential growth was a concept that found its way into many writings of different kinds. It was treated poetically by Browning in "Rabbi ben Ezra" and other poems and was developed as a truism in many novels. The idea is closely related to the Victorian work ethic that was given new life by Carlyle. You find your life's work and you do it. But each day you struggle to do it better. In that way you grow. Inevitably you will make mistakes as you struggle, but they will help you rather than hinder.

The imperfections of your work will show that you are trying to do better than your best. This in a nutshell is Ruskin's "doctrine of the imperfect," which Browning dramatized in another poem, "Andrea del Sarto." All these writers, working hard to make themselves heard, saw the need for struggle. To a person they paid homage to hard work and proved their allegiance to work by the sheer mass of their writings. In those days just the act of writing was hard work. They wrote by hand with a pencil or scratchy pen on recalcitrant paper and often rewrote. Pater who seems to have grown tired of the Victorian scene while still in his prime may have shunned the importance of struggle, and yet he too labored diligently as an author. After reading Carlyle he came to believed in the value of slow and steady work and gave many hours to exhaustive scholarship and literary labor.

Macaulay and Mill best represent the school of thought that Carlyle opposed. Known as "Utilitarianism," Jeremy Bentham and James Mill had established the doctrine in England some year earlier. As you get to know these writers, you will discover that several of them were sons of important men driven perhaps by family competition to excel in their chosen fields. The son of James Mill, John Stuart Mill, was carefully trained to lead the utilitarian movement and in later years outdid his father in the struggle to make a lasting mark. His *System of Logic* was one of the great books of 1843 and was used as a textbook for the rest of the century. His economic system, also logical, called for a practical procedure directly related to the general welfare. Its basic concepts were founded on a principle of universal happiness for all individuals, "the greatest happiness of the greatest number." Even though this doctrine reached into every branch of academic thought, its implications most significantly affected the realm of ethics. In philosophy the equivalent system, promulgated by Comte in France, was called "Positivism." It held that active, hands-on experience is superior to theory or deductive reasoning. The Positivists tended to oppose conventional religious thought and the intellectual murmurings of academicians.

Most of the Utilitarians and Positivists called themselves freethinkers regarding ethics, moral behavior, and religion. Before mid-century, however, in matters of religion few of them claimed to be atheists or even skeptics. In 1869 Thomas Huxley coined the term *agnostic* to describe more precisely their point of view. The word was quickly adopted to indicate a position of not knowing. Since the agnostic did not have the proof of a personal immortality or the existence of God, either negative or affirmative, it was necessary to confess, personally and painfully, "I do not know." This change in attitude toward Christian teaching was due in part to the influence of the emerging new science, but also to the insistent rationalism of the eighteenth century. The ring of rationalism sounded hollow to the average reader and had little appeal, yet readers could not ignore Mill's lucid, closely written arguments. His work provided the basis for the influential books of Herbert Spencer, who tried to expand upon Mill's thought under the title *Synthetic Philosophy*. Spencer believed the inductive method, touted as the new scientific method, was sufficient for all reasonable investigation. Till the end of his life he remained convinced that inductive reasoning used expertly could solve all problems, even explain the most perplexing mysteries of nature.

The Positivist point of view, presented as a basic principle by Mill, soon became associated with "the religion of humanity" earlier proposed by Auguste Comte in France. This system of thought wedged into a religious framework was meant to be a substitute for those creeds based upon divine revelation. In England the Positivist Society, which conducted services similar to those in a church, was led by a group of able though minor writers, such as Frederic Harrison and John Morley. They made their views known through the *Fortnightly Review*. A more important group attempting to reconcile science and religion was the Metaphysical Society founded in 1869. At its meetings many of the best leaders on either side of the controversy loudly debated their beliefs. At the time James Knowles was editing the *Contemporary Review* and later the *Nineteenth Century*, the discussions of the Society had a large audience. Another persistent opponent of orthodox tradition was Leslie Stephen. He was able to influence readers with a series of well-written books, particularly *An Agnostic's Apology*. George Romanes, a biologist by profession and a close friend of Darwin, published in 1878 an examination of religious belief and flatly asserted that no person who knew anything of science could believe in a beneficent God. Grant Allen, who was writing novels and books influenced by the new science and by many of Spencer's theories, without hesitation agreed.

Philosophical writing in England in the nineteenth century was largely divided between religion on the one hand and science on the other. The writing that dealt with religion was often concerned with problems and conflicts within the established church. The Oxford Movement with its ninety *Tracts for the Times* (1833-1841) attempted to resolve conflicting opinions within the church. A leading contributor was John Henry Newman, who sternly opposed liberal belief as undermining the authority of the church. He went on to write several important books that tended to negate the "higher criticism" of the Bible and the rational interpretation of scripture. In the scientific community many scientists were writing books so vivid and so compelling in their ideas that they were read eagerly by the general public.

Their books strongly influenced the thinking of writers in other fields, and their popularizers extended their fame. Hugh Miller, who published *Testimony of the Rocks* in 1857 (the year of gang riots in New York), was one such popularizer. Robert Chambers with his very influential book of 1844 was another. Both men paved the way for the more serious and more learned works that would come later from exhaustive scientific study. The scientists who wrote treatises that became literature were Charles Lyell, Charles Darwin, Alfred Wallace, Thomas Huxley, Joseph Hooker, and John Tyndall. Later in the century, as research turned from geology to human beings in the natural world, an important figure was Sir James Frazer. An early anthropologist, he devoted twenty-five years to the twelve volumes of a massive work, *The Golden Bough* (1890-1915). Later in the new century the book exerted a pervasive influence upon the thought and poetry of T. S. Eliot.

The leading disciple of Carlyle was surely John Ruskin. Beginning as a scholarly critic of art, Ruskin eventually turned to social criticism after he developed the theory that great art cannot flourish in a corrupt civilization. The drab industrial cities with polluted skies and the factory system that exploited its workers convinced him that his own age was pedestrian. He was a stern opponent of industrialism because its motives and methods seemed fatal to the human spirit. His literary style in the books on art was sonorous and musical. It became clear, direct, and simple as he began to express his social, political, and economic ideas. William Morris, a Pre-Raphaelite and medievalist, took a path very similar to Ruskin's.

At first Morris thought that high-caliber art should be above everyday life, but then he reversed his thinking and reached the conclusion that genuine art, even that of the masters, justified itself by bringing beauty into the average home. As Ruskin in his thinking had moved to socialism, so did Morris who expressed his socialist views in many volumes, including *News from Nowhere* (1891). Standing apart from the theorists, but deeply concerned with the direction his century seemed to be taking, was Matthew Arnold. With lucid prose he tried to probe the reasons behind the disputes. He called for sweetness and light to replace the heat and confusion of the iron times in which he lived. He placed himself as a mediator between those on the side of science and those fighting to preserve the religious way of life. As a phrasemaker he contributed permanently to the language.

Water Pater attended some of Arnold's lectures at Oxford and for a time agreed with some of his ideas. But as Pater's thought matured he began to separate art from life and turned his back on the frenetic activity of the Victorian world. Down through the century a multitude of panaceas came forward to improve the quality of life, and yet many problems persisted. There had been the democratic hope, the faith in machinery, Carlylean idealism, the trust in reason and progress, and Arnold's appeal to the need for individual self-development. The dreams and ideals that aimed for a bright and shining tomorrow had ended in mediocrity and monotony. The value system of pre-Darwinian days slowly disappeared, and only the fittest could survive.

The standards of the jungle were now in force, and the implicit brutality impelled men like Pater to look at art and literature as a refuge from the actual world. To many sensitive late-Victorians his writings had great appeal, for they emphasized the value of sensations, sharp human feelings, and vivid sense impressions in a jaded world. Carlyle had urged his contemporaries to find themselves in work, but Walter Pater's new Epicureanism sought withdrawal from the world. His followers delighted in the beauty of his style and his attempt to make art a religion. Gladly they went with him in quest of the exquisite moment, hoping to seize it before it quickly evaporated. His doctrine of beauty and subtle pleasure, however, lacked the power to move his followers in a truly positive direction. An age of great achievement was bidden to relax and take it easy, and that made for confusion.

Concerning the period itself, the sharper perspective afforded by time reveals one inescapable fact, that of change and adjustment. The Victorians, as we ourselves, lived in a time of unprecedented change.

Within a single lifetime they saw England move from stagecoaches to motorcars and trains. Even dreams of flight were soon to be realized. Change was a fact of life, and they were constantly adjusting to change. These attempts to adjust inevitably led to conflict in all areas of life. Conflict could be found in the economic arena particularly, but also in social, political, religious circles, and among those who viewed themselves as intellectuals. From their intense desire to reconcile conflicting forces came the spirit of compromise for which the Victorian Era is so well known.

Unlike our own time when compromise among opposing groups seems impossible to achieve, the Victorians learned to work together to achieve a worthy goal, and so the era has often been called "the Age of Compromise." The substantial citizens of the middle class felt the need for freedom of action but also a need for control and guidance. They were willing to listen to authoritative voices, weigh and consider, accept or reject, and they often struggled to reach a compromise. Most of them revered tradition but were charmed by innovation. They wanted to believe in the Book of Genesis but were fascinated by the theory of evolution. They looked for a compromise between religion and science, and those not able to find it suffered a spiritual crisis or loss of faith. It was a time characterized by serious and earnest work, by unceasing labor that brought satisfying achievement but ultimate disappointment. The searchers for light, often stumbling in shadow, explained in volume after volume what their search was yielding. To a large extent these writers of prose were at the center of it all.

Thomas Babington Macaulay

Those who didn't like him, and even some who did, called Thomas Babington Macaulay (1800-1859) Thomas Babbletongue. He was in his element when he could gain the center of attention and speak at length on any subject under the sun. Though talkative and expansive in thought, he exemplified the best qualities of the middle-class mind in England prior to mid-century. Near the end of his life he rose to the peerage and became Lord Macaulay. That identity was intensely ironical, for his social position was upper-middle class, and his literary endeavor ignored the aristocracy while celebrating the ideals and aspirations of the middle class. He was a perfect example of that kind of person whom Matthew Arnold would later call "Philistine." He was at all times a Whig, a liberal, and a great believer in the dogma of progress. Convinced that he was living in the best of all countries in the best of all times, he was consistently happy. He was complacent concerning England's prosperity and believed it would go on forever, and he was highly optimistic over what lay ahead for his country. In terms of mental capacity he was brilliant even though his thinking lacked originality and his vision was limited. Unable to distinguish subtle shades of gray, he tended to view the complex issues of a complex time either as black or white or something in between. However, he was gifted with a good mind and memory and with a special talent for making his views understood by others. His style was incisive and his knowledge abundant, but his critics claimed with some justification that he had "no philosophy, little subtlety, and a heavy hand."

Though contemporaries, Macaulay and Carlyle stand in vivid contrast to one another. To know their differences is to know them. Macaulay during most of his life was a public figure – a lawyer and a famous talker, a politician and a cabinet minister. Carlyle was somber, self-taught, moody, taciturn, and seldom in the public eye. Macaulay was rich, optimistic, triumphant, fortunate, and self-satisfied. Carlyle never seemed to have enough money, deplored the condition of England, wrestled with failure and fate, and developed in time a gospel charged with passion but veering away from the religion of the day. Macaulay's literary style, as readers were quick to note, was sonorous, rich, clear, and swift. Carlyle's style, much influenced by German prose, was often convoluted, obscure, and difficult. Macaulay held visionaries in contempt and developed no gospel by which to live; the banal world of commerce and politics was good enough for him. Carlyle was poet and prophet, a social philosopher, and a religionist of deep thought. Macaulay wanted to see people working hard to make money, for enough money would buy them a good life. Carlyle wanted to restore the faith of the people in something larger than themselves. Macaulay lacked a sense of mission but valued work. Carlyle also believed in work and had a deep sense of purpose. Both men were influential in shaping public opinion.

Thomas Macaulay was born in Leicestershire in 1800. His father, Zachary Macaulay, was editor of *The Christian Observer* and a leading evangelical. A precocious child, the boy planned at the age of eight a compendium of universal history. Before he was ten he was writing long poems in the manner of Scott, and displaying a remarkable memory. He entered Cambridge at eighteen, read voraciously on all subjects, and made influential friends. He left college a fervent and liberal Whig and in 1825 published the essay on Milton, which earned him entry into Whig circles. In 1830 he became a Member of Parliament. A year later he established his reputation as a public figure with his speech advocating passage of the First Reform Bill. From then until 1847 he was a full-time politician and bureaucrat of high position. In 1833, the English East India Company appointed him to the council that governed the British colony of India. From 1834 until 1838 he lived in India and served on the council. He earned as much as 10,000 pounds a year during his stay in India and returned to England a wealthy man. During the interval between 1847 and the year of his death he devoted himself to writing and publishing his masterwork, *The History of England from the Accession of James II.* A bachelor all his life, he lived in a quiet place with his sister who shared his literary interests. He died of heart trouble at the end of 1859 and was buried in Westminster Abbey in 1860.

2

"Southey's Colloquies" (1830) — Colloquies are serious discussions about important matters. They have nothing to do with collards (cabbages that don't develop a heart). In the book titled *Colloquies* Southey is presenting his views on "the progress and prospects of society." Macaulay, the foremost exponent of middle-class liberalism, speaks as a loyal Whig opposing the conservative or Tory point of view. Robert Southey (1774-1843) had been a Romantic poet of second rank and was the current poet laureate. As a young man he was something of a visionary, and had planned with Coleridge a utopian community on the banks of the Susquehanna River in Pennsylvania. Southey's politics, imagination, and criticism of the Industrial Revolution irritated Macaulay. Although his aim in this essay is to ridicule the Tories and elevate the Whigs, he scoffs at Southey whenever he can. He is not much concerned with assessing the literary merit of Southey's book. He is not a literary critic, and his purpose is more political than critical. His thoughts and opinions stand in contrast to those of Southey, but also to Carlyle, Ruskin, and Arnold. These same opinions may be placed side by side with the theories of John Stuart Mill to know Macaulay better. Both men were influenced by the rationalists of the eighteenth century.

To understand Macaulay's position, we need to look at what was going on at the time this review was written. In 1830 the Whigs wanted to equalize representation in Parliament by giving more power to the middle class. This would take away many of the traditional prerogatives of the landed aristocracy, and so the Tories were against it. Also the Tories felt that such a move would invite disaster. In their minds the authority of the state was divinely ordered, supernaturally ordained. Any attempt, therefore, to go against that divine authority was in effect going against God himself, and that was unthinkable. On the other hand, the Whigs believed the state was merely a social contract fashioned by human beings, and that contract could be broken at any time. They believed the secular state should be ruled by the people's representatives in Parliament, not by the church or by a supernatural power.

When they used the term "people," they were not referring to the entire population but only to those who were able to vote. They wanted the entire middle class to have the vote but not the working classes who were uneducated, indifferent to politics, and largely illiterate. They believed that in time the working classes could merit the vote but not until sweeping changes were in place. They believed in laissez-faire economics, and that system was largely responsible for holding the working classes in fetters. On most issues Carlyle and Ruskin steadily opposed the Whigs. In another arena, Newman and the Tractarians opposed their so-called Erastian views.

It could be expected that Robert Southey as a Tory would have views that would rub liberal and legalistic Macaulay the wrong way. Southey argues that a country should always be governed by its wisest and best. In this respect, even though he is speaking of the traditional aristocracy, he is quite close to Carlyle and Arnold in his thinking. Macaulay declares in rebuttal that no person whatever can be certain that aristocrats are really the best. Indeed, history has shown they are frequently weak in body, spirit, and mind. With this remark Carlyle, who had little respect for Macaulay but even less for aristocrats, reluctantly agreed. Southey, on the other hand, was unwilling to upset the old order of rule, and he looked upon the state as an organism closely associated with church and religion. Macaulay views the state as merely a collection of human beings in contract with one another to make life easier. Religion to his way of thinking should serve the state rather than attempt to rule it. This is the doctrine of utility advanced by Jeremy Bentham (1748-1832) and the Utilitarians. Macaulay is in sympathy with the Utilitarians, believing that use or usefulness is a touchstone by which to judge the merit of anything. He believes, too, that religion has its place in society because it keeps the people complacently in line.

Macaulay opposes the Tory attitude when speaking of America.

The Tories have always been contemptuous of Americans, he asserts, have traditionally looked down the bridges of their noses at them. But the Whigs feel no such prejudice because they know the Americans are relatives of the English and in their own right just as clever, capable, and industrious. While the Tories shun Americans as upstarts and vulgar boors, the Whigs view their brethren across the sea as equals and want to trade with them. Southey had attacked commerce and the manufacturing system, but Macaulay appreciates the wealth and comfort business has brought into the world. The present, he insists, is incomparably better than the past, even the recent past of fifty years ago. Southey looked upon the new mill villages as ugly and offensive to the eye. John Ruskin also found the ugly, cheap, jerrybuilt houses a shock to the senses. With something of a sneer, Macaulay wishes to know whether Mr. Southey believes the English peasants have ever resided in anything better. Have they at any time lived in idyllic, well-built cottages with lush flower gardens, beehives, and orchards? Macaulay is sternly pragmatic and will not allow Southey to dream or imagine or move his readers. The cottages of the workers may not be pretty, he declares, but they are functional and utility must come before appearance. In attitude two contemporaries of the same nationality could not be further apart.

The gulf that separates the two is wide and deep. Macaulay was a hard-nosed and realistic reformer firmly rooted in the present but keenly aware of the past. Southey was a moon-struck dreamer viewing his country as he thought it ought to be. Macaulay takes umbrage at the suggestion by Southey that the time of Sir Thomas More (the early sixteenth century) was better in some ways than the nineteenth. That offhand remark launches Macaulay into a lengthy comparison of the two centuries to illustrate the superiority of the nineteenth. He delivers in that clear style of his numerous advantages: better food and clothing for the poor, creature comforts not even known in More's day, medical attention superior to anything the king could have gotten from the best doctors, longer life, and greater security both day and night. To support his argument of greater security he cites a statistic: 72,000 persons were executed during the reign of Henry VIII. He doesn't mention the number of people who died of malnutrition in the early decades of the nineteenth century, or the ones struggling on starvation wages even as he wrote. However, he is not blind to the fact that the poor in England are suffering severe hardships. Yet they suffered more in the past, he maintains, and they suffer less in England than in other countries. Only in America are "the lower orders" somewhat better off than commoners in England, but that is because the population there is less dense.

England in 1830, he declares with fullest confidence, is the richest country in Europe, the most commercial country, and the country with the most productive manufacturing system. Working conditions are not always as good as they ought to be, and yet the English worker has it better than workers in any European country. Russia and Poland are the poorest countries, but in time they will inevitably grow richer because "this natural progress of society" will not be denied. On every hand the wealth of nations is increasing, the lives of citizens becoming better, and the arts of life that make living more pleasant coming closer to perfection. The present moment is one of great distress, he allows – 1830 was a year of political and economic unrest – but England undeniably is becoming richer and richer.

At this juncture Macaulay attempts to look into the future and compare 1830 to 1930. He will prophesy nothing, lest his readers think him insane, but will visualize the future. That disclaimer, a subtle mockery of Southey who dared to dream, allows him to list examples of the progress England will see in a hundred years. In 1930 the country will have a much larger population "better fed, clad, and lodged than the English of our time." Cultivation as lush as flower gardens will climb even the mountains, and farms will flourish in connection with trade. Efficient machines "constructed on principles yet undiscovered" will be in every house to make life easier. Railroads will be the highways of the future, and people will be able to travel from place to place at incredible speed. The steam engine will revolutionize transportation, and the use of horses for that purpose will in time disappear. Macaulay's predictions do not always hit the mark, but he scores a bull's eye when he sees new machines obeying new principles. The next century was to see greater material progress than he could possibly imagine.

The value of this essay as it relates to Macaulay and his times lies in the fact that he has expressed in no uncertain terms the creed of middle-class liberalism. That creed he places side by side with that of the conservatives to show their moodiness, uncertainty, and cynicism. The liberal creed by contrast is an expression of optimism in the present and hope for the future. It characterizes the middle-class mindset during the early and mid-Victorian decades. The essay provides a fundamental statement of "Whiggism," the attitudes and beliefs that motivated the Whigs. Their thought has been defined as illogical but practical compromise between two extremes that are logical but not at all practical. The Whigs set out to get things done and were impatient of dawdling dreamers. That is why Macaulay is sometimes ungenerous, even abusive, in his comments about some of the personal failings of Southey. He believed that Southey's serious meditations, like those of many other Tories, lacked substance. His own liberal position he thought superior. His over-bearing confidence, his consistent optimism, placed him in hot water with Arnold and later critics. He is a near-perfect example of the philistine chastised by Arnold. Macaulay's philistinism is alive and well today and exerting its force not just in Britain and America but on a global scale.

"Francis Bacon" (1837) — Basil Montagu's sixteen-volume edition of all the writings by Bacon, published in London over a period of several years, provided Macaulay with the chance to examine a well-known person living in a time he admired. Analyzing his subject, he reveals once again a great deal about himself: his practical and utilitarian bent, his enthusiastic support of material progress, his belief that Bacon as a philosopher was superior to Plato though lacking as a man. Many students of philosophy and history vehemently disagree with his estimate of Bacon. They also protest his attack on Plato and idealism. The essay injured Macaulay's reputation as a serious thinker, but one should note that he believed what he said and was sincere in his beliefs. One reader observed that he had a keen eye for business and politics but seemed almost blind in the presence of abstract truth. The value of the essay rests upon the second half, where Macaulay expresses the Whig ambition for the attainable and the workable and his own passion for the practical. To his mind heaven was not attainable in this life and neither was utopia. However, an effective implementation of Baconian philosophy could bring about in just a few years a condition of comfort and relative happiness for thousands of British citizens.

The ancient philosophers, he vigorously maintains, disdained to be useful. Their philosophy was therefore a treadmill (a metaphor often quoted), not a path. And so the human mind accordingly marked time instead of marching. On the other hand, the whole purpose of Bacon's philosophy was to produce fruit, tangible goods to improve everyday life. Used properly, it could mitigate human suffering, bring about an improvement in the conditions of life, and make people of all classes more comfortable. Utility and progress were at the heart of Bacon's philosophy. Progress resulted in better roads, better transportation, better food, better medical care, and better living conditions. Macaulay has no faith in those philosophies that promote only culture and the inward development of the individual. He places his faith in the dogma of progress and the concept of utility. He interprets Bacon as the far-seeing philosopher whose work established a path leading to the fruits of the present time (1837).

The essay presents a vivid and detailed comparison – Macaulay loved to compare – of Bacon and Plato. All that is positive and constructive he sees as Baconian; everything opposite is Platonic. In a famous passage he sums up his remarks: "The aim of the Platonic philosophy was to exalt man into a god. The aim of the Baconian philosophy was to provide man with what he requires while he continues to be man . . . . The former aim was noble, but the latter was attainable." This spurs him to make the statement seen by most readers as the main point of the essay: "An acre in Middlesex [a county containing part of London] is better than a principality in Utopia." Near the end Macaulay praises the progress that has taken place in the interval between his own time and Bacon's. And what are the lasting results of Bacon's philosophy? It has lengthened life, mitigated pain, extinguished diseases, increased the fertility of the soil, given greater security to the mariner, furnished new arms to the warrior, spanned rivers with great bridges, lit up the night with the splendor of day, extended the range of human vision (not through imagination but through better eye-glasses), and it has made for wondrous machines that presently serve all mankind. Its law first and foremost is progress. The value of Macaulay's essay is the expression of a point of view that won prevalence and dominance later in the century and was passed on to us through the twentieth century to the present.

"Lord Clive" (1840) — This essay was published in the January number of the *Edinburgh Review*. In form it is a review of Sir John Malcolm's *Life of Robert Clive* (three volumes, 1836). Macaulay could thoroughly admire a man like Clive, a military man of high achievement known for his courage, self-control, and firmness of purpose. The book by Malcolm, he tells us, could have been more skillfully arranged and could have been improved by giving it a tighter structure. It presents, however, a better picture of Clive than James Mill's *History of India* (1818). Unrestrained admiration prompts exaggeration when Macaulay identifies Clive as "the founder of the British empire in India," and yet Clive's exploits in India were highly valued. Born in 1725, Robert Clive went to India as a minor clerk at the age of eighteen, arriving in the distant country more than a year later. Twice in the sweltering heat he attempted suicide by placing a gun to his head. When the pistol failed to fire the second time, his despair evaporated and "he burst forth into an exclamation that surely he was reserved for something great." At twenty-one he became a soldier in the service of the East India Company and immediately began to show qualities of leadership. By the time he was twenty-five he had risen to the rank of Captain, and in 1751 commanded a successful raid on a military garrison at Arcot. Then for fifty days he and his men defended the city against a vastly superior force of French and native soldiers. In the final struggle more than four hundred of the enemy fell, but Clive reportedly lost only five or six men.

After this notable feat he rose rapidly in rank and fame, got married, and returned to England at twenty-seven to be honored as a hero. His family found it hard to believe that in scarcely ten years "their naughty and idle Bobby had become a great man." In 1755 he again sailed for Asia, and in 1757 he avenged the tragedy of the Black Hole of Calcutta by defeating Surajah Dowlah in the great victory of Plassey. Extensive areas of India were now under the control of the English and were possessions of the British Empire. Clive became the governor of Bengal in 1758, and in 1759 suppressed a Dutch attempt to colonize part of India. He returned to England in 1760 with a fortune of 300,000 pounds (fifty-seven million in today's dollars) and became a member of the Irish peerage in 1762. He was a Member of Parliament from 1760 to 1764, and in 1765 returned to India as governor and commander in chief of Bengal. He put an end to the disorder and corruption that had developed while he was away, restored discipline to the armed forces, and reformed the civil service. His greatest achievement during this third period in India was to extend British influence into other regions and to establish the Empire of British India. He resigned his office reluctantly in 1767 because of poor health, returned to England, and was charged with malfeasance. Although Parliament cleared him of all charges in 1773, he felt disgraced by the charges. Though still a very wealthy man who could have lived in luxury anywhere he chose, he died by his own hand in 1774.

Even though Macaulay felt sympathy for the renowned soldier, in this essay he censures him for taking bribes from native potentates. Such actions, he contends, display a moral weakness and embarrass the British people. Macaulay is doing more than merely telling the story of Clive. He is laying down policies for the ethical conduct of British colonialists all over the world. In a wretched place where millions suffered the worst kind of poverty, greedy Englishmen from the other side of the world were reaping in the preceding century obscenely huge fortunes. He condemns the rapacity of the military and the oppression visited upon India by the English. In his own day, he asserts, the administration of India is much better than it was in Clive's time, and conditions are better than in the past. As late as 1840 India was not yet officially a part of the British Empire, but to all practical purposes it was a possession of England. The essay made English citizens swell with pride. They were proud to have shouldered "the white man's burden," for they had done it with unfailing competence.

In the essay Macaulay skillfully justifies his nation's imperialism and offers excuses for the bloody conquest of India. The Indian had to be saved from himself, for he was unable to maintain order in his own land. Civilization had to be carried to this backward country, and England was the one to do it. India had long been in a state of chaos, had been worse governed than any of the nations of Europe. Indian rulers were feeble of mind, lived in indolence and debauchery, and were not fit to govern. English officials could bring honesty into government and could improve economic conditions. "There never existed a people so thoroughly fitted by nature and habit for a foreign yoke." All these excuses are Macaulay's moral and ethical justification for the conquest of India. They are blended with expressions of pride in the British race: "With the loss of twenty-two soldiers killed and fifty wounded, Clive had scattered an army of near sixty thousand men, and subdued an empire larger and more populous than Great Britain." He viewed the conquest of India as greater than the exploits of the Spanish conquistadores: "The people of India, when we subdued them, were ten times as numerous as the Americans whom the Spaniards vanquished, and were at the same time as highly civilized as the victorious Spaniards." No Englishman was more proud of his race than this Englishman.

History of England (1849/1855) — When Macaulay came back from India in 1838, he expected to give up political life, retire to a quiet place in the country, and devote his days to writing his masterpiece. But again he was caught up in political affairs and was not able to spend his full time on this work until 1847. The history was to run from 1688 to 1832. He thought he could do it in five volumes. He later discovered that to carry out his original intention, he would have to write fifty volumes in 150 years. As the dates show, his purpose was to vindicate and glorify the position of the Whigs. He wanted to put on parade the progress that England had made under the rule of Parliament dominated by Whigs. He wrote the first lines of the *History* on March 9, 1839. In June of that year he was elected to Parliament to represent Edinburgh and was subsequently caught up in political affairs. Three months later he became Secretary of War in Melbourne's cabinet. In 1842, although his health seemed to be in decline, he published while continuing work on the massive *History* a collection of poems he called *Lays of Ancient Rome*. Coming from a pragmatic writer of prose, they were not poems of high caliber, and yet for a time they were very popular.

Near the end of 1848 Macaulay published the first two volumes of the *History* and dated them 1849. Because of the method he had adopted, he wrote slowly and produced only two pages a day. He read all he could find on his subject, visited scenes of importance, and accumulated an impressive number of facts that he stored in his prodigious memory. He wrote with great care and read his day's work aloud to his sister every evening. He strove for clarity of style, simplicity, and directness. His audience was the middle class, and yet he wanted to be easily understood by any concerned person who could read. The first two volumes were enormously popular. He got what he wanted, a wide and profitable distribution in both England and America. In 1855 volumes three and four were published, and they too enjoyed great popularity. At the time of his death he was working to complete the fifth. The five volumes covered fifteen years from 1685 to 1700. Even for Macaulay, energetic and expansive, the plan was far too ambitious for completion and was in time truncated by his own mortality.

Those familiar with the man's work often wonder what Macaulay hoped to achieve by writing this history? To say he simply wanted to inform his readers, as I am doing here, is not to see the whole picture. Prompted by confidence in his own ability and by an overriding ambition, he was seeking more than that. He wanted to show that England became a great nation not through kingship, as many supposed, but through the rule of Parliament. So in a sense he was abating the value of the royal family while praising the work of politicians. He put on display the tremendous progress England had made from the time Parliament took over in 1688 to the time of the First Reform Bill in 1832. And he insisted the progress was the result of capable men working together to achieve a common good.

Entertaining a concept unusual for his time, he said history should be made as interesting as fiction but should rest entirely on fact and never veer for any reason from the truth. The historian should establish in every chapter a vivid background and then trace the lives of real people in front of it. The writer of history should work in much the same way as the writer of novels, but with two main differences. In the historical work the background would not be imaginary, and the people in the foreground would not be fictional. He was moved by what he perceived as truth and was perhaps not conscious of any bias as he wrote. Yet he sees the past solely from a liberal point of view, believing all blessings flowed from the Glorious Revolution.

Chapter III of the History is the one most often read today. It requires some specific attention and some detailed discussion. At the beginning Macaulay writes, "I intend in this chapter to give a description of the state in which England was at the time when the crown passed from Charles the Second to his brother." To explain, Charles II had died in 1685 at which time the crown went to James II, who ruled for only three years until deposed by the Bloodless or Glorious Revolution. The focus throughout most of the chapter is upon the year 1685. He sets out to paint a vivid picture of the era as represented by that one year, but his main concern is to show its differences when compared to the present. Mid-Victorian England, he insists, is infinitely better off than England in the seventeenth century. The many creature comforts enjoyed by the nineteenth century, he reminds his readers, are directly traceable to the Whigs. Without their progressive leadership such improvements would not have been possible.

Lovingly he runs through the catalogue of good works attributed to the Whigs. Thousands of square miles, once moorlands and fens, are now rich with undulating wheat and dotted with villages. Instead of a few huts covered with thatch, the countryside teems with manufacturing towns and seaports and the wealth of these places. With material prosperity has come improvement in manners and taste. The typical English gentleman of 1685 was gross, uneducated, untraveled, and given to a stifling view of life. His wife and daughter in taste and accomplishment were inferior to upstairs servants in the affluent houses of the nineteenth century. In 1685 London had only half a million people; in 1851 the city could boast 2,300,000. London was filthy and primitive, dark and unsafe. Nineteenth-century London by contrast is clean and orderly and ablaze with light. Anyone who reads knows the seventeenth century was morally corrupt. Brothels flourished in all the cities, and girls in scanty costume repeated suggestive lines on the stage. By contrast, the nineteenth enjoys vast improvement in morality (no mention of the vice dens in London). In the seventeenth century scientific investigation was in its infancy, but the nineteenth has opened many secrets of nature to improve human life. In every way that matters the average citizen of the nineteenth century, particularly in England, is better off than his counterpart at any other time in history. Deliberately he doesn't mention the exploitation of workers in the cities in his time and the thousands of prostitutes.

In all his writings Macaulay displayed a staunch belief in laissez-faire economics, rugged individualism, self-interest as a motivating factor, and the doctrine of utility. He championed whenever he could the liberalism and secularism of the middle class and its optimistic apprehension of the future. This spirit of secularism and optimism went hand in hand with the spirit of compromise. For the first time in history thinking persons were attempting to view society and the affairs of life independently of the church and its influence. This frame of mind would have seemed puzzling, even impious, to the people of Shakespeare's day, but after the Age of Reason and the advent of the Industrial Revolution the secular spirit, gaining momentum, was not to be resisted. Macaulay truly believed he had caught a glimpse of Bacon's brave new world. Sustained and organized scientific thought would give to mankind the power to learn the secrets of nature and use them to advantage. Secularism, rationalism, and liberalism, grounded in the new science and the new criticism of the Bible, promised to make the here-and-now world a heaven on earth. Happy and rational people could improve themselves in a gentle, caring, affluent society without interference from the church or government or any dominant authority. Macaulay's views were attacked by orthodox believers such as Newman and by idealists such as Carlyle. If not for the voices of opposition, the liberal position would have triumphed quite early to become the dominant point of view in the minds of citizens

3
Thomas Carlyle

Thomas Carlyle (1795-1881) gained admiration from some of his contemporaries as "the Rembrandt of English prose." As we know, Thomas Macaulay was a Whig, but Thomas Carlyle was an unyielding Tory. That is a main distinction between the two and one to remember. It is a distinction that places them worlds apart. If you remember this one fact, many of the differences between the two men will easily explain themselves. At the same time it's important to remember a few significant similarities. Both authors, for example, published essays in the *Edinburgh Review*, the official voice of the Whig party. Carlyle would have been expected to publish his work in the *Quarterly Review*, the organ of the Tory party. Perhaps to see if it could be done, however, Carlyle published two important essays in the publication of the opposing party. They were "Signs of the Times" in 1829 and "Characteristics" in 1831. These two articles appeared after the essays on German literature and thought in the same review. He was sending Tory articles to a Whig magazine, believe it or not, and getting them published. Eventually Whig readers loudly protested, and Carlyle turned elsewhere to publish his prolific work. He was a dour man not without humor but also not given to frequent laughter. When the Whig readers blasted him for his boldness and prolonged the attack, calling his efforts egregious effrontery, Carlyle smiled at their discomfiture and perhaps laughed a little as well.

We know Macaulay was the apostle of liberalism until the middle of the century. He presented in a clear and readable style the rationalistic, materialistic, and pragmatic view of the world that was typical of the Victorian middle class. Carlyle, on the other hand, was a romantic, an idealist, a transcendentalist with a world view just the opposite of Macaulay's. To look carefully at his background may help us understand some of his basic beliefs. He was born in 1795 (same year as Keats) at Ecclefechan, Scotland. He was the second of ten children born to James Carlyle and his second wife Janet. Only crude contraception was available in those days. Moreover, Scotch Calvinists, believing in the biblical injunction to be fruitful and multiply, used no contraception. Carlyle's father was a puritanical stonemason and farmer gifted with glowing speech but often irascible in temper and unpredictable in behavior. The mother, we are told, was a woman of gentle and quiet nature. The boy himself was raised in an atmosphere of frugality, discipline, labor, and religion. From an early age he was taught the principles of Scotch Calvinism and never quite lost those early teachings. In grammar school he read all the books he could lay his hands on and soon began to learn Latin, French, and Greek. With family encouragement, he decided to become a clergyman. At the age of fourteen, to realize that goal, Carlyle walked more than a hundred miles to Edinburgh University and was able to enroll there. Though he didn't become an orthodox clergyman, he became in later years a powerful preacher seeking to revitalize the old religion.

At the university he quickly became a leading student in mathematics under Professor John Leslie, perhaps a model for Teufelsdröckh in *Sartor Resartus*. As a college student he continued to read enormously and became an intellectual leader among his peers. The powerful influence of Hume and Locke and the French skeptics shook his religious convictions and made him question the orthodox Christianity of his parents. He left the university in 1814 without a degree to become a teacher of mathematics. He had already begun to doubt his fitness for the ministry, but he shuddered at the thought of spending his life as a schoolmaster. Losing himself in his reading, he began to dream of authorship, intellectual greatness, and fame. Two years later he met a young woman named Margaret Gordon and fell in love with her. So far as we know she returned his love, but her stuffy guardians frowned upon her suitor's peasant background and interfered. Margaret later became a model for Blumine in *Sartor Resartus*. At about this time (1818) he abandoned his divinity studies and the career of schoolmaster and sank into extreme unhappiness, becoming lethargic, depressed, and indifferent of both present and future. Also he began to suffer from dyspepsia, a stomach disorder that might have been partly psychosomatic and partly hereditary. That condition – now we call it acid reflux – plagued him for sixty years.

During the time he was searching for a suitable life work, he began and soon abandoned the study of law, learned German, and turned to translation. Jane Welsh, a young woman strong in mind and character whom he met in 1821 and married in 1826, encouraged him. By now the ideas he had found in the writings of Goethe, Schiller, Fichte, and the other German philosophers and thinkers enabled him to interpret in a new way his native Calvinism. He had found his mission to popularize German literature and philosophy in England. He had to find a better way to carry out the mission, however, than merely translating the words and thoughts of others. At Craigenputtock, the lonely farmhouse isolated on the moorlands, he lived in tumultuous marriage with Jane but also completed *Sartor Resartus* there in 1831. In vain he tried to sell the book to publishers in London. Eventually *Fraser's Magazine* accepted it for serial publication during 1833 and 1834. Emerson helped bring the book out in America in 1836, and in 1838 the London edition appeared. That brought an end to the years of literary apprenticeship. Carlyle was now living in London with Jane and deeply immersed in the labor of presenting German thought, and his own thought, to the English-speaking world. Near the end of his life he was offered a British title but turned it down. He refused also a pension and a pompous burial in Westminster Abbey. He died at the age of eighty-five in February of 1881.

This overview of Carlyle's background, though not as detailed as it could be, may help us understand his basic beliefs. As we have seen, he was brought up in the strict burgher sect of the Scottish Church. The group preached the Bible as the literal word of God, as the only true explanation of the universe and all it contained. It was a faith based on Calvinism; today we would call it fundamentalism. A basic tenet of that faith was the belief in the trinity, or God the Father, God the Son, and God the Holy Ghost. Three other important tenets of Calvinism were the doctrines of depravity, election, and predestination. The first held that man is God's creature and must perform God's will. But in all his fleshly appetites he is the child of the devil because he inherited depravity from Adam and Eve. The second tenet held that God in his mercy extends his grace to "the Elect," who have within them a God-given inner light or guiding principle. Even though the children of God are tainted and live in the fallen state, God nonetheless selects a few for salvation who become "the Elect." These chosen people and also those not elected live their lives as predestined by God, the purpose of life being to carry out God's plan on earth until the Kingdom of Heaven arrives. The world is therefore governed and guided by the will of a stern but loving God.

When Carlyle went away to college, Calvinism was the force behind his daily life. Then his reading of the rationalistic thinkers of the preceding century began to undermine his religion. He read Gibbon, Hume, Locke, and Voltaire. He absorbed the thoughts of the deists who held that God rules the world by means of natural law, but does not himself live in the world. These deists held the belief that God was comparable to a great watchmaker. He made a finely ordered watch, tuned it carefully, set it running, and put it aside to make other watches. This famous extended metaphor comes from the work by William Paley, *Evidences of Christianity* (1794). The book is a seminal statement of deistic beliefs. The deists did not believe in the divinity of Christ or the inspiration of the Bible. They looked to nature for their inspiration. Their beliefs comprised a "natural theology" based on reason and methodical proof of God's existence in nature. This view stood in opposition to the older and more orthodox concept of "revealed religion" which had been set forth in the Bible and taken primarily on faith.

Deism was a rationalistic point of view, reliance upon reason rather than revelation. It was in part the logical result of the new knowledge that had come from the theories and discoveries of Columbus, Copernicus, Galileo, and Francis Bacon. In many respects it stood in opposition to Calvinism and was more optimistic than Calvinism. It had a strong appeal to questing intellectuals in Europe and also in this country. Near the end of the eighteenth century deism influenced such men as Thomas Jefferson, Benjamin Franklin, and Thomas Paine. It began to lose ground when the leaders of the Romantic Movement objected to an absentee God and tried to bring a living God once more into the world. The transcendentalism of Carlyle was intended to combat deism, and Wordsworth's pantheism had a similar goal.

At this time Carlyle also read Jeremy Bentham, who wanted to get rid of God altogether. His reading among the rationalists led him to doubt the tenets of Scotch Presbyterianism, and encroaching doubt slowly eroded faith. When that happened he gave up his aim to become a minister in the Scottish Church. As a teacher of mathematics, he worked hard to master Newton's *Principia* (1687) and placed high value upon it. If Bacon's *The Advancement of Learning* (1605) advanced reasonable knowledge, Newton's important book advanced the cause of mechanical science. Carlyle believed these rationalistic books helped to improve the human condition, but later had second thoughts. On closer analysis they seemed to make the world merely a mechanism with no purpose at all. One phase of Newton's thinking, however, seemed quite positive and had a lasting influence. He postulated that time and space appear to exist on three different planes. In the first instance, the geometric or three-dimensional world can be known through the senses. In the second, the abstract world, apprehended by intellect or reason, lies in the realm of physics. Beyond these two is transcendental space and time on a much higher plane, transcending altogether the world we know through our senses and intellect. This concept, ironically coming from an eminent scientist whose view of the world was severely mechanistic, contributed importantly to Carlyle's conversion from rationalistic skeptic to transcendentalist. His reading of German mysticism was another significant influence. At length, as he wrestled with doubt, Carlyle came to the conclusion that not even the wisest among us can prove that God does or does not exist.

For him the truth had to rest on deeper foundations than those presented in Paley's *Evidences of Christianity*. He needed a theory of the world that would include all the sciences and at the same time justify Calvinistic morality as the one true path. At this time he began to read the German philosophers, devouring the writings of Kant, Hegel, Fichte, Schiller, Schlegel, and Goethe. After forming a synthesis of their thought, he found a basis for reinterpreting his Calvinistic faith in new and vital terms. He would no longer seek as a reasonable and methodical researcher evidence or proof of God's existence. He would trust his own soul, the Geist within, to help him find a transcendent reality essentially spiritual and purposive. In the Germans he found justification for some of his earlier beliefs. By 1826 he had worked out a doctrine that guided his thinking with some modifications for the rest of his life. On his journey to search for the light, with some difficulty he conquered his skepticism and doubt. He went on reading the Germans in order to fashion his new faith into a philosophical system. At the core is the transcendentalist view that ultimate reality is spiritual.

Readers of Carlyle often want to know the sources that stimulated his thought. From Goethe he took the concept that all nature is the living garment of God. Fichte's concept that spirit is idea or thought is the source of Carlyle's Divine Idea. This Divine Idea is eternal mind that is forever thinking and while thinking creates the world of phenomena. Through this Divine Idea the world is constantly realizing itself in infinite forms eternally. The world is the web that God weaves in the loom of time and space. From the web we may surmise the nature of the weaver. The natural world is therefore not static and mechanical, but a living organism and the vital expression of eternal spiritual force. In this scheme man is the living, palpable instrument of spirit because the breath of God is within him. Ultimate reality, however, is knowable only through intuition, or the spirit dwelling within the human mind. This indwelling spirit, inner light to the Calvinists, is a fragment of the Divine Idea that permeates all nature. The outer world of matter is a garment or a word or a symbol uttered by the Divine Idea.

The obligation of human beings, tutored imperceptibly by the Divine Mind, is to decipher the message as thoroughly as they can. Yet because our minds are finite, the mystery of the Infinite can never be fully understood. We are like soldiers fighting in a foreign land, performing individual acts of heroism, but without knowledge of the entire campaign. We are not capable of seeing the vast design of the Divine Mind, but like soldiers we know what has to be done for the moment. If the Divine Mind speaks to all of us, how does Carlyle justify the existence of evil? He asserts that evil in the broadest sense is chaos which man must conquer and control. The situation comedy *Get Smart*, long past its prime but enjoying re-runs on cablevision, has the good agents of Control battling the bad agents of Chaos. The central idea behind all the nonsense is Carlylean, even the limited intelligence of Smart himself, who works hard at what he does but often in a state of unknowing. To use Carlyle's own words, "Evil is the dark, disordered material out of which man's Freewill has to create an edifice of order and Good." This perpetual struggle to stem pervasive disorder is the progressive unfolding of the Divine Idea in the world. The struggle involves suffering, but to suffer is to grow. All comedies that come out divine, he says of Dante in reference to *La Commedia Divina*, are wrought after long suffering.

Another important component in Carlyle's philosophical system is the doctrine of work. He believed that while matter and the physical world may be an illusion of the senses, it is also an expression of Universal Will at work. Since the working of the Divine Mind creates the world of matter, the act of working among human beings becomes essentially religious. Through long, hard, sustained and positive work, men and women may save themselves. Moreover, by working the individual comes into the presence of the Creator himself. In this context the aim of human life is not happiness, but the state of being blessed by divine favor, and that comes of labor constant and unremitting. Work is the force that brings order to the chaotic external world and to the internal mind. Happiness, therefore, is merely a byproduct of work well done in the world. Here is Carlyle's remark that best sums up his doctrine of work: "If at the end of your life you can turn upon yourself and ask, 'Have I done good and useful work in the world, and have I done it well?' And if you can answer saying 'Yea,' there will be no need to ask yourself whether you were happy."

3

Now you may ask how did he view the state? Like Southey who was castigated by Macaulay, Carlyle saw the state as a living organism that drew its life from vital principles. Unlike Southey, he went further to embrace organized society as the embodiment or expression of the Divine Idea. For him the state was much more than a mere aggregate of individuals living in accordance with a dull contract. His view of the state includes his theory of the hero, for he believed that only heroes are capable of guiding the destiny of a nation. He insisted that the hero is the dominant force in the making of history, which he termed "the biography of great men." He could have included women, but Carlyle was dyspeptic Carlyle and lived in a different time. At some risk I shall interpret his thought while attempting to be more expansive and more inclusive. The great man or the great woman, therefore, is the one able to probe reality with keener attention and greater vision than other men or women, and by consequence has a duty to lead. All persons hear the voice of God, but some hear the voice much plainer than others. These are the ones we respect as heroes. They are closer to divinity and are therefore natural leaders. Their main trait is sincerity and they have a talent for silence, for listening to the promptings of the Divine Mind to receive inspiration. Heroes are in fact agents of the Divine Mind, and the citizens of any state should follow them with loyalty and obedience.

Carlyle's position in his most famous work, the book you will see examined shortly, is mainly Hebraic and Calvinistic. His transcendentalism to a large extent is the old Calvinism of his youth dressed in new clothes. The doctrine of predestination, for example, is now presented as the progressive unfolding of the Divine Idea in history. The doctrine of the elect is now the hero who works close to God to bring order out of chaos. Even the Calvinist doctrine of depravity is not entirely abandoned by Carlyle. Because he sees much corruption in the world around him, he reasons that man's inner self must also be corrupt. People must therefore strive to banish this corruption from themselves and from the world around them. Transcendent reality, that other world beyond the senses, has become the equivalent of the Calvinistic heaven. The stern God of the Calvinists while demanding dutiful obedience had always seemed inscrutable and remote, strong and unpredictable, sometimes in the world and active but sometimes out of it and passive. Carlyle's Divine Idea brings God back into the world, for his spirit runs in and through all things. His divinity mysteriously works in all forms of nature, as well as in mankind, to carry out the divine plan.

"Characteristics" (1831) — This essay is one of Carlyle's most significant and should be read carefully. It may not be, as his biographer maintained, "more profound and far-reaching than *Sartor*," but no study of Carlyle is complete without it. You will find that it contains in little the essence of most of his major ideas. By the time it appeared in the *Edinburgh Review,* he had completed his study of the German philosophers. Also he had finished *Sartor Resartus* but had not found a publisher. The essay was ostensibly a review of Thomas Hope's *Essay on the Origin and Prospects of Man* (1831) and Friedrich Schlegel's *Philosophische Vorlesungen* (Philosophical Lectures) of 1830. The speculative work by Hope he dismissed as drivel, but the essay is not about either of these books. Its subject is mainly the social and political confusion England was enduring in 1831, as moodily viewed by one who thought he might be able to offer a remedy. In some respects "Characteristics" presents in more compressed form the ideas of *Sartor Resartus* and "Signs of the Times," published in the *Edinburgh Review* in 1829. It reflects many of those ideas that were beginning to snap into place in Carlyle's mind to form a philosophical system. It is a scornful attack on rationalism, utilitarianism, and materialism – everything Macaulay had praised – in favor of transcendentalism.

He begins with an analogy between the health of the human body and the health of society. A healthy society has balance, organic unity, and performs its work without self-consciousness. But England in the 1830's is intensely self-conscious, and that is a sign of weakness and sickness. If mankind is to come into harmony with the Divine Idea, this pervasive egoism must be eradicated. Our lives are not given to us merely for living, for selfish satisfaction of the appetites, but for a nobler purpose. Man is the instrument of the Divine Will and must live for the realization of the Divine Spirit within him. The hero is the spokesman for the Divine Idea, for he is able to transmit its lessons without distortion. Admonitions of the Divine Will teach us what we ought to do with our lives. We have the freedom to obey these admonitions or ignore them, but when we disobey we are brought to certain misery. It is our duty to listen intently to the great leaders in loyalty and obedience, for they know best. All institutions die when they cease to perform for the good of the Divine Idea; even the state sickens when it ceases to be loyal to the Divine Idea. There is only one remedy that works: *find the hero of either gender and follow the chosen one.* The wisest persons often emerge when the times need them most, and they must not be rejected.

Early in the essay Carlyle touches on his cyclic theory of history. Societies grow and develop only to a certain point and then enter a period of decline. From the collapse of the old order a new order rises and begins to move upward through struggle and growth. Periods of growth are characterized by a strong and stable faith. Periods of decline are marked by confusion and unfaith. In the nineteenth century religion has become mere lip service, is not concerned with the creative shaping of life, and the era clearly needs revitalization. To build a new order from the ashes of the old requires unremitting labor, but there is endless salvation in work. The blessed and the specially chosen are the ones who work the hardest to discover the Divine Idea and cooperate with it. Can mankind, according to Carlyle's theory, attain a permanent utopia in the future? The answer is no; that will never happen. But all people can strive to reach perfection and in the struggle may be able to purify themselves. Any society of any worth whatever is always becoming, never being. It is always in flux and change and struggling upward from the old to the new. The best society in Carlyle's view must be based on spiritual principles, not economic or political concepts.

The old order in the western world ceased to exist after the French Revolution and is now dead. The new one is struggling to be born. Carlyle puts it this way: "The doom of the Old has long been pronounced, and irrevocable; the Old has passed away: but, alas, the New appears not in its stead; the Time is still in pangs of travail with the New. Man has walked by the light of conflagrations, and amid the sound of falling cities; and now there is darkness, and long watching till it be morning." Human thought that separates men and women from the animals must necessarily be doubt and inquiry before it can become at a later time affirmation and sacred precept. In the darkness and confusion lurks evil, and people must summon the courage to stand against it and put it down. Again Carlyle is speaking: "Evil, in the widest sense we can give it, is precisely the dark, disordered material out of which man's Freewill has to create an edifice of order and Good. Ever must pain urge us to

Labour; and only in free Effort can any blessedness be imagined for us." This concept was later taken by one of Carlyle's earliest admirers, Robert Browning, and developed into one of the dominant ideas of Victorian literature. Look for it in the poetry and fiction of the day.

Near the end of "Characteristics" Carlyle offers a solution to England's current economic distress by suggesting a more even distribution of the population over the land. Too many people are crowded into the industrial cities where there are not enough jobs for them, but the countryside goes begging for workers to till the soil. Also in a world so huge the millions need not cramp themselves in the confines of a little island. An Englishman does not lose face by emigrating and finding fresh air to breathe and room to grow. "Must the indomitable millions, full of old Saxon energy and fire lie cooped up in this Western Nook, choking one another, as in a Blackhole of Calcutta, while a whole fertile untenanted Earth, desolate for want of the ploughshare, cries: 'Come and till me, come and reap me?'" If contemporary leaders are incapable of implementing a massive program that involves displacement of many thousands, new leaders should be found. "If the ancient Captains can no longer yield guidance, new ones must be sought after," and they will become the heroes. The difficulty lies in knowing exactly what to do and how to do it, and the hero will know.

Sartor Resartus (1833) — This is surely one of the most important books of the nineteenth century, and people continue to read it and form reactions to it even today in the twenty-first century. Not long ago I read in a magazine that a middle-aged woman, coming upon the book in her local library, was astounded by what she found in its pages. All her life she had been thinking similar thoughts in similar language and wanted to write them down. Now someone she had never heard of had published long before she was born a book containing the essence of every thought she ever had in a style that seemed her own. With tongue in cheek she asked her friends and then a lawyer whether she could sue.

She might have asked why the Scotsman wrote the book, and why he clothed his thoughts in such an odd style.

Perhaps we have the answer here. He looked upon society as sick and suffering and trying to help itself by means of quack remedies. Quick and quack remedies – Band-Aid fixes we call them today – were clearly ineffectual and temporary and had no power to save the country or even to cure its scrapes and bruises. The political economists were on the wrong track, and so were the Whigs who wanted to extend the franchise. The Utilitarians (Mill's group), who believed nothing was valuable unless proven useful, were a gang of misguided galoots. In dark confusion, the nation had little need for all these unworkable remedies. It needed above anything else a restoration of a living faith to replace the one that was dying. So without delay Carlyle the visionary penned *Sartor Resartus* to provide a new religion for the western world. A more grandiose purpose for writing a book is surely impossible to find. However, in the spirit of sharing he wanted to give to his generation and those coming afterwards the positive faith and the peace of mind that he himself had found.

What would you say is the theme of the book? Lurking behind that picturesque, half humorous and half tragic, gnarled and convoluted and mock Germanic style, it can be hard to find. Yet the theme is partly revealed by translating the book's Latin title, which means "The Tailor Retailored." Owing to advances in thought and science, mankind's beliefs and dogmas have yielded to confusion and erosion. Man's conception of himself as he relates to the nation, the world, and the universe has been reduced to tatters. As a shaken victim of circumstance he desperately needs new apparel to clothe his shivering frame and supply him with new confidence. All that men and woman have made to express themselves (language, art, science, traditional learning) represents the garment of the spirit that must be replaced with a new garment. The unique style of *Sartor Resartus*, we might say, is the garment of Carlyle's thought, or more precisely that of his persona, a wild and chaotic German professor. This, then, is the relatively simple theme that underlies the eloquence and profundity of the book.

Now what can we say about its structure? The work is divided into three sections, or "Books" as Carlyle called them. The first and third are somewhat rambling and discursive while the second assumes the guise of biography. Book I is where we find the best explanation of the famous clothes philosophy. It is made up of the meditations of an eccentric German professor with the unusual name of Diogenes Teufelsdröckh. He is Professor of Things in General at the University of Weissnichtwo (know-not-where). The English editor of the professor's papers (Carlyle himself) has taken upon himself the task of sorting through a mind-boggling mass of disorganized materials to try to make sense of them (struggling to bring order from chaos). He manages to insert comments here and there, but the passages on the significance of clothes, the spiritual nature of the world, and the superiority of Reason over Understanding are the thoughts of Teufelsdröckh. "Reason" as here understood means intuition, and "Understanding" means the logical faculty. The semantics tend to twist the usual meaning.

Book II is the biography of Diogenes Teufelsdröckh pieced together from the philosophic fragments of the professor, and from the notes sent to the indomitable editor by a friend, Heuschrecke (grasshopper in English). From these notes Carlyle pretends to derive both a philosophy and a biography. Arriving in six paper bags crammed with everything from laundry bills to abstruse philosophical ideas, the notes represent an overwhelming disorder. The undaunted editor, through hard and persistent labor, is able to bring the papers under control and present them to the world as a systematic philosophy. Obliquely Carlyle is illustrating one of the main tenets of his own philosophy, that of bringing chaos under control though hard work. Book II also details his own spiritual journey from everlasting 'No' to 'Yea.'

Book III returns to Carlyle's "Clothes Philosophy" with emphasis on the application of Teufelsdröckh's ideas to religion, politics, starvation wages, social regeneration, and the new attitude toward God and nature suggested by German transcendentalism. It is written mainly by the English editor of the papers. Carlyle has created two fictional characters to be his spokesmen. The first is a romantic, excitable, absent-minded, chaotic, and cerebral German professor. The second is a calm, rational, methodical, workmanlike yet sensitive English editor. The clever device of "editing" an imaginary person's papers allowed for extravagant humor, pedantic posturing, scholarly allusion to esoteric learning without fear of censure, and frequent digression. Also anything outrageous could be attributed to Teufelsdröckh.

What can we say about the impact and meaning of this important book? A latter-day critic, attempting to assess its influence, called *Sartor Resartus* (1838) "the second most important book of the century." The one of first importance in his judgment was the *Origin of Species* (1859) by Darwin, and the third was *Culture and Anarchy* (1869) by Matthew Arnold. Carlyle's book, though puzzling to some, was certainly a significant document of the time. To understand it, begin with its theme as reflected by the translated title. Try to identify Sartor. Who exactly is the tailor? The reality we know through our senses? The state? The outworn institutions of a state in trouble? All of mankind in a troubled world? Is the tailor perhaps the Calvinist religion, crammed with Hebraism, which in Carlyle's time had become tired and taken for granted? The tailor's identity would seem to be synonymous with all these, but we need to be more specific. Perhaps the title has to do primarily with dressing all people in a new suit of clothes, even those who make the clothes. Carlyle is stripping away the old, uncomfortable Hebrew clothes and supplying his generation with new clothes. They are cut pretty much from the same pattern, but he is using different and better cloth.

Now what about the meaning of that strange, half-comical, hard-to-pronounce, polyglot name Diogenes Teufelsdröckh? The first part is Greek for "god-given," and the second is German for "devil's dung." So clearly the German professor, a curious blend of pathos and comedy, is seen by Carlyle as both spirit and flesh. Outwardly he belongs to the world of time and is not free of evil, but his untainted inner self is heavenly and eternal. God-given, he came into the world from the lap of God. If all people are children of God, then everyone belongs to the same family, a universal brotherhood. This is why Carlyle insists that the mill owner owes more to his workers than mere cash payment. This is why he maintains that society is more than a social contract, as the Whigs had termed it. *Sartor Resartus* is mainly Tory in its point of view, but at a time when religion was seriously being called into question its mystical transcendentalism, intended to restore an ailing faith, goes beyond politics.

Some questions to explore are these. How can one fully explain the clothes philosophy? What does Carlyle mean by "The World in Clothes," the title of one of his chapters? Perhaps the world as we know it is clothed in apparel created by man over a long period of time. The world is clothed in its institutions, habits, manners, customs, and traditions. Such clothing is necessary, to be sure, but as times change the clothing of one age may not serve another. When the ideas and beliefs of the past no longer serve us in the present, they should be discarded lest they strangle us. When they become uncomfortable clothing, they hamper the circulation and cause rashes on the skin and threaten to harm us with headaches rather than help us. It is only through clothing that civilization is possible, Carlyle asserts, but clothing tends to wear out with time and use. Even so, people often develop warm affection for the old, worthless, worn-out clothes and are reluctant to replace them. The time arrives when it becomes essential to strip off the old clothes, albeit reluctantly, for a fresh examination of self in new clothes.

What does he mean by the title of another chapter, "The World Out of Clothes?" When we are most deeply immersed in worldly affairs, he maintains, we are sleeping and unconscious. When we are silent and meditating, we are closer to the transcendent world and the Divine Idea. This transcendent world is the world out of clothes. It is the world of spirit that lies above and beyond the world of matter. Through the exercise of the Intuitive Reason we are able at times to look through the garment of nature and all the apparel created by man into this world of spirit. We are able to glimpse through the clothing to see for a fleeting moment Ultimate Reality in its naked beauty. Or to put it another way, through the use of the Imagination we are able to experience rare moments of insight that supply glimpses of the white radiance of eternity. "The beginning of all Wisdom," says Carlyle, "is to look fixedly on Clothes till they become transparent." The eye of vulgar logic, looking at a man, sees only "a Biped that wears Breeches." The eye of Pure Reason, or intuitive reason, sees a divine apparition, a fragment of the Divine Idea, because it can look through the clothes to the real person. The most insignificant tinker, animated by spiritual reality, becomes in this perspective a creature wondrous to behold.

In Book II of *Sartor Resartus* Carlyle examines his own spiritual journey in those three chapters beginning with "The Everlasting No" and concluding with "The Everlasting Yea." Teufelsdröckh's conversion is to a large extent what happened to Carlyle himself in Edinburgh in the summer of 1822. The chapter titles are names for the state of spiritual negation Teufelsdröckh feels when he loses his young sweetheart, Blumine, to a close friend. In his suffering, "The Everlasting No," he discovers he has no faith in himself or anything else. The universe is merely a machine and people the victims of unalterable law. Rambling lost in "The Centre of Indifference," he stumbles through an uncaring world in resigned sadness unable to construct a new life or a new faith. "The Everlasting Yea" comes about when he discovers that duty and suffering have a higher reality than self-indulgence and pleasure. The world now seems less hostile, his sense of alienation is slowly lifted, and disgust becomes pity. The final step in this phase is the will to act, to labor and produce. The crisis has taken him from a negative rejection of the world through total indifference to a very positive understanding of what he can do to make the world better. He has given new garments to his religious convictions. Through suffering and searching he has saved his own soul.

He now begins to feel the presence of God in nature and in himself. He is able to see that blessedness in human life is far more important than happiness, and blessedness comes from working. From this point to the end of the chapter we get a full explanation of Carlyle's doctrine of work. The dramatic injunction, "America is here or nowhere," is important in this connection. It first appeared in Goethe's *Wilhelm Meister* (1796) to signify greener pastures, or that ideal utopia which lies ever beyond the horizon. It has to do with that timeless yearning on the part of sensitive young people everywhere to build for themselves a better life in a better place. That better life, Carlyle insists, has to be built by hard work in the here and now, not in some dream world of the imagination. America, that fabled land of milk and honey, is wherever the divine plan has placed you in life. "Yes, here in this poor, miserable, hampered, despicable Actual." It is here in the world of matter that the young person is called upon to work to improve himself and all that surrounds him. *Amerika ist hier oder nirgenst* is the command in the original German – *America is here in your own backyard or nowhere.* The key to finding your America is to build it with your own hands. Make it your own personal reality of blue skies, fleecy clouds, fair winds, and fruited trees by working hard wherever you happen to live.

Book III is where one finds that important chapter called "Natural Supernaturalism." By this phrase Carlyle means that he considers nature marvelous or miraculous in her own right. This position differs from the older doctrine that looked upon nature as rather humdrum, but held the belief that a glorious super nature had the ultimate power of miraculous intervention in the workings of plain and dull nature. When we see a rainbow or a sunset time and again, we cease to think about it and take it for granted. But does that make it any the less miraculous? Spring, for example, comes every year just like clockwork, and so this miracle that ought to stagger the mind we take for granted. "Custom," Carlyle typically proclaims, "doth make dotards of us all." Then he adds, "Innumerable are the illusions and legerdemain tricks of Custom; but of all these perhaps the cleverest is her knack of persuading us that the Miraculous, by simple repetition, ceases to be Miraculous." He wanted his readers to work silently in the world in order to come closer to their God and realize their destiny. Of equal importance was the wish to have them wake up and see the world as in itself it really is.

A question that comes up in any discussion of *Sartor Resartus* is the one concerning style. Though phrased differently by different people, it generally asks why did Carlyle choose so strange a style? Contemporary readers were quite puzzled by what they saw as perverse and persistent obscurity. Some were even offended by the difficult German-like style, which in time came to be called "Carlylese." When the book appeared serially in *Fraser's Magazine,* many readers believed literally in the existence of the nutty professor and were not able to recognize the satire. The words used by a critic to describe the book's initial reception were "unqualified and universal disapprobation," but within a few years it became a bestseller. In choosing such a style Carlyle is attempting to move his readers, stir their imaginations, and instruct them. One should remember also that he viewed style as a form of clothing, and so he created, as Emerson explained, "a splendid rhetoric to clothe the truth." He is attempting to present his version of truth as attractively as he can in clothing that will amaze and startle his readers. It is a style that brings the reader in touch with the writer's personality. It is brilliant and original and surprising in its turns and twists. It appeals to the senses as well as the imagination. It is vivid and humorous. At times one can see the revivalist preacher in resolute battle against complacency.

5

The French Revolution (1837) — When *Sartor Resartus* was published first in a magazine and later in book form, readers at first didn't know what to make of it and the reception was at best lukewarm. This historical account of a famous revolution, however, was more than warmly received. It quickly brought Carlyle literary fame and placed him among the greatest of living writers. Some years before, as seen in the essays on Voltaire and Diderot (1833), his imagination had drifted toward revolutionary France as the possible subject for a major work. The very next year, when Mill encouraged him to use a collection of materials he had gathered, Carlyle began to write. On this work he built his reputation as both historian and artist. In it he takes the raw material of history, runs it through his imagination and philosophy, and turns it into exciting and moving drama. His aim is to make readers see what is happening as if they were there. His method is almost that of a cameraman who uses the panoramic view, zooms in for a vivid close-up, and then focuses upon the human quality of the scene. He brings into the narrative a multitude of characters who demand to be heard, but not once in the welter of voices does the ever-present narrator lose his own voice. It is audible and strong, commenting here, lamenting there, pontificating, and always sustaining high pictorial power. Even more remarkable is to know Carlyle had to rewrite the entire first volume. He had loaned the manuscript to Mill for review. A maid burned it by mistake to rekindle a fire.

We laugh at that familiar human blunder now, but when it happened Carlyle surely wasn't laughing and neither was Mill nor his maid. Remarkably he forgave her, and she remained in his service. Southey read the history with great enthusiasm and pronounced it splendid. Mill gave it a favorable review and so did Dickens and Thackeray. Others of lesser note took up the volume and passed it on to their friends. In no time at all everyone seemed to be talking about the book, and it provided impetus for the study and writing of history. Carlyle interpreted the revolution as the vengeance of the Divine Idea upon a parasitical and tyrannical aristocracy. For the first time, persuaded by a sympathetic and powerful voice, English sentiment seemed to favor the revolution. The Whigs were pleased by the attack on the aristocracy, and the conservatives were soothed by the condemnation of the revolution for losing its idealism and failing to achieve lasting objectives. The four chapters on the taking of the Bastille are a good example of how Carlyle makes the reader see, hear, feel and become involved. The chapter on the execution of Louis XVI in 1793 is yet another good example. Carlyle covers events from the death of Louis XV in 1774 until Napoleon's triumph in 1795 and illustrates his philosophy of history and heroes as he does so. While the urgent voice of the narrator is exciting, even moving at times, his romantic reading of history never won the full favor of scholarly historians.

Carlyle's Concept of Historical Periods — This philosophical concept, carefully formulated by Carlyle over a number of years, had tremendous influence upon just about every thinker of the nineteenth century. The concept didn't originate with Carlyle, however, but rested on a synthesis of thought taken from several sources. He derived from his native Calvinism the basic idea that history is a fulfillment of God's will. He acquired from Fichte the concept that to do God's will is to nurture the Divine Idea. From Herder he received support for the belief in a beneficent Creator who works through natural law and progressive change to have only the best survive. His countryman Coleridge supplied him with the important distinction between the Reason (intuition, creative imagination) and the Understanding (the logical faculty). From Goethe came the idea that two conflicting forces in the world, ultimately shaping its destiny, are faith and skepticism. Epochs of faith are splendid and fruitful while those of skepticism are bleak and barren. From the Saint-Simonians came the concept that history exhibits periods of growth (when directives and doctrines approach fulfillment) and periods of decay (when earlier principles are held as dogma and faith degenerates into formalism). The Saint-Simonians were the followers of Claude Henri Saint-Simon (1760-1825). He set forth his theories in a series of writings that led his disciples to form a cult of well-educated believers, found a magazine to publicize his thinking, and seek converts.

The Saint-Simonian theory of history postulated historical progress to take place in cycles. They saw a cycle of unity and growth in the Greek and Roman polytheism that reached its highest perfection in the time of Pericles in Greece and Augustus in Rome. This cycle slowly began to decay with the period of Socrates in Greece and Ovid in Rome; it fell into disunity and collapse during the European dark ages. Another cycle was the growth of Catholic Christianity and the feudal system that reached its point of highest development in the period of Pope Leo X (1521) in religion and of Louis XIV ("L'etat, c'est moi") in secular policy. The cycle began to decay with Luther, the Reformation, and the rise of individualism. It decayed rapidly in the eighteenth century under the attacks of Voltaire and the philosophes and fell into fragmentation and collapse during the French Revolution.

That paved the way for a new era of positive achievement to begin, but the march of change in the nineteenth century stifled unity and growth and remained a critical seedbed of ideas rather than a period of growth. The theory of society endorsed by the Saint-Simonians was based on ideas comparable to those of communism. Their theory of religion looked to science rather than to theology for doctrine, and as new Christians they sought to improve the lot of the poor. They established a utopian experiment at Menilmontant, a colorful neighborhood of Paris, but the French government objected to their practices. After a trial in 1832 the cult was dissolved.

In his synthesis of these ideas, Carlyle included Goethe's analysis of the history of the Hebrews into a period of growth through faith to unity and triumph, and then decay through skepticism to disunity and collapse. Carlyle supposed each Saint-Simonian high point to be the result of a struggle upward toward fulfillment of the Divine Idea. The struggle moved as far as the theories, principles, and doctrines formulated in the period of organic growth would allow. Collapse began when new facts were discovered that would not fit into the old doctrines. Collapse continued until all ideas were obsolete and no principle of any kind ruled the world. Then occurred palingenesia (the phoenix rebirth). The new facts that had challenged the old doctrines slowly became the seeds for new doctrines that led from the past into the future. In the new birth, new world theories and directive principles take shape and provide the framework for organic growth toward a new peak of faith and unity. This new peak, superseding the previous one, is a closer approach to fulfillment of the Divine Idea. But it too eventually collapses as new facts challenge its tattered truths, and society again collapses. In this way our cultural history is forever moving through periods of faith and unfaith toward fulfillment of the Divine Idea. The cyclic movement reaches higher and farther in each cycle but never completely embodies the infinite.

As he fused these ideas from many sources, Carlyle concluded that each organic epoch, guided by Intuitive Reason, was a period of growth and momentary perfection, faith and loyalty, unity and trust. Each critical period he saw as an era of decay and collapse, a skeptical, rebellious, disruptive, and mordant era trusting only the Understanding. He viewed the French Revolution as the absolute destruction of the feudal system; yet it was a "Death-Birth," palingenesia. The seeds for the new world order seemed to include the new literature of Germany as well as democracy. This democracy he saw as a disintegrative force that fragmented society, but it was only transitional.

As the world in collapse struggles to its feet and begins to formulate new doctrines, democracy will serve its purpose and disappear perhaps in 200 years. Inevitably and with excitement Carlyle expected the new society to be built on the ashes of the old. The new order would have unity (a centralized government), industrial development (perhaps under Captains of Industry), a hierarchic social system (with men of wisdom as rulers), and a universal religion to bring about a renewal of faith. He believed that the skeptical ages, though negative, were necessary to destroy inadequate beliefs so that new ones might grow to be challenged in turn by newer facts and brought to collapse. He believed this cyclic historical process would continue year after year ad infinitum to bring mankind closer to the Divine Idea.

6

On Heroes and Hero Worship (1841) — This book, which explains Carlyle's theory of the hero in modern society, is surely one of his most readable. It is based on a series of lectures in which he examines the historical hero in six memorable identities: as divinity (the Norse god Odin), as prophet (Muhammad), as poet (Dante and Shakespeare), as priest (Luther and Knox), as man of letters (Johnson, Rousseau, Burns), as king (Cromwell and Napoleon). Although each of these heroes is very different from the others, each in his own way is a manifestation of the Divine Idea in gifted human beings. For that reason they have certain traits in common. They are wholly sincere: unimpeachable sincerity is the hallmark of the hero. They have a deep awe for the mystery of life and the wonder of the universe and see farther and deeper than ordinary persons. They are resolute in seeking the unvarnished truth, and they handle the truth better than ordinary people. Carlyle's central contention is that heroes, inherently modest, never demand worship from anybody. And yet they deserve to be worshipped because they themselves worship the Divine Idea that runs like pure energy through them.

Until this time (1841) Carlyle's heroes (like those of Emerson in America) had been representative men, not demigods or supermen. Later he tended to glorify force for its own sake and to believe that the end justifies the means. This is what the critics call "the later Carlyle," and it was the later Carlyle who appealed so much to the Germans in both world wars, particularly the second. Carlyle's intense biography of Frederick the Great, which took him thirteen years to write, was said to be Hitler's favorite book. Carlyle's convoluted prose wielded considerable influence upon the German philosopher Nietzsche, who died in 1900. Nietzsche in turn influenced the thinking of those who became leaders of the National Socialist German Workers' Party, founded in 1919 and brought to power in 1933 under Adolf Hitler. Members of the party were called Nazis, and the party advocated state control of the economy, racist nationalism, and imperialist expansion that promoted aggression. The war that resulted from these policies wreaked devastation upon the world. It has been said that all wars have an economic basis as strong as the political, for all wars are fought to control markets or to extend territory. While that theory may be largely true, German expansionism, incredibly destructive, was motivated in part by the utterance of theoretical thinkers, Carlyle among them, broadly misinterpreted.

"The Hero As Poet" — The essay quickly makes the point that the great man who becomes a hero can excel in all pursuits, and yet the time into which he is born inevitably shapes his destiny. In the twentieth century Sir Winston Churchill emerged as a great statesman. In another century he might have become a great poet or a great king. A splendid, all-feeling heart and a "clear, deep-seeing eye" characterize the hero of Churchill's stature. He is able to see the truth when other persons cannot see it, and this makes him a natural leader. Seeing deeply, he is able to think deeply, and so his thoughts are musical. What the ancients and moderns alike call poetry is neither more nor less than musical thought. "A musical thought," says Carlyle by way of definition, "is one spoken by a mind that has penetrated into the inmost heart of the thing; detected the inmost mystery of it, namely the melody that lies hidden in it." If a poet is incapable of musical thought, incapable of detecting the melody that lies behind reality, he is no poet.

Carlyle has high praise for Dante. The Italian poet's great work, *Commedia Divina,* is the most sincere of all poems because the poet himself is marked by sagacity and intensity. "He is world-great not because he is world-wide, but because he is world-deep." In Dante – the medieval poet died in 1321 – ten silent centuries found a voice. Shakespeare, emerging at the beginning of the modern era, may be the voice of ten centuries to come. Shakespeare's dominant trait is a great intellect, "a calmly seeing eye," which is able to penetrate the inmost mystery of things and disclose their inner harmony. Dante gave the world faith and soul while Shakespeare gave it practice and body. Yet Carlyle judges Shakespeare greater than Dante. An artist as brilliant as Shakespeare is without a doubt the most priceless possession any country can boast. Some day the Indian empire will go and the United Kingdom will shrink to a tiny isle, but its poet will endure. It is a great and wonderful thing for any nation to find its voice, and the English have found theirs in Shakespeare. "We cannot give up our Shakespeare!"

"The Hero as King" — Carlyle chooses for discussion two men who were not hereditary kings. Cromwell and Napoleon, he asserts, became rulers because they were eminently qualified to rule, but history shows that kings who inherit their kingdoms often are not qualified for leadership. The king is primarily the able man, the man who is capable of cutting through complexities and getting things done. Through an outdated etymology, now shown to be false, he construes the word *king* to mean one who *can.* But the word really comes from the Old English *cynn,* meaning race, plus the patronymic *ing.* The two when put together form *cyning,* which means "a man of noble race." Carlyle is distorting the meaning of the word, but out of ignorance rather than a lack of intellectual honesty. Philology in his time, led by the Germans, had many discoveries to make. Trusting his definition, Carlyle asserts that the king is right because he has the might to prove it. It is thinking of this sort that becomes strident in later writings, particularly the *Latter-Day Pamphlets* of 1850, where he calls for a national dictator with the power to override Parliament. Such thinking threw him out of favor eventually, and yet he himself had a deep-seeing eye, a prophet's vision of decay at the core, and with deep sincerity he thought he was offering good advice.

As he spoke of heroes in history, Carlyle presented no lectures on the hero as philosopher, as man of science, painter, musician, or sculptor. In this respect his plan falls short of Emerson's *Representative Men* (1850). A careful comparison of this work with *Heroes and Hero Worship* could lead to a better understanding of these two influential thinkers who were friends. They are similar in their dislike of "Mammonism," or the fanatic worship of materialism in England and America, and both are transcendentalists in their religious views. Yet by and large Emerson's cogent lectures stand in vivid contrast to Carlyle's. Emerson criticized the undemocratic culture in England, but Carlyle opposed whenever he could the advance of democracy. Emerson chose Plato as a representative poet and philosopher and placed him second only to Christ in the influence he wielded. Carlyle did not choose Plato as one of his heroes, but did name Shakespeare the greatest and deepest of all poets. Because Shakespeare seemed to Emerson neither profound nor even sincere at times, he called him the "master of the revels of mankind." Carlyle's understanding of the poet-dramatist was closer to the mark than Emerson's. If Shakespeare had belonged to America, Emerson's view might have differed. They both agreed that a well-developed society needed a voice to be heard and heroes to work on its behalf.

Past and Present (1843) — This remarkable work is Carlyle's first and greatest piece of social criticism of considerable length. The book attacked the social, political, and economic injustices of the Victorian Era, which Carlyle considered to be the worst of times. It urged action to correct the social and economic condition of England, and it called for a hero to mitigate the country's present predicament. In the midst of his labors on *Cromwell*, he observed that two million able-bodied men were sitting in Poor-Law Bastilles and asking with a plaintive cry, "Hast thou no word to say for us?" After its publication in 1843, *Past and Present* became one of the great weapons for social reform. Carlyle's reputation as a thinker and moral leader, made secure by *The French Revolution* of 1837 and the *Miscellaneous Essays* of 1839, was now so powerful that the book immediately exerted an influence on political and public affairs. An important document of the time, it may be read as a book that speaks also to our time.

Carlyle interrupted his work on the life of Oliver Cromwell to compose with a sense of urgency this book with its powerful though simple title, *Past and Present*. While working on Cromwell he found it necessary to travel about England to find source material. He was therefore able to see at firsthand the hopeless condition of the poor. As many as thirteen people were living like animals in a single room. In the mines and factories men, women, and children as young as nine worked seventeen grueling hours a day at low wages and starved as they worked. Thousands of unemployed men were sitting on the curbstones of the cities, ready to take the place of any worker who died on the job. Hungry, miserable, inarticulate workers were attempting to address abuses, trying to gain strength in numbers by holding mass meetings. Each assembly they organized was quickly and brutally broken up by armed troops. The Corn Laws made wholesome bread too expensive to buy, and bakers were selling bread laced with alum, chalk, and plaster to the poor. It clogged their bowels, made them sick, and sometimes killed them. "My heart is sick," Carlyle wrote in despair, "to look at the things now going on in this England." The present at that moment was unmistakably more important and more painful than the past.

Book I of *Past and Present* is placed somewhat illogically in the present. It deals with the condition of England in the early 1840's. The nation, as the middle-class Whigs were so proud of proclaiming, was exceedingly wealthy and a leader of the entire world. Yet in the workhouses, or "Poor-Law Bastilles" as Carlyle called them, one and a half million paupers, more than ten percent of the population, were slowly starving to death. These workhouses, an old institution, were given new life with the passing of the New Poor Law of 1834. It was a law quickly put into effect by the political economists, who were much influenced by Thomas Malthus and his principle of population. The law required that subsistence in the workhouses could not be better than that afforded by the meanest job a person could find. In other words, the workhouses couldn't be set up in competition with the wage scale of private business. However, the wage scale was already at starvation level and when the workhouses made it even lower, certain starvation was the result. This is why Dickens wrote against the workhouse and why it was anathema in the minds of the people. To go there meant surrender, misery, and slow death in prison-like surroundings. In most cases to refuse the workhouse also meant to die slowly, but at least one could die with dignity breathing free air.

Carlyle viewed the workhouses as a quack solution of the grossest sort. The only remedy, he explains in Book I, is to find a responsible leader who can do something and do it fast. A hero-king is the solution, not Corn-Law repeal, more workhouses, and more ballot boxes. Book II, which has to be read entirely to be understood, is an illustration of what the hero-king can do when times are bad. It is largely a translation of a Latin manuscript, "seven centuries old," written by Jocelyn de Brakelond and published in 1840 by the Camden Society. That rare manuscript told the story of the Abbot Samson and how he brought order and prosperity to a twelfth-century Benedictine monastery after it had fallen into ruin.

Carlyle's vivid portrait shows a paternalistic administrator dispensing justice and efficiency right and left. When Samson became abbot, he acted with vigor to get rid of the conditions that threatened the future of the abbey. He exacted complete authority with a heavy but just hand, demanding and getting obedience, and he brought order out of chaos. Himself a hero, he was inspired by other heroes or leaders. It was easy to see that the medieval abbot illustrated the kind of wise and energetic hero-leader whom Carlyle thought England desperately needed to solve the problems of the present. A real historical figure and real events surrounding him made clear the definition of the hero at work.

Books III and IV apply this lesson of the past to the present. What

England needs, Carlyle insists in Book III, is a true aristocracy because the class that claims to be aristocratic has resigned its time-honored right to rule. In their selfish, indulgent idleness they have fallen into "do-nothingism and have ceased to rule." A true aristocracy, he urges, can be found among the "Captains of Industry," for they have energy and will and know how to get things done. They are the able people, persons of action, and they could become a reservoir for capable leadership. Yet before they could serve as efficient leaders, they would have to change some of their attitudes and ideas.

Book IV exhorts the present leaders of England to do something soon to correct intolerable social conditions. You have it within your power to mend society, Carlyle preaches, and you must do it without foot-dragging delay. The captains of industry must assume the duty of making goods and not merely money. The people must seek blessedness and not mere happiness. Everybody must be educated to the utmost limits of their intelligence in schools that teach the trades as well as in the universities. Oxford and Cambridge and lesser universities must extend their curriculum to meet the needs of the present. They must reach out and accept all students of talent, not merely the sons of gentlemen, and move away from the dead past. Over-population could be alleviated by emigration to the colonies, to the wide-open spaces of the world. Books III and IV eloquently preach the gospel of work, obedience, duty, renunciation, and responsibility.

The chapter "Gospel of Mammonism" is one of the most important in the entire work and the one most frequently read today. Here we find Carlyle's famous contrast between the Christian hell and the English hell. With Christians, hell is "the infinite terror of being found guilty before the Just Judge." For the English people, hell has become "the terror of not succeeding, of not making money." Heaven, of course, is the opposite – making money and plenty of it. Yet somehow people must be made to understand that money has no power to produce the heavenly paradise of their dreams. Mammonism is Carlyle's target here, a dogma that preaches worship of money and materialism. But since it also preaches the doctrine of work, Carlyle doesn't wholly condemn it. "There is endless hope in work, were it even work at making money." The mill owner, however, should do all he can to help his workers (Carlyle's paternalism) because he owes them more than mere cash payment.

"Gospel of Mammonism" should be compared to Dickens' "Gospel of Podsnappery" set forth in *Our Mutual Friend* (1864). Charles Dickens was Carlyle's dedicated disciple.

Near the end of the chapter Carlyle vividly pleads the case of the poor Irish widow dying of a fever. "I am sinking bare of help," she calls out to her affluent neighbors, "ye must help me! I am your sister, bone of your bone; one God made us; ye must help me!" They ignore her cries at first but eventually make answer: "No, impossible; thou art no sister of ours." Yet having infected seventeen others, who also died, she has proved her sisterhood. "They were her brothers, even though denying it! Had human creature ever to go lower for proof?" This poignant story and Carlyle's book in general had a profound effect upon Herman Melville in America during the 1850's. After reading *Past and Present* the American author penned "Bartleby the Scrivener," a moving and brilliant story about a young man who dies not from a disease, but simply because he prefers not to go on living in a society that cares so little for the individual. Woven through the story are themes of renunciation, responsibility, and brotherhood taken directly from Carlyle, and reminding one of the Irish widow.

In the chapter entitled "Happy" Carlyle sternly minimizes the emphasis the Benthamites had placed on being happy. He argues that blessedness is the end of human life, not happiness, and blessedness is living in harmony with one's God. The only happiness we need trouble ourselves with is happiness enough to get our work done. All work adds value to life, and work will bring us closer to God. That experience brings joy, and to know joy is better than to be happy. In the chapter titled "Labour" he preaches one text, "know thy work and do it," for work is sacred. If you find your work and do it, you will not have to worry about being happy, for happiness is a by-product of work well done in the world. Then he introduces Plugson of Undershot, his name for the rising middle-class merchant. Plugson has one outstanding virtue: he is able, ready, and willing to work. He is not very bright, but he has courage and energy and is no fool. In Plugson there is hope for the future, but at present there are those who hamper him, making it difficult for him to get his work done.

In "Captains of Industry" – the phrase is now part of the language – Carlyle predicts that the leaders of the nation, the rulers of the nation because they work, may one day become a true aristocracy. But he cautions once more, in that repetitious manner of the fire-and-brimstone preacher, that the love of men cannot be bought by cash payment alone. Instead of cash payment, the relationship between employer and worker should be one of mutual trust, loyalty, respect, and brotherhood. The worker should know that his employer has his welfare at heart, is willing to look out for him when times are hard, is in fact paternal in his care.

Any person who brings other persons together for any purpose whatever, Carlyle asserts, should remember this one thing: "Without love people cannot endure to be together." It's an interesting comment coming from him because readers generally think of Carlyle as paying little attention to love in human life. However, his wife Jane, a capable and sensitive letter writer, stood behind him for forty years. Though we are told of tender moments, their marriage was often tumultuous and unhappy, dry and sterile. She died in 1866 and her husband outlived her fifteen years. After reading her diary, he published without delay and out of guilt, some have said, *Reminiscences of Jane Welsh Carlyle* (1866).

To a large extent *Past and Present* did what Carlyle hoped it would do. It had a lasting influence upon thinking persons of the time, upon such men as Tennyson and Browning, Froude and Forster. Also it influenced Dickens, Ruskin, Kingsley and the Christian Socialists, Disraeli and the Tories. It wielded power to undermine the Whigs because it weakened many of their arguments. Macaulay, for example, had defied anyone to show him a century better than the nineteenth. Carlyle showed him in vivid prose the twelfth century, a time inspired by a strong and abiding faith. That purposive faith the nineteenth, fumbling in darkness and confusion, had lost.

"Shooting Niagara and After?" (1867) — This bitter essay is often cited as one of the century's most severe indictments of democracy. Carlyle wrote it in reaction to the Second Reform Bill of 1867, which doubled

the number of men who could vote. To pass the bill, he argued, would be as dangerous as shooting Niagara in a barrel devised by fools dreaming of heroes. He believed that ordinary men were incapable of ruling themselves, and so the rule of democracy would bring about massive irresponsibility and confusion. Elected leaders, no better than the ones who elected them, would become steadily unfit and eventually bring ruin and chaos. In an age weak in faith and moral stamina the leveling effect of democracy would be disastrous. Society needed leaders of strong character, strong moral integrity, and undisputed intelligence. Democracy, or "swarmery" (putting one's trust in the opinion of majorities), would lower cultivated taste to the point of total vulgarity, and its spread would greatly augment contemporary problems. To some extent his predictions have come true, but on the other hand his Niagara has not proved so dreadful or so dangerous as he imagined.

Carlyle rebukes Disraeli for passing the Reform Bill and censures influential groups for allowing themselves to be led by the nose down a dangerous path. He predicts that once the Niagara leap has been made, the better kind of nobility will withdraw into private life and relinquish any right to rule. They will leave politics and the ruling of the nation to those vulgar classes who have demanded the rule, and the result will be disintegration and chaos. A vital and sustaining faith has already been sacrificed to Mammonism, and now rule by Demos is being proposed. In a limited time democracy will run its course (his theory of history), but by then the church and all religion will have degenerated into hypocritical and foolish jabbering about "Liberty of Conscience" and other phantoms.

The tendency of the age is to slap a coat of varnish on structures that should be torn down and built anew. The varnish solution of his time is the band-aid solution, the quick fix, of our time. Both put off to a later date what should be done now. Carlyle has hope, however, in the eventual coming of heroes to rectify the wrongs. There will be no end of work for them. They must annihilate the soot and grime and squalor that deface the nation. They must ignore an out-dated moral sense and be guided by intelligence and will as they work to improve all matters social, economic, and political. If they are to do their work, the least they can expect from others is obedience. In our time, mired in the democratic miasma, many thinking people do not see genuine leaders rising up to lead. As Carlyle predicted, our leaders at present are in no sense better than the people who elected them.

Carlyle's intense spiritual journey moved from Scotch Presbyterianism to eighteenth-century rationalism through German mysticism to a personal transcendentalism and to an earnest attempt to lead his people out of the wilderness. His reputation over the years has gone up and down and up again. As the ideas in any work of the past cease to apply to the present, that work often ceases to be read unless its style provides satisfaction to the reader. That point is particularly applicable to Carlyle because of the decline in reputation that he suffered after the turn of the century. Even before then his ideas were being vulgarized and misinterpreted by the popularizers, and some readers proclaimed themselves shocked by the latter-day writings. By then Carlyle, like his disciple Ruskin, had become bitter and disillusioned.

It is entirely possible that much of the extreme language in these writings was quite deliberate, for English society seemed to be going rapidly from bad to worse, and that disgusted him. As his reputation slipped in England and America, the Germans adopted him almost as one of their own. They felt an affinity for the substance of his work and revered his style as reflecting their own. The literary style that many English readers found curious and difficult was based to some extent upon Germanic sentence structure. That made his work easy to translate into the German language, and in the 1930's German doctoral theses sought to explain his ideas. That trend brought him to the attention of Nazi leaders, and their enthusiastic acceptance precipitated a decline in reputation. In later years new generations discovered the work of this earnest Victorian prose artist, and with a resurgence of interest his reputation began to rise. Every generation eventually finds Thomas Carlyle because in a style that piques their interest and hones their intellect he has something to say to all of them.

John Henry Newman

When we look at the work of John Henry Newman (1801-1890), we see in action another sensitive, important, and deeply involved thinker of the Victorian Age. While Carlyle was trying to revitalize the old religion by giving it a new set of clothes, Newman struggled to do much the same thing but in a different way. His mission was to defend the traditional religion against the onslaught of liberal opinion. He was convinced that liberal thought was breaking up ancient institutions in church and state and would not end until those institutions were paralyzed or destroyed with little to replace them. If he could strengthen and spiritualize the traditional theology of the English Church, his mission would be accomplished.

He wanted to impart intellectual depth to Anglican dogma and renew its kinship with the mother church. He set himself the task of scrutinizing every basic tenet, every shred of truth taught by the church. This microscopic examination of doctrine ultimately shook the very foundations of the Church of England and unsettled his faith in its teachings. Intensive study convinced him that the Roman Catholic Church was closer to the true religion than the Anglican Church, and it alone could stand against the forces of unbelief. Reluctantly and painfully but in good conscience, he became a Catholic. His conversion from Anglicanism to Catholicism shocked many people of the time, and some never forgave him. As sincere in his beliefs as Carlyle, he felt it was the only course he could take. Years later in a book that moves readers even today he defended his conversion.

We have seen that Carlyle believed vital faith had degenerated to mere ritual. He wanted to revitalize and restore faith with a system of philosophical ideas that came to be called transcendentalism. He urged all people to recognize the reality of a world that transcends space, time, matter, and logic. Newman, however, could not accept either Carlylean or German transcendentalism as a religion, and for a number of reasons:

It was mere opinion without substance, footless and rootless.
It was devised by man and did not develop over the years.
It was outside the church and the fabric of sacred writings.
It was a mystical view of the world not easy to understand.
It was not truly a religion founded by a prophet of old.

Newman, I should stress, was a traditionalist in matters of religion. He believed that God was in the world through his church, but God's presence had to be accepted mainly through faith. The trust in human reason, the rationalism that Newman called "Liberalism," was undermining faith. This secularism he countered with dogmatic Christianity. Materialism, gaining ground every day, he utterly rejected as a false perception.

John Henry Newman's life span, even longer than Carlyle's, embraced every decade of the century. The eldest of six children, he was born into a middle-class, evangelical family (his father was a London banker) in 1801. As a boy he read avidly the novels of Scott, the work of the Romantic poets and essayists, and the *Arabian Nights*. When only fifteen he experienced an epiphany that vividly revealed to him the reality of God. The experience strengthened his faith then and for the remainder of his life. During his undergraduate years at Oxford, 1816 to 1820, he was known as a puritanical, hard-working student who was always reading. He was not unfriendly, we are told, but didn't display the usual college-boy conviviality.

Quickly he gave up thoughts of becoming a lawyer and for a time yielded to the influence of liberal theology. As an Anglican cleric he was swayed by his friends Keble and Froude, and drifted from evangelicalism into clerical traditionalism and conservatism. On a Mediterranean cruise with Froude in 1832-1833, he wrote the hymn "Lead, Kindly Light" and was drawn closer to Catholicism. When he returned to England, he wrote more than a third of the pamphlets titled *Tracts for the Times* (1833-1841). R. H. Froude, who died three years later and should not be confused with his brother J. A. Froude, wrote only three of the tracts. As vicar of St. Mary's, the university church, Newman quickly became the leading spokesman for Anglo-Catholicism. Many prominent people journeyed to Oxford to hear his sermons, his "Romeward" followers crying *Credo in Newmannum.*

When *Tract XC* (1841) caused a storm of protest, he retired in 1842 to Littlemore and the next year resigned his vicarage at St. Mary's. In 1845, just two days after Ernest Renan in France publicly renounced the Roman Catholic priesthood to embrace atheism, Newman was admitted to the Roman Catholic Church. In Rome he was ordained a priest and granted an honorary Doctor of Divinity. Returning to England, he joined a monastic order near Birmingham, where he remained for nearly forty years. Though isolated from London, he soon became the most influential Roman Catholic voice in all of England. The years from 1845 to 1864 have been called years of eclipse because of high opposition to his Catholic pronouncements and some personal failures. In 1864 he vindicated himself with his famous *Apologia*, and circumstances turned in his favor. In 1879 he was promoted to the rank of cardinal and for the next ten years was a vociferous opponent of liberalism in all its forms. At the time of his death in the summer of 1890, he enjoyed a high place in British public opinion. Carved on his tombstone at Rednal is a Latin inscription that sums up his spiritual journey in just a few words. It reads in translation, "from shadows and semblances into the truth." He was indeed searching in shadow to find the light, and he died believing he had found it. Those opposing him believed it to be a false light.

2

In the closing pages of the *Apologia*, Newman vehemently made reply to eighteen principles of liberalism to help his readers understand an attitude of mind that was sweeping the nation. When taken together they form the best definition of liberalism to be found anywhere. If I condense and simplify, I should be able to give you the list and perhaps maintain the mocking tone of voice that Newman employs throughout.

- No religious tenet is important unless sanctioned by reason.
- No one can believe what he does not understand.
- No theological doctrine is anything more than mere opinion.
- No person can believe anything on faith but needs proof.
- No person should believe anything not congenial to his nature.
- No revealed doctrine may stand in the way of scientific conclusion.
- Christianity changes to accommodate civilization and the times.
- Other major religions may have more truth than Christianity.
- Each person may judge for himself the validity of the Bible.
- Any person may teach what is wrong if he believes it is right.
- There is no such thing as a national or state conscience.
- Breaking religious rules is no crime and not punishable by law.
- Utility and expedience guide and limit behavior, not God's laws.
- The state may dispose of church property without sacrilege.
- The state has the power and right to meddle in church affairs
- It is lawful to rise in arms against legitimate princes.
- The people have ultimate power and suffrage is a natural right.
- Virtue is the child of knowledge and vice of ignorance.

Newman viewed these eighteen precepts or propositions, reflective of current popular thought and eagerly endorsed by thousands, as fatuous and absurd. For thirty years, he tells us, he has opposed them. Yet he knows well enough that most of the members of his own class believe in them and live by them instead of the long-established tenets of religion. By 1864, the time of civil war in America, these attitudes had subverted religion. Do any of them sound familiar today? Do most of them describe a mentality that seems all too prevalent in our time? To answer yes is to see the triumph of liberalism before we were born. The list will help us learn more of Newman.

As an Anglican he believed in the old-time religion and was thoroughly orthodox. The creeping infidelity brought on by liberal attitudes disturbed his peace of mind. He soon came to believe that unless the church were revitalized, it would not be able to compete with rationalism, materialism, and the wide-spread lack of faith in religious matters. Something had to be done to revitalize religion and restore the church's authority. This was the intention of the Oxford Movement. The absorbing story of how the movement began is told in one of the early chapters of the *Apologia*. Newman, Keble, and Pusey – all of them dons in Oriel College at Oxford – were the leaders. Because of the ninety tracts the movement published to make its voice heard, it is sometimes called the Tractarian Movement.

What were the principal aims of the movement? It wanted to assert the independence of the church and its separation from the state in church affairs. It opposed rationalism and stressed the divine origins of the Anglican Church. It wanted to show that the church in all respects was "more than a merely human institution." It sought to strengthen the authority and spirituality of the clergy. How were these aims to be carried out? Religious tracts addressed mainly to clergymen, and carefully written to be understood, would be distributed throughout the land. All of the tracts would emphasize the need to root out liberalism in the so-called Broad Church. They would emphasize also the need for unity in the full Church of England.

To achieve this unity they would have to find a way to dissolve the Low Church as well as the Broad Church. Inveterate dreamers, they would do this while revitalizing and giving more power to the High Church. The tracts were published regularly from 1833 to 1841, gained a wider audience than only clergymen, and were sold as fast as they could be printed. They varied in length from as few as three pages to long books. Tracts 67 through 69 comprised a book by Dr. Pusey on Baptism. When he added his initials to a tract on fasting, some readers began to call the movement "Puseyism."

So by then there were three names for the same movement. It came to be called the Oxford Movement (because its headquarters was Oxford University), the Tractarian Movement (because it made itself heard through the publication of pamphlets or tracts), and Puseyism (after one of its leaders). Though it was Newman's intellect that gave impetus and direction to the movement, his name was never attached to it. The ninety tracts covered every topic that could be related to religion, and they were at times opinionated if not dogmatic. Number 36, for example, classified the religious sects in England on the basis of truth. The Anglicans had the truth though it was somewhat warped; the Dissenters in their confusion had only part of the truth; and the Catholics in their zeal taught more than the truth. The Jews, Hindus, Buddhists, Islamists, and all religions apart from Christianity flatly failed to find any truth at all.

The separation of church and state in the minds of the Tractarians was a topic of main concern. As detailed in Tract 59, they wanted the church to have supreme authority in all matters concerning religion, but they did not want to lose the revenues that came from the state. Tracts 4 and 5 remind the clergy that their authority comes directly from Christ, and they should make themselves worthy of that authority. The power of Christ was transmitted through the years in the same way a flame is passed from torch to torch. Christ handed down his authority to the apostles. They in turn gave it to the church fathers, who passed it on to present-day officials. This doctrine of apostolical succession was a major argument in support of church authority. It supported, too, the emphasis on ritual and tradition.

The church is not to be guided, according to Tract 3, by what the people like. Sermons should not be made shorter to accommodate busy people, and clergymen should not lard any of their sermons with numerous exempla. These exemplifying stories attract attention, but some people get into the habit of listening only to the stories rather than pondering the text of the sermon. The tracts dealt with the minutiae of everyday life at times but also delivered religious opinion on dogma, ceremony, and anything else affecting the church. They were mainly concerned with shaping an attitude toward life throughout the nation, with establishing a whole way of life to be governed by deep religious feeling. Presented in plain English that was "pure and lucid," said one critic, for a time they kept at bay the hounds of rationalism.

In all these tracts one may see a brand of thinking that is anti-liberal, anti-worldly, anti-sentimental, and anti-materialistic. As they came out year after year, they set into motion a minor movement with the mouth-filling name of *Antidisestablishmentarianism*. Surely one of the longest words in the language, and a splendid example of sesquipedalianism, the term means Newman and his group were against those forces that sought to disestablish the established or state-supported church. The liberals, Newman believed, were gradually subverting the divine power of the church as they promoted the civil power of the state. If unopposed, they would eventually succeed in disestablishing the sacred institution, separating it entirely from the government, and cutting off its funding.

None of the Tractarians wanted to see the government meddling in church affairs. The so-called Erastians believed the state could dabble in church matters with impunity because it had power over the church. The Tractarians argued for a hands-off policy, but made it clear that the legitimate Church of England was entitled to state revenues and state protection. The movement toward disestablishment, which came to be called Disestablishmentarianism, alarmed the Oxford group and drove them to muster a counter movement, Antidisestablishmentarianism. For the Victorian family the foot-long word became a favorite tongue twister to rattle off fast at the dinner table or in parlor games, and it brought merriment. Word-conscious Victorians made fun of polysyllabic, verbalistic, bombastic language.

The Tractarians sought to define the Anglican Church as the *via media* between the Reformers and the Romanists. During most of the 1830's Newman believed the Church of England had broken from the Roman Church when the latter became corrupt. The Anglican Church preserved the truth while the Roman Church allowed accretion to dim and distort its vision. By 1839, however, Newman had come to believe that the English Church was not a true church in its own right, but only an offspring of the mother church and a rebellious one at that. In 1841, when *Tract XC* was published, Newman was contending that the split with Catholicism was harmful to both churches. That was so because only the whole institution without fragmentation could withstand "the league of evil."

To many interested persons at Oxford and elsewhere it appeared that these men, brilliant in so many of their arguments, had been seduced by circularity of argument. Several groups rose up to oppose them and began to call them Roman Catholic wolves in sheep's clothing. *Tract XC* on the compatibility of the thirty-nine articles with Roman Catholic theology brought clamorous dissent that signaled the abrupt end of the movement. Stunned by the uproar and denounced as a traitor to his church, Newman sadly went into retirement at Littlemore. On October 9, 1845 (the day he would long remember) he became a Catholic. Not one of his colleagues in the original movement went along with him, but his defection was decried by Gladstone and Disraeli and regarded as a national disaster.

What now were some of the general effects of the movement? In a manner of speaking, it had attempted to lift religion from a smelly swamp to a plateau where the air was pure and pristine. Though opponents had other opinions, those in sympathy with its aims believed it had done what it set out to do. A religion rapidly becoming vulgarized was given new spirituality and greater dignity. The dominant pragmatic influence that valued only the here and now yielded to some degree to an unworldly idealism. The cold and brittle dryness of the High Church gentlemen gave way in some measure to warmth of soul and religious passion.

It checked to some extent the runaway rationalism and naive emotionalism in church matters. It invigorated the clergy, revived a sense of mission within the church, and made the church aware of the human condition in the great cities. Little by little (in the minds of the people if not in actuality) the lean, austere, self-effacing, soft-spoken, and ubiquitous clergyman of the High Church replaced the solid, worldly, well-fed, pompous and vocal Evangelist. On the other hand, the movement increased the distance between the English Church and the dissenting sects. It tended to drive the Evangelists to nonconformity and intensified the dissidence at the heart of middle-class life. It split the country into two hostile camps, Anglicans and Dissenters. Also the Tractarians had ignored the great European movements of thought and science. Insular in their thinking, they had left unconsidered theological problems in Germany that eventually would rob many of their religious certainty. When the wave of "Higher Criticism" swept across England, the entire nation was startled and unprepared for it.

3

For twenty years after the movement collapsed Newman's reputation was in eclipse. In 1850 he delivered a series of well-crafted sermons on *The Difficulties of Anglicans*. In the following year he became involved in a libel suit brought against him by a person calling himself Dr. Achilli, a man who had once been a Dominican friar. The disgruntled ex-Catholic had made anti-Catholic utterances, and Newman in an uncharacteristic reply had accused him of gross immorality. To his surprise, Newman lost the court case and was fined 100 pounds and costs of 14,000 pounds! Catholics in America and England paid the sum with enough left over for him to buy property at Rednal. In 1852 he became involved with the establishment of a Catholic University in Dublin and began his lectures on the *Idea of a University*. The project was a failure but the lectures were not. In 1857 he was asked to edit a new translation of the Bible but also abandoned that project. In 1860 he was made editor of *The Rambler*, a liberal Catholic magazine, but was compelled to resign his post within two months. Except for the establishment of a school for the sons of gentlemen in 1859, he was experiencing during these years one failure after another. He was in constant trouble with his superiors, forgotten by the world at large, and suffering from a need to vindicate his chosen career. At the end of 1863 he walked into the light again and remained there for the rest of his life.

By accident he came across Charles Kingsley's trenchent review of James Froude's *History of England* in *Macmillan's Magazine* for January 1864. A passage easily missed by most readers but incendiary to Newman caught his eye: "Truth for its own sake had never been a virtue with the Roman clergy. Father Newman informs us it need not be, and on the whole ought not to be." Newman exchanged letters with Kingsley, who made under pressure a reluctant, half-sincere apology.

Then shortly afterwards Kingsley published a sarcastic pamphlet with the peevish title: *What, Then, Does Dr. Newman Mean?* Furious but in careful control of his anger (lest he be sued again), Newman replied to Kingsley in a series of seven pamphlets of his own. Each Thursday, from April 21 to June 2, a pamphlet appeared. A few months later all but the first two were published the book, *Apologia Pro Vita Sua*. After 1865 more and more people eagerly read Newman's clear and direct prose, listened to his eloquent and sometimes passionate sermons, and spoke in praise of him as a deeply sincere religious prophet.

Charles Kingsley (1819-l875) was an outspoken Protestant who had never been in sympathy with the Oxford Movement or its aims, and now thirty years later in 1863 his opinions were unchanged. He was educated at Cambridge, came under the influence of Carlyle, and involved himself in social reform. At the time he and Newman were at sixes and sevens he was a professor of modern history at Cambridge. He was known as a practical-minded man in spite of the Carlylean influence upon him. The importance Newman placed on spirituality seemed over-stated to him and unworkable in the modern world. He felt that Newman's brand of Christianity, even before the latter became a Catholic, was namby-pamby, ineffectual, elitist, worn-out, and beyond repair. Something stronger was needed.

Kinglsley headed a vigorous religious movement called "Christian Socialism," which advocated a "muscular Christianity." In his work and writings he attempted to apply the ethics and precepts of Christianity to improving the horrible living conditions of the poor. He believed that the main value of Christianity lay in a set of moral maxims by which to live. He was convinced that if the poor obeyed these maxims, they would be able themselves to alleviate much of their distress. As a poet, essayist, and novelist Kingsley left behind a legacy of good works, but intellectually he was no match for Newman. He attempted to argue without success that Newman was a fool if he really believed his own teachings. By seriously underestimating Newman, it was Kingsley who proved the fool. Overnight Newman was in favor with the English public again.

In this conflict of opinion we see that Kingsley's values are the values of reason. He looked upon the Roman Catholic Church as a human institution, but Newman contended that the church was divinely founded and divinely guided. The influence of the rationalistic writers prompted Kingsley to say that good works will guarantee a place in heaven. Newman replied that the important thing is the condition of the human heart. Kingsley had attacked the august power of the Pope, but Newman, defending that power, argued that the Pope is here to oppose and control evil. Kingsley declared that the Catholics, while mouthing platitudes about the *souls* of parishioners, often ignored their *soles* but never their money. Newman replied that even though the Church's primary function is to prepare people for the hereafter, it has never ignored the present or the human condition in either present or past. These arguments and more may be found in Part VII of the *Apologia*, which has the title "General Answer to Mr. Kingsley."

Apologia Pro Vita Sua (1864) — The Latin title means "A Defense of My Life." The first word, though almost identical to the English word, should never be read as "apology." Newman is defending his sincerity as a man and his reputation as a teacher and preacher. He is not apologizing for anything. His purpose is to explain his position and the reasons for his conversion from Anglicanism to Catholicism. In the first two of the seven original pamphlets he wrangled with Kingsley, but in book form these two parts were omitted. In the revised edition of 1865, now the standard text, Kingsley's name is not even mentioned. The finished book transcends refutation of Kingsley to relate with simple honesty the author's quest for spiritual peace. In the careful revision Newman seems to have consciously cast his material into that five-part structure characteristic of Shakespearean drama. His critics have charged that the act of composition gave his spiritual crisis a dramatic form that was lacking in real life. Also he may have diminished the importance of certain psychological factors in the development of his career. They all agree that the quarrel with Kingsley in letters and the open press inspired the book. Those contentious remarks by Kingsley were the catalyst that Newman needed to exonerate himself in the eyes of the world.

Part III with the title "History of My Religious Opinions" deserves special attention. Notice how clear the style is and how quiet the tone. Notice how certain passages seem to cry out for the emphasis of underlining, and notice too how memorable are so many of these passages. All this, of course, made the book very effective in Newman's time. It is classic autobiography with a philosophical twist. The clarity and simplicity of this section obviate any need to summarize, but I can point out a few passages often mentioned in just about any discussion. Note that as a boy Newman's view of the world seemed quite similar to that of Carlyle. But at an early age, without knowing anything at all about Catholicism, he was drawn to certain doctrines of the Roman Catholic Church. On going into the dark, for example, he would cross himself. In a copybook he drew a picture of a rosary. Then at fifteen he "fell under the influences of a definite creed," and for a time believed that he had been elected to eternal glory. He saw himself "predestined to salvation" while others were passed over. Later he came to view those narrow Calvinistic beliefs as "detestable doctrine." In other passages he gives credit to several of his teachers – Hawkins, James, Whately – who taught him that the church, more than a mere institution, is a spiritual organism.

What is Newman's attitude toward miracles? Half way through Part III you will find the answer. He tells us that he has written two essays on the subject of miracles and that he accepts the literal meaning of miracles. Other authors were writing about miracles, and their different opinions created a controversy. Carlyle, as you remember, had urged his readers to see nature and the whole world as miraculous. Even a child will tell you that the wondrous planet on which we live is bathed in celestial light. The sunsets so many of us take for granted are miracles, and so is springtime. Miracles, according to Carlyle, are all around us and such miracles do not involve supernatural intervention. But according to Newman the term "miraculous intervention" is the very definition of miracle. Newman accepts miracles in the traditional sense because the church for centuries has taught that such things exist in the world. If thaumatologists, the so-called experts, tell us that miracles involve supernatural intervention and are probable rather than possible, we must accept what they say on faith and deny the tendency to rationalize. Matthew Arnold, who had a genuine respect for both Carlyle and Newman, did not accept miracles as either man defined them. In *Literature and Dogma* (1873) he rejected both miracle and prophecy and offered a rational explanation. That did not end the controversy; it continues in our time.

Also in Part III Newman tells us it was the will of God that he should lead a single life, that his calling in life should require celibacy. He confesses that until 1829 he found it hard to maintain a celibate existence, but after that year "without any break at all" he conquered the flesh. In these remarks he is deeply personal, but he is also touching upon a genuine problem that has always bothered the priesthood. He is not arguing either for or against celibacy; he merely accepts it as an inviolable rule of the church not to be contested. He goes on to say that as his thinking grew more mature, he began to have "fierce thoughts" against the liberals. He began to oppose those liberals in the church who wanted to change it to reflect the times. He traces the beginning of the Oxford Movement to July 14, 1833 when Keble preached a sermon at Oxford entitled "National Apostasy." In this context "apostasy" means a total desertion of principles or ethical rules by which to live. So Newman, like Carlyle and others, was disturbed over the loss of faith in his time. Unlike so many of the others, however, Newman's personal faith remained intact from an early age. In those troubled times after he became a Catholic his religious faith was unassailable. Near the end of the *Apologia*, he announces that after his conversion to Catholicism he experienced "no anxiety of heart whatever." In later years he lived in spiritual peace with no regrets after years of crisis.

Idea of a University (1852) — This book is Newman's most popular work. It is made up of nine lectures delivered at Dublin in the spring and summer of 1852, between May 10th and June 7th. The lectures were published the same year and called *Discourses on the Scope and Nature of a University Education*. In Newman's collected works the book was given the shorter and pithier title that it has now. It is a timeless discussion of the aims and goals of a higher education. It speaks to us today, with the same salient points, as surely as it did to those mid-Victorians who heard the lectures or read the book. What can we say about its background? What can be said about those events that led Newman to prepare and deliver these discourses, which later became a remarkable book? What should we know about the intellectual atmosphere in which the lectures were prepared and delivered?

To answer the last question first, Newman wrote these lectures in the midst of circumstances not at all to his liking. He wrote them in a climate of envy, indifference, ignorance, and hostility. At every turn he found himself up against obstacles adverse to his aims. He had been invited to Dublin in 1851 to guide the founding of a Catholic university. Pope Pius IX had approved the project and had assured those involved that funding would be available. But the Irish bishops couldn't agree on how to do the job. When Newman wanted to move ahead, because of petty rivalries he found himself twisting in the wind. Here was the opportunity to establish a great Catholic university that could take its place beside Oxford and Cambridge. Though it would focus on Catholic theology, the curriculum would include all the subjects offered by any great university. The bishops, however, wanted merely an institution to train young men for the priesthood. They wanted not an all-embracing university, in Newman's opinion, but a narrow technical college or training school. Everything he saw quickly convinced him that the Irish had no clear understanding of the idea or essence of a university. They would have to be taught, "educated" as we say today. So he prepared, delivered, and published these lectures to achieve that purpose.

The people listened politely, shrugged their shoulders, and walked away. Not one word Newman had said seemed to have any effect upon them. The ideals he proposed somehow didn't stir even the Irish imagination. There was apathy then in Ireland, hunger and suffering, and the stark remembrance of relatives who had died in the great famine. Even to dream of a great university their sons might attend was a luxury they couldn't afford. To be asked to pay for such a project was out of the question. The Pope had said funding would be available, but he failed to say most of it would have to come from Ireland and not from Rome. So Newman was called upon to raise enormous sums of money in a country with very little money.

He exhausted himself in the attempt and received no thanks for his efforts. Eventually the bishops approved the project but offered no substantive help. In time he was named rector-elect of the university, but the appointment was never confirmed. Plans were made to hire key faculty members to fill important positions, but Newman was not allowed to select them. In time the Catholic Church donated 2,000 pounds to realize the effort. Although he still had to work under great difficulties, the money boosted morale and gave the project validity. By 1854 Newman had workers remodeling some large houses that would become university buildings. Also by this time some professors had been hired to form a skeleton faculty.

In November when Newman opened the Department of Philosophy and Letters, the university became a reality. He later built a university church and set up a newspaper. In 1856 he bought a building for the medical school. In the midst of these positive developments he continued to face opposition, apathy, and a lack of funds. Only a few students were taking courses. At one point Newman had twenty-three professors and fewer than one hundred students. The university had virtually no support from either the church or the people and no real source of income. The Irish bishops had insisted all along that it be a place for training ecclesiastics. Unable to contend longer with such problems, Newman resigned as rector in 1856, and the dream evaporated. Without his leadership the university soon fell apart and ceased to exist. Newman had given more than five years of his life struggling to establish this university. It was an interval sometimes painful and often exasperating, and yet the challenge was important to him. The venture sapped his energy, was very time consuming, and deprived him of sleep but was by no means a lost cause. It produced a book that anyone associated with higher education in our time or any time should read carefully.

The lectures that comprise the *Idea of a University* continue the attack on rationalism set going with *Tracts for the Times* twenty years earlier. The book clearly defines a liberal education in the old sense of the term. Ironically it was published at the same time the Royal Commission was recommending liberal and secular studies as the main curriculum to serve both Oxford and Cambridge. The traditional "education by the parsons" intended to train new parsons at the two great universities was to be superseded by secular instruction delivered by lay specialists. Earlier in both universities students spent hours translating Latin and Greek texts in addition to their religious studies meant to train them to become clergymen. All of the students upon graduation did not become classical scholars or clergymen, and that generated concern over the years as to what was missing in higher education.

The focus now would be on modern studies in the sciences and humanities. While Newman had no quarrel with that plan, his view of liberal studies was more traditional and more conservative. He sought to reinvigorate the concept of education that he had found at Oxford in his youth. Its aim was cultivation of the intellect and cultivation of the gentleman without regard to a stated purpose. He said the prestigious Oxford diploma, along with family influence, would insure any graduate a living. The kind of teaching that expanded the minds of students was therefore more important than mere training for a job. His critics maintained that in their experience very little expansion of the mind had taken place at either university, but that Newman ignored. His university was to be a teaching institution with a favorable ratio between teacher and student. The professors were not asked to lose themselves in research but required to pay particular attention to each student. The subjects to be taught would be history, literature, the arts, and science.

5

Education, Newman insisted, can never be equated with training. Education is the production of a philosophic mind, and should be an end in itself while training never is. Education with the aim to produce excellence of mind should never be degraded to the level of mere training, he told the Irish bishops. Newman was not at all interested in utility, which of course is the essence of training. He viewed education in much the same light as Matthew Arnold. When Arnold speaks of the children of light, he means those people liberally educated in the humanist tradition. In this respect both men are traditionalists and place their faith in the best that has been known and said.

I should emphasize, however, that Newman didn't oppose technical schools. They serve a good purpose even though their instruction is practical and utilitarian and directed toward securing certain goals that are mainly material. Such instruction falls short of the major aim of any great university, which is to stretch the mind and cultivate the intellect. The aim of a competent university can be achieved with students actively pursuing all disciplines and exchanging different points of view. To exchange ideas is very important because it hones the mind to a fine edge. The student who is exposed to a liberal education forms a habit of mind that can balance opposing points of view with calmness and moderation. Moreover, the young person's acquisition of knowledge satisfies a direct need of human nature.

We don't go to a university, however, to acquire a lot of facts. One can do that by traveling or by reading an encyclopedia or, as we know today, by going online. We come to learn how to handle facts, to see relationships and resemblances between them, to make connections so as to synthesize them and use the whole structure later. Only then does learning take on meaning and become the knowledge expected of educated persons. Only then does one achieve the discipline that makes for true excellence of mind that is surely the aim of genuine education. Religious training, Newman observes, is of great importance and should be a part of every university's curriculum but never the entire curriculum.

Expansive liberal education cultivates the person who pursues it. Such education "makes not the Christian, not the Catholic, but the gentleman." He goes on to say that regardless where or when the aspiring young man lives, or what he plans to do with his life: "It is well to be a gentleman, it is well to have a cultivated intellect, a delicate taste, a candid, equitable, dispassionate mind, a noble and courteous bearing in the conduct of life." Newman is clearly a traditionalist on the subject of higher education and also the making of the gentleman. Much of what he says in this passage had been said more colorfully by the great humanists of the Renaissance, and by such people as Lord Chesterfield in the eighteenth century. Newman is clearly a descendant of those early thinkers who wrote conduct books for future leaders. Ironically, those conduct books to a large extent were training manuals.

In the passage just cited Newman stands in opposition to Carlyle, who advocated universal education reaching the limits of a person's intelligence. Carlyle knew from history alone that great leaders, the heroes of our society, do not always come from the upper classes. Therefore, any person of any class ought to have the opportunity to develop his potential by attending school not as long as he wishes, but until he reaches subjects he can no longer master. In these remarks

Carlyle is revealing his peasant background even as Newman reveals his upper-middle-class origins. Newman's university education is for the sons of gentlemen in the act of becoming gentlemen themselves. That had always been the mission of the two great universities in England, both of them in the hands of the clergy.

However, by mid-century these sons of gentlemen came not so much from the aristocracy as from the middle class. Members of the lower classes were better fitted for technical schools, Newman thought. They ought not be denied such training, for no social class should be consigned to ignorance, but on the whole, he thought, members of the working class have no place in a university. The snobbery that Thackeray railed against is clearly evident in Newman, who was otherwise an admirable person. His style is plain, persuasive, pleasant to read even though some of his thoughts and attitudes do not rest comfortably with us today. However, the argument that people need education for development of the mind is sound and powerful.

In the *Apologia Pro Vita Sua* we heard Newman saying that as his conservative career progressed he began to develop fierce thoughts against the liberals. In the *Idea of a University*, Discourse V, we see him opposing the position of Macaulay in regard to Aristotelian deductive logic. Macaulay had viewed himself and Bacon (both were lawyers) as Utilitarians. Macaulay had agreed with Bacon that Aristotle's idealistic philosophy began in speculation and ended in speculation without moving anywhere. He praised the utilitarian philosophy of Bacon, the so-called father of inductive logic, because it got results. In Section 7, without referring to him by name, Newman directly answers Macaulay. In Section 8 he declares that the philosophy of utility has done its work, but only because its goals were within easy reach. It aimed low and hit the mark. Is it not infinitely better, he suggests, to aim high and miss the mark? The person who places the target forty feet away will score a bull's eye. The few among us who aim for the moon will never hit it, but it's the attempt that matters. "A man's reach should exceed his grasp," Robert Browning said at about the same time (1852), "or what's a heaven for?"

Newman's clear thinking and plain writing offered readers a better understanding of what higher education can do for the individual in a complex society. As a traditionalist he favored those institutions that insisted on serving human beings so as to bring them richer lives. For that reason he was an outspoken churchman, and he was equally outspoken in the area of public and university education. He believed in religion and education as two great sources of human improvement, but more than once he insisted that neither could be taken as a panacea for all troubles. His literary gifts, combined with incisive thinking, secured for him the attention of the entire nation, and before he died he had the attention of the English-speaking world.

The habit of detecting distinctions, which he acquired as a student from Hawkins and Whately, sometimes placed him at odds with his superiors. The habit of unceasing labor (acquired possibly from reading Carlyle) gave him the strength to carry on. He was fair in his treatment of others, yet unswerving in his convictions. Always he placed high value upon principle. In his own day even those who disagreed with his ideas often mentioned his acuteness of mind as one of his best qualities. In our time we speak of Newman as a stylist, as a lover of language who put the right word for the right thought in the right place. That talent didn't go unnoticed in his own time. "Cardinal Newman," a contemporary critic observed, "himself fixes on one of the most striking of his literary gifts, the delicacy of this feeling for words and for the fine distinctions between related words." The word, however, was always less important than the idea, for Newman was a man of ideas. Some of those ideas presented in a style of writing very readable to us today are with us still, and quietly they exert their influence among Catholics in their daily life as well as in the secular world.

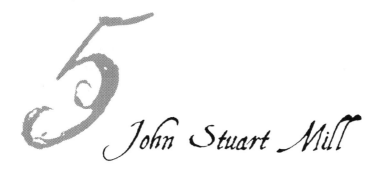

John Stuart Mill

John Stuart Mill (1806-1873) is a Victorian philosopher who differs markedly from Carlyle, Newman, and even rationalistic Macaulay. In his rationalism he is similar to Macaulay, but the depth and range of his thinking make him a philosopher. What would you say is the difference between a philosopher and a thinker? A philosopher is seminal in his thinking, originates new thought, and is studied by other philosophers. A thinker, on the other hand, uses philosophical thought with some modifications of his own and perhaps extends it but doesn't change it radically. A philosopher is expected to assimilate the thought of other philosophers and advance it a stage further to a different plane or frontier for examination and use by others.

In some areas Mill seems to have done that, and yet modestly he viewed himself as a thinker while looking upon Coleridge and Bentham as true philosophers. As a thinker he stands for the perpetuation of eighteenth-century rationalism in the nineteenth century. Newman, as you remember, defined liberalism, or rationalism as it was sometimes called, and argued that it was the strongest enemy of the Tractarian Movement. Mill agreed with Newman's definition of liberalism but had difficulty understanding how a person with such a good mind as Newman could take so much on faith. He thought it was a kind of weakness of mind to accept religious doctrine that one could not prove by means of reason. Unlike so many other Victorians, he never lost his religion because he never had one to lose. By the same token he didn't have an unhappy boyhood, as some have said, for he was never a boy.

John Stuart Mill is a good example of the child prodigy who accomplished much in later life. Psychologists rank his native intelligence with that of Newton, Leibnitz, and Einstein. Born in London in 1806, he was a brilliant and precocious child – the eldest of the nine children of James Mill. His father, a strict disciplinarian, was a well-known historian and utilitarian philosopher. Mill is the rare example of a son who gained fame equal to that of his father in the same career. A disciple of Jeremy Bentham, champion of English utilitarianism, James Mill eagerly began the education of his son in accordance with the principles of rationalism at a very early age. He taught the child to read Greek at three, and then went on to teach him Latin and the sciences. He would take the boy on long walks and afterwards have him write lengthy essays on what he had seen. In that way he learned to write as well as to think but underwent more than his share of scolding when he was careless with language or even with commas. Because his father thought modern literature and religion worthless, the boy spent most of his time pursuing a program of reading that omitted them altogether. At eight he was reading the Greek and Roman classics and translating Greek prose writings into English. Soon after he began to teach Latin and Greek to his younger brothers and sisters. By thirteen he had mastered history, mathematics, and philosophy, and by sixteen a great deal of science and political theory. He was taught to examine facts and to accept no opinion on authority. His father sought to develop in the boy an appreciation for hard work and positive service. His adult happiness, Mill soon came to believe, would come from steady and unceasing service and a struggle to improve himself.

So in 1823 at the age of sixteen, after deciding not to become a lawyer, he became a clerk in the East India House where his father was an official. He remained with the company for thirty-five years and climbed to its second highest office, perhaps with some help from his father, before its dissolution in 1858. In the meantime he became active in utilitarian circles, established the Utilitarian Society for Discussion and Debate, and contributed articles to the *Westminster Review*. He was being groomed to become the next leader of the Utilitarians, but then in

1826 he suffered what we would call today a severe nervous breakdown. He himself called it a period of crisis.

In large measure the trouble seems to have come directly from a very strict, all-work-and-no-play upbringing. As a healthy and normal child he seems to have had none of the usual childhood experiences. The fantasy life of children was denied him. No one ever told him a good story, or encouraged him to read good stories. The book that fascinated Newman as a child, the *Arabian Nights*, was not among the many books in the Mill household. They had any number of heavy tomes detailing the principles of complicated subjects, but nothing that could stir the imagination. As he entered manhood at the age of twenty, Mill realized that he had no spiritual riches he could rely on. He believed he could only think and not feel. In the famous fifth chapter of his autobiography, he tells us that his discovery of Wordsworth in a time of great despair taught him how to feel for the first time in his life.

During this crisis he began to modify many of his views and came under the influence of Carlyle, Goethe, and the Saint-Simonians. He expanded, for example, his narrow view of human happiness and began to read poetry for its own sake. All the books he had read since childhood spoke to the head, but poetry touched the heart and gave him pleasure. Wordsworth's poetry in particular had a healing effect upon him. It made him rethink his mechanical view of human nature and freed him. It opened the door of the dark room and pointed the way out. Once he knew he could feel, he cultivated feeling in the same way that he had earlier cultivated thought. In his intense relationship with Harriet Taylor he proved himself capable of strong, sustained, and controlled feeling. She was a married woman with children when he met her in 1831 and fell in love with her. She was something of a radical, an exponent of Shelley's thought, and careless of public opinion. The relationship was highly emotional on both sides, but they gave little thought to marriage. Harriet lived apart from her husband, however, and for twenty years the affair endured. When Harriet's husband died in 1849, they finally married in 1851. Then Harriet died in 1858. They had known each other for twenty-seven years, but were man and wife for only seven. For fifteen years, until he died in 1873, he mourned her death.

Harriet delivered human emotion and grace to Mill's existence. She brought poetry into a life that had been for too long entirely prosaic. She influenced his attitudes toward the individual and toward society. She gave him a number of good ideas on women and liberty and directly influenced the essays *On Liberty* (1859) and *Subjection of Women* (1869). Mill described her as "the inspirer, and in part the author, of all that is best in my writings." Under her influence he became dissatisfied with the narrowness of Bentham's starchy utilitarian theories and developed a broader and more sympathetic understanding than Bentham ever had. Unlike Carlyle, he supported the reform bills. He favored granting women the vote, and his support gave tremendous impetus to their movement.

He wanted to grant women more liberty in all areas of life, and while this pleased the women it earned Mill no merit points among the men. For a time he and Carlyle were good friends, but eventually their views became so divergent that the friendship could no longer be sustained. On the matter of work, however, he was in full agreement with Carlyle. He earned his living doing meticulous work in the India House. In 1858 he retired with a good pension that allowed him to work full time at his writing. A book he wrote while working on projects he considered more important, *System of Logic* (1843), was recognized as the best book in the field for almost a century, and was used in schools as a textbook. Mill was the least literary of the prose writers we are viewing here but without a doubt one of the most influential. His style was clear and persuasive. His thinking gave credence and power to much of the liberal thought of the day.

European critics view John Stuart Mill as the most representative English thinker of the nineteenth century and as the foremost exponent of empiricism. Despite the break with his father's teachings, he remained essentially faithful to the principles of utilitarianism and was deeply imbued with the philosophical principles of rationalism. Yet in 1862, on moral grounds, he favored the Northern side in America's Civil War, even though most of England was on the Southern side. England's leaders had utilitarian reasons for their alliance – the rising cost of cotton because of the Northern blockade of Southern ports. Mill believed, however, that the conduct of human beings should not be judged entirely by utilitarian standards. The South was ignoring the human factor as it tried to save its economy. The North was on the side of good when it acted to eradicate slavery

A rational agnostic, he dismissed religious and intuitive thought altogether. He embraced the inductive method of reasoning as the only way to determine truth. The human mind alone has the power to discover man's duty in the world and his relationship to the universe. The moral and physical sciences are based on causation, and the study of cause and effect will ultimately reveal the secrets of nature. Pursuing self-perfection in the everyday world, instead of Carlylean blessedness, defined as being favored by a divine being, ought to be the ultimate goal of human struggle. Individual pursuit should be extended to society and the world to bring lasting improvement. Because human behavior is predictable, our species in the present can control its destiny in the future.

"Nature" (1874) — This highly influential essay was published after Mill's death in a volume entitled *Three Essays on Religion*. The essay had been written twenty years earlier or more, perhaps in 1854. The other two essays in this volume were entitled "Theism" and "Utility of Religion." They make up Mill's attempt to apply right reason and logical definition to an area where there was much confusion. Mill asserts that as long as man has been on this earth he has misinterpreted the character of external nature. The neo-classical writers who urged man to follow nature as a guide to worthy and right action misunderstood nature. In modern times Wordsworth has felt a presence in nature that he interprets as deity. He has urged mankind to come closer to God through nature, but sadly the poet-philosopher also misunderstands nature. Byron and other Romantics have looked upon nature with a sense of awe and reverence, particularly those elemental forms of nature such as mountains and waterfalls, but they are also mistaken in their views of nature. The mistake has been to see mind and consciousness, human attributes, either in nature or behind nature. It is a regrettable mistake because the forces of nature are unconscious.

Because nature is without consciousness it can only be indifferent toward human beings and all that we hold dear. It cannot guide men and women, cannot teach or lift them morally because as a raw force it has no mind and no heart, no intelligence and no feeling. Nature is force operating primarily in accordance with the laws of cause and effect, or what has been called natural law. Nature will kill the person who gets in the way of these laws or breaks even one of them, and will do it without hesitation and without compunction. If you jump from the top of a seven-story building and expect to float downward like an autumn leaf, your act will defy several laws of nature, and the law of gravity will crush you. Assume that you change your mind half way down and scream, "Let me live, please! I made a mistake!" Do you suppose nature, or God, or some other living force will hear you and intervene? Do you suppose you will be lifted gently back to the rooftop? Mill didn't believe in miracles, and one of his most memorable statements is this: "Nature pardons no mistakes." Raw force such as nature is neither moral nor immoral, but amoral. It is neither good nor bad; it is simply there. It can never serve as a guide to human conduct. Instead of attempting to live in harmony with nature, Mill suggests that we should struggle to know as much about it as we can. The important thing is to know the laws of nature to avoid injury and perhaps use them when possible.

That, of course, is the doctrine of utility being put into practice. It is an idea that increasingly changed man's attitude toward nature in the nineteenth century. The earlier, Wordsworthian teaching was to listen to nature and be guided by nature. "One impulse from a vernal wood," said Wordsworth, "may teach you more of man, of moral evil and of good, than all the sages can." Mill found it hard to believe that someone so gifted as Wordsworth could have been so false in his thinking. Nature, he insisted, cannot teach us moral lessons because it has no mind and no morality. If nature, therefore, possesses no morality, it is the duty of human beings to impose their own morality upon nature. That can be done only when men and women have learned how nature operates. Mill calls for understanding the laws of nature and using them for the benefit of mankind. Man can never really harm nature, for man is petty and the natural world gigantic, but he can use it to his advantage. The shakers and the movers must learn to exploit nature wherever and whenever they can. By doing so, all of humanity may benefit. This is the idea that motivated the many engineering projects near the end of the century. It has to do with harnessing nature to perform as men would have it perform to make for a better world. It is one of several Victorian gospels we are beginning to resist in our time.

As you become acquainted with Mill's ideas, it's important to keep in mind the enormous influence they had upon other thinkers. As with Carlyle, we need to know Mill well in order to evaluate the ideas presented by other writers of the Victorian Period. Too often what seem to be original ideas in the work of Darwin, Spencer, and Arnold are really ideas taken verbatim from Mill. The date of the essay "Nature," said to be on good authority between 1850 and 1858, is significant. The arbitrary date of 1854 places Mill's essay on nature in the pre-Darwinian era. Mill is not taking ideas *from* Darwin as he writes this essay as early as 1850. In articles published prior to 1859, in fact, he may have imparted ideas *to* Darwin. He is certainly anticipating Darwin's scientific view of nature. Tennyson also got the jump on Darwin to some extent when in 1850 he referred to nature in his masterwork, *In Memoriam*, as "red in tooth and claw." That is the exact view of nature put forth by Mill at about the same time. Tennyson seems to have formed the idea from reading Lyell's *Principles of Geology* (1830), and Mill's thoughts on nature may have been stimulated by similar sources.

A little-known fact is that many writers of the time looked at Darwin in the light of Mill's thought. An important development near the end of the century was literary naturalism, drawing its name from the assumption that everything that our senses perceive as reality exists in nature. That basic assumption, contrasting with Carlyle's super nature, is Mill's position. His view of nature as seen in this essay and elsewhere gave impetus and philosophical soundness to the naturalistic movement. Many of the theories presented by the naturalistic writers can be checked off point by point in Mill's essays. Scientific determinism, which may be defined as a kind of predestination without religious overtones, is strongly prevalent in the naturalistic novel. It is present also in Mill's writings. The irony that a good action may produce a negative or evil result while a bad or evil action may bring a good result is at the heart of naturalistic writing. The essence of the irony, the idea, may have been taken directly from Mill. Other thinkers such as Newton, Marx, Freud, Taine, Comte, and Zola also helped shape the movement. But the greatest single influence upon literary naturalism was Darwin (from whom it took its metaphor of the lawless jungle). Even so, the interpretation of Darwin could have been colored by Mill's thought. Thomas Hardy, foremost among naturalistic writers and a great novelist of the time, is said to have known Mill's "Nature" almost by heart. Hardy took his view of nature directly from Mill with little modification.

On Liberty (1859) — While *System of Logic* (1843) and *Principles of Political Economy* (1848) are seen as Mill's masterworks, the piece we want to examine now is the philosopher's most famous essay. In length the essay is a book of five chapters:

1. Introductory
2. Of the Liberty of Thought and Discussion
3. Of Individuality As One of the Elements of Well-Being
4. Of the Limits to the Authority of Society Over the Individual
5. Applications.

The chapters in the middle are the ones most often read today, but the first and final chapters are equally important. The first chapter explains why he decided to write on this subject and the final chapter is an application of the principles discussed earlier. Because the book is carefully structured to reiterate its main points, and because so much of what he says applies to us today, one should read it all. Mill reported that it was more a joint effort of himself and his wife than other writings bearing his name. "I had first planned and written it as a short essay in 1854. It was in mounting the steps of the Capitol [in Rome] in January 1855 that the thought first arose of converting it into a volume. None of my writings have been so carefully composed or so sedulously corrected as this."

On Liberty was published in 1859, the *annus mirabilis* of Victorian literature, and so was up against some stiff competition. In that year the scientific book that shook the century was published, Darwin's *Origin of Species*. Also published in that memorable year were Fitzgerald's *Rubaiyat*, Tennyson's *Idylls of the King*, Eliot's *Adam Bede*, Meredith's *Ordeal of Richard Feverel*, and Dickens' *A Tale of Two Cities*. In that same year, on the world scene, the Suez Canal was opened (the attempt to tame nature had already begun). In this country the first supermarket was founded. Also in this country Joseph Jefferson published *Rip Van Winkle*. It was a fertile year with numerous good minds at work on a rich and bountiful harvest. The years that followed saw the publication of provocative books that were eagerly read by thousands, but for sheer quality the literary output of 1859 stands alone. Competing with so many outstanding books, Mill's slender volume might have been ignored if his name had been less known. By that year, however, his reputation as a Victorian thinker/philosopher capable of expressing deep thoughts in a clear and pleasant style was well established. He had a following of many readers, for his audience was the entire middle class. These were the people Matthew Arnold would later call philistines.

Students of Mill have said that many of the most striking ideas in *On Liberty* came from Harriet Taylor, his wife, who died less than a year before the work was published. She may have helped in the organization and composition as well. Certainly she was a patient listener and critic as Mill read aloud each sentence he had written and weighed it carefully. Its final revision was scheduled for the winter of 1858, but Harriet died before that could be done. There is little doubt that she influenced his thinking in regard to the individual and society, but the reasoning here is Mill's own. His contention is that the best interests of an advanced society should encourage minority opinion and should never attempt to suppress the rights of the free individual. This emphasis on individualism is the keynote of the entire essay. It is a defense of minority groups against majorities of every sort, and it defends also the individual's place in society. It is a major document in the long and continuing debate on how the individual relates to the group and how the largest group tends to dominate.

Mill decries "the tyranny of the majority," saying this is the greatest threat to liberty, this and what Bagehot called "the cake of custom." Fertile minds, he insists, are almost always a part of the minority, and they should never be intimidated by the majority. Mill termed his book "a kind of philosophical textbook on a single truth." The emphasis in almost every paragraph is on free discussion of one's thoughts. Society must ever encourage not only freedom of thought, but free discussion as well. Only from this will come the truth. Only from truth discovered will come improvement in the daily affairs of life. The difficulty is that truth is very complex and takes many forms. A detested doctrine may contain part of the truth. An opinion being suppressed may be true. Both Socrates and Christ were killed as heretics. Each of the five chapters underscores this insistence on freedom of mind and thought. Mill believed that all human beings are born free and must have basic rights as they live their lives. With this idea Carlyle disagreed, saying more than once that we must earn our rights through blood and sweat and tears – work and sacrifice and suffering.

However, Mill argued that social progress and personal happiness can be secured only when the individual has the right to search for his destiny and development. In all matters that affect the individual personally there should be complete freedom. The state should intervene only when the individual's conduct is such that it tends to harm others. Here are some main questions relevant to the issues of the day that Mill attempts to answer:

- What exactly is individual liberty and what should be its limits?

- In what way is individual liberty good for society?

- Why is it important for adult human beings to have full liberty?

- How complete is the liberty that does not harm others?

- Is it ever feasible for a majority to impress its will on a minority?

Most of these questions Mill had little difficulty answering. Even his critics were willing to admit that his conclusions were doggedly sound. The fourth question, however, stimulated strong and lasting response and remains essentially unanswered today. Readers saw this as a severe restriction, for almost everything we do has some bearing upon others. Therefore, they were quick to point out, there is no such thing as complete individual freedom. In our time as more laws are made and more people break them, individual liberty is compromised and perhaps diminished. The fifth question is also troublesome to us today. What does a society do when the tyranny of the majority is superseded by the tyranny of the minority? When a minority seems determined to impress its views upon the majority, what is to be the solution? Can the majority justifiably and legally take steps to suppress the minority? Does the majority have the power to suppress the expression of minority views? If so, what form should the suppression take? And how would it stay within the limits of the first amendment to the constitution?

As he discusses freedom in the conduct of human affairs, why does Mill repeatedly emphasize adult human beings? You could say an enlightened thinker dares to include women in plans for mankind. Your answer would be partly right, for Mill does believe that women are fully capable of pursuing careers outside the home and solving some of the problems of public life. In speaking of adults as the only persons qualified to accept the responsibilities of free behavior in a free society, Mill is not inclined to exclude women. He is thinking, however, of those not qualified for such responsibility by virtue of age or mental capacity. Individual freedom can never be granted to children, for they have not reached the necessary maturity to govern themselves. And for obvious reasons, if the mentally ill are not able to control their actions and therefore pose a threat to others, freedom should not be granted to them either. This same principle applies to the so-called backward nations of his time, such as India. Liberty and maturity go hand in hand. If the people of a nation are not mature enough to use their liberty responsibly, a more advanced nation has the duty (though perhaps not the right) to look after them. In this way Mill justified the imperialism and empire building of the liberals, who welcomed his support. As the political economists relied on thinkers to validate their actions, so did the imperialists.

The term "utility" as used by Mill is sometimes confusing. Even a cursory reading of this work and others will turn up the word many times. He was, after all, a utilitarian of high rank in Bentham's camp. Baconian utility or usefulness was as dear to his heart as it was to Macaulay. But when Mill used the term he was often thinking of self-interest, that kind of self-interest that guides the individual as he works to improve his condition and position in life. He meant that kind of progressive development, say improving one's economic status, which most individuals seek. In later years the journalists picked up the concept and began calling it "getting ahead." Coupled with getting ahead was the hypocritical keeping up appearances even when a family was not getting ahead. Ruskin said the English worshipped the "Goddess of Getting-On" and were often excessive in their reverence. If indeed they did worship a goddess at the core of materialism, it was a debasement of Mill's concept. And why? Because it was not entirely productive either for the individual, his family, or society. The individual, said Mill more than once, must genuinely improve himself in order to improve conditions close to him and ultimately the state. "I regard utility," he declared, "as the ultimate appeal on all ethical questions; but it must be utility in the largest sense, grounded on the permanent interests of man."

The Subjection Of Women (1869) — Mill was persuaded to be a candidate for Parliament in 1865. Although he refused to conduct a campaign, he was elected and held his seat for three years. During that time he helped to organize the first Women's Suffrage Society, and he presented its petition to Parliament just as the lawmakers prepared to pass the Second Reform Bill of 1867. During intense debate the petition was thrown out, but Mill continued his work in support of women's suffrage. At the instigation of his wife Harriet, he began to think about the condition of woman in Victorian society and came to support the cause of female emancipation. This pamphlet with the powerful title – subjection seemed perilously close to slavery – was the result. If the title pulled no punches, the contents of the essay were even more persuasive in the cause of women. Its purpose was to show that the principle that regulates social relations between the two sexes, "the legal subordination of one sex to the other," is not only morally wrong, but one of the chief hindrances to human improvement. The wrong could be set right by replacing it with "a principle of perfect equality." That way neither sex would be able to claim special privileges or power over the other. Mill wanted to change public opinion so that half the human race might be liberated from intolerable second-class citizenship.

He argues that any system that entirely subordinates the weaker sex to the stronger is archaic. It harks back to a primitive age, "the very earliest twilight of human society," when women were held in bondage by men solely by reason of superior strength. This primitive state of slavery is a relic of the past and discordant with the future. The inequality of rights existing between men and women has no other source than the law of the strongest, and that belongs to the past. In earlier ages the law of force was the rule of general conduct, but in modern times this law has lost its power except in the subjection of women, where it remains an anomaly. Some protest that the rule of men over women is not one of force. Mill answers that increasing numbers of women from all classes, and particularly the middle class, are filing complaints, demanding better treatment. What is more, greater numbers would complain if they were not afraid of reprisals. It is illogical and immoral in modern times that half the population should be subjected to the other half simply because it is physically weaker.

In Chapter II Mill discusses the marriage contract of his time. He maintains that it is unfair because it places the woman in the position of bondservant to her husband. The wife as soon as the marriage vows are said becomes the total property of her husband. She can do nothing without his permission and must obey his every command. She can acquire no property of her own, and even her children belong to the husband. Her body belongs to him, and he may force her any time he wishes to become "the instrument of an animal function contrary to her inclinations." The wording here is starchy, pompous, and borders on circumlocution. The language he uses sounds a bit strange to us today. But as a good Victorian writing for Victorians, Mill was compelled to beat around the bush when talking about sex.

In Chapter III he insists that women should be admitted to occupations traditionally open only to men. There is no great mental difference between the sexes, he argues, and any job requiring mental capacity instead of brute strength can be done by women as well as by men. Also if women were free to work at jobs of their own choosing, they could improve their condition economically and that of their family. Thousands of women dependent on male relatives could become independent, and that would improve the individual, the family, and society at large. Working for wages would improve the individual woman, and that in turn would improve society.

In Chapter IV of the essay he recognizes an important change that has taken place in domestic life with the passing of time. The association of men with women in daily life is more common in the last third of the nineteenth century than ever before. In former centuries women were always concerned with the home and largely confined to it. Their men, on the other hand, came and went at their pleasure and seldom participated in family affairs. In the eighteenth century, for example, the coffee houses were often centers of social life for men. There they wined and dined, wrote letters, read the current pamphlets, and discussed the important matters of the day while the women cared for the children at home and remained ignorant of the world.

Mill's progressive age, on the other hand, is beginning to frown upon that way of life. Men who work in the noise and confusion of the market place are looking to the home for refuge and for personal and social pleasures. Even though for centuries the role of husbands has been legally that of tyrants, Mill asserts, Victorian middle-class wives have gained a practical equality with their husbands. Is it not possible, therefore, for these women to enjoy similar equality on jobs away from the home? Mill employs this argument to justify the introduction of women into the work place. Dismissing the myth of woman's inferiority to man, he insists that women are fully capable of assuming positions side by side with men in the world of work. They ought to be granted equal opportunity with men to hold office positions and to enter any of the professions, including medicine. They should be allowed to sit side by side with male students in a university.

The essay generated angry rebuttal from conservatives. Herbert Spencer said in reply that equality between men and women isn't possible because nature has decreed many differences that weigh against woman. Carlyle reminded loyal readers that woman's place has always been the home. Tennyson and Ruskin asserted that broader culture should be granted women, but not higher education, the vote, or any of the professional careers. Other critics proclaimed that admission of women to mercantile offices would mean working in the same room with men, and that would surely bring about an undesirable familiarity between the sexes. Opponents of Mill's liberalism and specifically the women's movement, including Queen Victoria herself, were outraged at the thought of women being admitted to the study of medicine. "To propose that they should study with men things which could not be named before them, certainly not in a mixed audience, would be to disregard the rules of morality." The Queen was not at all in sympathy with the women's movement. She called it in a moment of pique "the mad wicked folly of my poor weak sex."

At length the fervor diminished and eventually women were admitted to the professions – to university teaching, the law, and even medicine. Near the end of the century thousands were becoming nurses, and after 1878 many women enrolled at London University to become doctors. Through his wife Mill was closely attuned to "the Woman Question."

He took satisfaction in knowing that his book and his work helped the cause of women in one of the great movements of the century.

Autobiography (1873) — In our time, with the exception of *On Liberty*, this has become John Stuart Mill's best-known book. It was published in the latter part of 1873 after his death in the south of France in May of that year. Part of the book had been written in 1861 and the remaining chapters after 1870. Before his death he gave instructions to his stepdaughter, Helen Taylor, concerning when and how the autobiography should be published. He asked her to bring it out "without alterations or omissions within one year after my death," and she complied. The book revealed freely and frankly the personal side of Mill's life and made him seem more human than any of the many writings he had produced during his lifetime. It showed how serious and simple was the life of this "saint of rationalism" whose reasonable faculty was carefully developed at an early age at the expense of other faculties. And yet one can say from reading these pages that Mill's life was strengthened by incessant education. Until the day of his death he went on exploring all the nooks and crannies of a particular question, resolutely unwilling to accept any part without seeing clearly how it related to the whole. Again and again he found himself returning to puzzling questions until eventually their mystery began to reveal itself.

Coming from one who influenced his contemporaries so profoundly, this story of his mental and emotional history is curiously lacking that kind of egotism that marks the entire genre of autobiography. In this remembrance of things past, Mill displays superb mastery of mind or self-control, but little pomposity or self-importance. Carlyle, once a close friend, labeled the book "the autobiography of a steam engine" but only in jest. Divergence of thought and opinion is the source of the remark, not bitterness or scorn as some have said. Carlyle simply felt that Mill was too mechanistic in his thinking, and he deplored what he thought was a lack of spirituality. Yet Chapter V of the autobiography is very similar to the spiritual crisis Carlyle himself passed through in what he referred to as the "Everlasting No," the "Centre of Indifference," and the "Everlasting Yea." This particular chapter is also similar in substance as well as tone to Newman's defense of his life in the *Apologia Pro Vita Sua*. In a very real sense we have in the body of Victorian prose three great spiritual autobiographies. An intriguing question is why these men saw fit to reveal themselves in so personal a way to the entire world? Could it be that the spirit of Romantic confessionalism, which informed so many writings of an earlier era, still persisted in the Victorian Era? Perhaps with Carlyle we could say that, but Newman and Mill seem to have been driven by an urgent need to explain and perhaps justify.

There is little doubt that Mill's book is one of the most revealing documents of a highly trained human mind at work in the nineteenth century, and for that reason it remains valuable to us today. The opening section may validate to some extent Carlyle's pungent description. Here in meticulous detail Mill explains his father's impact upon his mental growth, the rigorous inculcation of concepts in these important areas:

- Politics — Representative government, the democratic system, is the best way to govern a nation. It is the only viable system and supreme. Mill was an earnest democrat. He didn't like Carlyle's concept of the strong man, for it seemed to veer in the direction of dictatorship. One of his most important books, published in 1861, had the title *Representative Government*. That book repeated opinions found in many of his essays, for example the need for complete freedom of thought and expression to make a representative government work. In line with this is Mill's belief that people working to improve themselves will improve their nation.

- Religion — Mill states with disarming frankness that as a young man he never suffered the doubt that plagued his contemporaries and never lost his religion because he never had one to lose. From an early age his father taught him to accept nothing on faith. He was agnostic and anticlerical all his life. He placed his faith in the ability of the human mind to find the truth through analysis and reason. He never went to church and never felt the need to do so. He believed that the church could never expect equality of power with the state. There ought to be separation of state and church, and the church had to accept a subordinate position in political affairs.

- Psychology — As with the Romantics Wordsworth and Coleridge, Mill was influenced by the associationism of David

Hartley (1705-1757). The term refers to Hartley's theories dealing with the association of ideas. A physician, he repudiated the view of Shaftesbury, which held that the "moral sense" within us is instinctive and intuitive. Hartley believed that men and women could know right from wrong and come closer to God by means of reason and thought that associates and refines ideas. Mill applied Hartley's rudimentary psychology, or philosophy, to the education of young persons in a proper environment. That kind of education suggested unlimited possibilities for improving the moral condition of mankind.

- Ethics — The heart and soul of James Mill's stern convictions, which he attempted to pass on to his son, was Benthamite utilitarianism. In his dour *Analysis of the Human Mind* (1829), he provided by his theory of association a psychological basis for his mentor's utilitarianism, and he taught his son how to use Hartlean association in the logical working out of ideas. He believed strictly in facts, and he tested all human knowledge in terms of its utility or usefulness. In his novel *Hard Times* (1854) Charles Dickens satirized James Mill in the character Gradgrind, an eminently practical man who believes in facts and figures and nothing else. Thomas Gradgrind brings up his children accordingly, suppressisng the imaginative and spiritual sides of their nature with grim results.

Chapter V, titled "A Crisis in My Mental History," is that portion of Mill's Autobiography most frequently found in anthologies. It is generally recognized as the most human and most moving passage of anything Mill wrote. For that reason anthologies pick it up while excluding many worthy passages from Subjection of Women and Representative Government. Anthologies that are frequently revised are beginning now to include excerpts from the first title, but none that I know of have seen fit to print those fine summary passages in the latter work, which bring into a system the opinions expressed in earlier essays. My point here is that more samplings of Mill's work are needed in the prose anthologies available today because his thinking was vastly influential then and should be now, because he said little that was unimportant, and because nothing in his work is frivolous. His style may be dry and unemotional, but his mind is vigorous and keen and always probing. To read Mill may do little for the human heart, but to read him sympathetically and with concentration is to come into the presence of a superlative intellect. Mill is man thinking. Energetic and profound thought suffuses his work, and he is always honest.

In 1826 at the age of twenty, as I have mentioned earlier, Mill suffered what we would call today a severe nervous breakdown. It was marked by feelings of hopelessness, lethargy, alienation, and depression. It became so bad at one point that he even contemplated suicide. The breakdown possibly came from overwork, but more likely it was the result of the stern training he received from his father from the tender age of three. James Mill was convinced that even the best schools in England were not capable of developing a child's mind either fast enough or early enough. He demonstrated his conviction by requiring his son to follow a rigorous program of studies many hours each day seven days a week. When the boy should have been outside playing with other children, he was in the half gloom of his father's study perusing books intended for older minds. There was nothing in them to stir his imagination or set going a dream. Surely the mental burden imposed by his father had much to do with the crisis Mill was forced to endure at about the time he was becoming a man. Jesuit scholars in our time have suggested that Mill placed a wrong label on his crisis when he called it mental. They would call it an intense emotional crisis generated by spiritual dryness. Its result was to awaken a soul.

It has been said that Mill himself offered no explanation. Yet if you read his remarks carefully, you will see that without understanding his predicament he is attempting to explain it. In Chapter V he tells us that at an early age he decided to become active in the cause of reform. His personal happiness would be dependent upon his work and would express itself through achievement. He reasoned that he had placed his happiness in an enterprise that could never be exhausted in a single lifetime. There would always be work to do, and the work would insure a sense of well-being. With each achievement he would feel happy, and that happiness would inspire him to future achievements. That state of mind sufficed for several years. Then in the autumn of 1826 he awoke as from a dream and asked himself whether he would be happy if all his goals were then and there instantly achieved. The answer he clearly received was a resounding No. "At this my heart sank within me. The whole foundation on which my life was constructed fell down." That realization made him unhappy, in fact miserable. The lines on grief from Coleridge's "Dejection Ode" he later found to be an exact description of his case:

A drowsy, stifled, unimpassioned grief,
Which finds no natural outlet or relief
In word, or sigh, or tear.

The suffering that Coleridge was able to capture in these lines had somehow reached out to explain Mill's suffering as well.

Carlyle's formula for happiness – find your work and do it – for a time seemed quite effective, but then it lost its hold upon Mill and ceased to influence him. He was thinking there had to be more to human life than work and struggle toward a goal. But what, he asked himself. Finding no answer, it seemed to him that life had lost its meaning, that he had nothing for which to go on living. "I became persuaded that my love of mankind, and of excellence for its own sake, had worn itself out." In vain he sought relief by reading his favorite books. He read them without feeling, for they could offer no pleasure. Two lines from another poem by Coleridge, discovered later he tells us (for as yet he had not read any poetry), seemed to describe exactly his dilemma:

Work without hope draws nectar in a sieve,
And hope without an object cannot live.

He felt a strong need to talk with someone about his condition and to seek advice, but couldn't be certain that anyone he knew would understand. He knew he wouldn't be able to broach a problem such as this before his father. Even if James Mill could be made to understand this "mental malady," he was not the physician who could heal it. "I saw no use in giving him the pain of thinking that his plans had failed." Yet his own pain was overwhelming.

Then one day quite by accident he came across a passage in Marmontel's Mémoires d'un Père (1804), which he saw as a small ray of light breaking upon his gloom. The passage moved him to tears, and from that moment his burden grew lighter. The capacity to feel emotions other than grief was not dead within him. He was now convinced that he was not a freak, not "a stock or a stone" in the guise of a tormented man, but a normal human being able to feel sympathy for the suffering of others. That brought him into the light. "I gradually found that the ordinary incidents of life could again give me some pleasure; that I could again find enjoyment in sunshine and sky, in books and conversation." As could be expected, he struggled intellectually with the idea of human happiness in general and his own happiness in particular. He didn't waver in the conviction that "happiness is the test of all rules of conduct, and the end of life." However, he now began to see that happiness could be attained only if it were not a direct end. People are happy only when their minds are fixed on something other than their own happiness. If you ask yourself whether you are happy, you cease to be so. "This theory now became the basis of my philosophy of life," he concluded in a tone of triumph. The passage shows Mill arriving at Carlyle's "The Everlasting Yea." It shows too that as both men of widely divergent views contemplated happiness, their thoughts were similar.

Mill was now able to feel deeply and now placed high importance on feeling. "The cultivation of the feelings became one of the cardinal points in my ethical and philosophical creed." At about this time (1828) he began to read the Romantic poets. He read through the whole of Byron to see whether his poetry could rouse positive feeling, but found the reverse. Byron through too much living had worn out all pleasures: "The poet's state of mind was too much like my own." Then quite by chance he came upon Wordsworth in a two-volume edition, and reading that poet became a pivotal event in his life. Wordsworth's poetry had a strong impact upon him for several reasons, but Mill places emphasis on two:

- The poems paid attention to rural scenes and to the beauty of nature. They appealed to the sense of pleasure he had always felt while taking long walks in the countryside. They expressed in memorable passages high praise of mountains. Mill had come to love mountains during an excursion to the Pyrenees while living for a year in France. Mountains had become his ideal of natural beauty, and now he was discovering that high mountains had awed and inspired Wordsworth too.

- The poems expressed not mere outward beauty but internal states of feeling and thought, particularly feeling colored by excitement in the presence of beauty. They said what he had often felt and struck a sympathetic note in his nature. He came to believe that Wordsworth was a kindred spirit. England has produced greater poets than Wordsworth, he declares in a famous passage, "even in our own age," but Wordsworth somehow touches deep chords of feeling. He had discovered Wordsworth at the perfect time, for his poetry in plain English exerted a peculiar appeal and filled a genuine and desperate need. "Poetry of deeper and loftier feeling could not have done for me at that time what his did."

Mill was mistaken in his assessment of Wordsworth. Time has shown that no poet who lived during the nineteenth century, with possibly the exception of Keats, was greater than Wordsworth. The reason for his greatness rests upon many subtle qualities of his art and philosophy, but a main reason has always been the poet's healing power. "I needed to be made to feel," Mill explains, "that there was real, permanent happiness in tranquil contemplation. Wordsworth taught me this." The poet also taught him that human beings share common feelings and a common destiny and often experience crises like his own. Mill discovered that he was not alone in the world. In Wordsworth, who had suffered in similar fashion, he had found a brother. Matthew Arnold would later recognize this same therapeutic value of Wordsworth. When the laureate died in 1850, Arnold wrote these lines in tribute:

> Time may restore us in his course
> Goethe's sage mind and Byron's force;
> But where will Europe's latter hour
> Again find Wordsworth's healing power?

Himself an accomplished poet, Arnold saw in Wordsworth qualities that would be difficult for the world to replace. It was diminished by his death.

Mill's mental or spiritual crisis had now run its course. From that time onward he would be able to accomplish prodigious labor, but he would also find the time to read great works of the imagination and to appreciate the artistic impulse living in men and women. He would modify and soften the unyielding Benthamism taught by his father. Eventually he would come to realize that social progress inevitably rests upon "the internal culture of the individual." His crisis was painful and hard to endure, but in some ways it was a blessing. He gained a sense of independence as he broke away from his father's regimen and began to think for himself. The experience taught him to extend his reading and social contact far beyond the Utilitarians who gathered around his father. He explored Coleridge and the German thinkers and talked for long hours with Carlyle, who failed to make him a disciple. He read the French philosophers such as Saint-Simon and Comte. His break with his father helped him reach a philosophical conclusion that colored all of his writings in later years. He believed that earnest seekers after the truth manage to pin down part of the truth. When the fragments are carefully assembled, mankind reaches a fuller truth.

John Stuart Mill was schooled in the sternest rationalism ever conceived, but in young adulthood was able to break away from its trammels to view wider horizons. Later a loving wife helped him in this journey, plainly and powerfully set forth in the *Autobiography,* and so did the poetry of Wordsworth. Both brought human emotion to a brilliant man trained to be an engine dispensing thought but no feeling. In his thought Mill became a competent philosopher and vastly influential. In *On Liberty* he vigorously pleads the case for complete freedom of thought, assembly, discussion, and action. His belief in the unrestrained liberty of the individual is soundly based on liberty of thought and feeling, including freedom of speech and freedom of the press. Liberty to frame the plan of our lives to suit ourselves and to pursue our goals as we choose so long as we do not harm others. Liberty of behaving as we choose, even foolishly, so long as we do not harm others. Liberty to assemble or unite for any purpose. Today any country that calls itself a democracy places a high premium on these principles of freedom. And today all women who cherish their freedom owe a debt to John Stuart Mill.

John Ruskin

During the Victorian Era numerous persons came forward to criticize art and society, but the foremost among them was John Ruskin (1819-1900). During the first part of his long career he was an indefatigable art critic, focusing on painting and architecture, but during the second half he turned his telescopic sight on the way people live and became a social critic. His works were edited during the first decade of the twentieth century in thirty-nine volumes. Just a glance at the index will reveal to you the incredible variety of his range as a writer. Guided mainly by what happened to interest him at the time, he labored earnestly in many fields. He wrote on art, architecture, economics, education, geology, literature, manners, morality, mineralogy, mythology, pollution, religion, road-making, national affairs, the conscience of the nineteenth century, and himself. He was enormously productive as a thinker and writer of poetic prose, and yet he developed no one consistent point of view or philosophy. As a writer with a romantic impulse he had little respect for the principle of consistency. That deeply ingrained trait in Ruskin spurred a critic of the time to call his collected works, perhaps with tongue in cheek, "thirty-nine volumes of sheer confusion."

John Ruskin was born in London in February of 1819, the only child of James Ruskin, a prosperous and puritanical Scottish wine merchant. Precocious and sensitive, he was brought up in a rigorously pious household under strict supervision. He was not allowed toys to play with and was not able to romp and play with other children.

When he got out of line (and a few times he managed to do that), his unpredictable parents didn't hesitate to give him an old-fashioned whipping. At other times they doted on him. Both parents had the ambition to make their son a genius and were on alternate days indulgent and austere. They began to teach him when he was quite young to love literature and painting, but he was also subjected to daily Bible lessons and required to memorize passages. He later termed this Bible study "the one essential part" of his early education. Another essential part was instruction in how to observe natural objects, how to listen to music, and how to appreciate art. As he grew older he polished his education by means of extensive travel, first in the British Isles and later on the Continent. When he was thirteen he was given a copy of Samuel Rogers' *Italy* with pages of subtle watercolor vignettes by J. M. W. Turner. The gift proved a landmark in the lives of Ruskin and his parents. It awakened an enthusiasm for Turner that ultimately led to the writing of *Modern Painters*.

In 1836 in Paris he met and fell in love with Adèle Domecq, the daughter of his father's French partner. She was lively and flirtatious but treated him at times with indifference. At other times she ridiculed him for being egoistic, not so civilized as the French, and too much the haughty intellectual. It was his first love affair and not a smooth one. Moreover, because her Catholicism jarred his Anglicanism, marriage was unthinkable. In the next year he matriculated at Oxford, his father hoping he would become a bishop. He remained at Oxford, his mother living nearby to supervise his activities, until 1840. In that year he was threatened with tuberculosis, met Turner, learned of the marriage of Adèle which made him sick, traveled with his parents for his health, returned to Herne Hill (the village where the family home was located), and in 1841 met Euphemia Gray. In better health, he returned to Oxford and received his degree in 1842. By then the first volume of *Modern Painters*, written to defend Turner who needed no defending at all, was almost finished. Ruskin was an undergraduate of twenty-three and Turner was a famous, well-established, and widely accepted English landscape artist. In 1843 the first of five volumes was published anonymously by "A Graduate of Oxford." Painters, even Turner himself, received the volume coolly, but the new reading public liked it for its style and simplicity. At twenty-four, just out of college, Ruskin found himself famous.

He took his first Continental trip without his parents in 1845 and greatly increased his knowledge of Italian art. As he traveled he worked on the second volume of *Modern Painters* (1846) and introduced his new enthusiasm regarding things Italian. In April of 1848 he married Euphemia Gray, who was ten years younger, because the two families wanted to gain a son and a daughter. The marriage was arranged by the parents on both sides and from the beginning was not a good one. There was no love between them, even though they traveled together, attended social events, and were often seen in public as a happy couple. Practicing hypocrisy by keeping up appearances was common at the time, and they were not exempt. As the weeks passed he began to lose himself in the study of Gothic architecture, while she enjoyed social popularity. During 1849, after publishing *Seven Lamps of Architecture*, and also for a time in 1850 they lived in Venice where Ruskin began *The Stones of Venice*. In 1851 he published the first volume of this impressive work with limited success, partly because the illustrations made the book too expensive for the average buyer. Enthusiastic response came from Carlyle, who staunchly agreed with the thesis that a people's architecture closely parallels its morality. Also in 1851, the year that Turner died, Ruskin became the champion of the Pre-Raphaelite artists and wrote powerful letters in their support. In 1851 came another crisis. The "dreadful hammers" of the professional geologists began to chip away at his faith in the dogmatic, uncompromising religion instilled by his parents.

In 1853 he published two more volumes of *Stones* and spent several weeks with his wife in the company of John Everett Millais, the Pre-Raphaelite painter. Euphemia and Millais developed a relationship, which they did not attempt to hide. The following year Ruskin's marriage was annulled on grounds that it had never been consummated. A year later Effie married Millais. Again Ruskin went on tour with his parents, returned to London to become interested in the newly founded Working Men's College, gave some lectures on art there, and reached the end of an epoch in his life. From 1854 until near the end of his life he would dedicate himself to social and economic criticism. He was thirty-five at the time and deeply upset over the way his personal life was going. In 1858 he met Rose La Touche, a child only nine years old, and fell tragically in love with her. The same age as Dante's Beatrice, some think she may not have been a real person at all. They argue that Ruskin drew a painful parallel between himself and Dante as both men wait, not always patiently, for the objects of their unnatural love to grow up. Ruskin, they contend, may have manufactured the rose-like little girl with tactile appeal to ease the "unendurable solitude" and bring solace.

Yet tangible evidence of the girl's sad existence stands in the way of that theory. We know too much about her to view her simply as a figment of Ruskin's imagination. She was a strange and brilliant child often quite perceptive in her discussions of life and art with the master. As she entered adolescence she understood the special power she held over Ruskin and sometimes flaunted it. She played word games with him and games of wit and led him on flirtatiously. At length she came to know that he was desperately in love with her. In 1865, the year he published *Sesame and Lilies*, she refused to marry him. In 1869 she refused him again, primarily because he was not orthodox in religion while she had developed an almost morbid religious fervor. During the 1860's allusions to Rosie came unbeckoned into his books, but her fullest portrait is to be found in *Præterita*, the rambling yet beautiful autobiography written after he lost her. After her second rejection of him for a time they broke off relations, but in 1870 they were reconciled. The strange friendship continued until Rosie died insane at twenty-six in 1875. Afterward Ruskin himself began to suffer intervals of mental illness.

With the legacy left by the death of his father in 1864, Ruskin had become independently wealthy but had suffered pangs of guilt and self-reproach. His mother died at the age of ninety in 1871, leaving him with feelings of emptiness from which he never recovered. While his attitude toward his father had been ambivalent, he viewed his mother as a fountain of strength and the source of all that was good in his life. He was unable to see that her relentless domination had warped him emotionally, had perhaps made him unfit to be a husband. In 1875 the girl of his dreams, the person who had toyed with his affection for seventeen years, died a tortured and untimely death. Never entirely stable, the loss of the three people he loved most in the world left Ruskin shaken and miserable. In addition to the emotional distress, enormous labor in many fields of interest was beginning to undermine his health. Another thorn to rend and tear was the unpopularity of his economic theories. Then in 1877 when it seemed he was mending, James Whistler sued him for libel. He was fined only one farthing, but the conflict drained him terribly. In 1878 he suffered the first of seven attacks of madness to be experienced over the next decade. In the autumn of 1889 he was broken by the most damaging of all attacks and wrote nothing thereafter. Except for short periods of lucidity, he was mentally deranged for the last fifteen years of his life. He died at eighty-one of influenza early in 1900.

As an art critic Ruskin was often fresh and original. Yet even in the books on art and architecture perceptive readers could see the influence of Carlyle. As he shifted to social criticism in 1854 and thereafter, the influence was even more obvious. Even though the autobiography minimizes the master's influence, it is apparent that in much of his thinking he was a disciple of the older and stronger thinker. A comparison of the two should tell us much about Ruskin and at the same time refresh our memory of Carlyle. It will help us see, I believe, the impact of Carlyle's thought upon a sensitive person of the younger generation.

- Ruskin's theory of art was shaped by a moral though not entirely religious bias. So was Carlyle's. Ruskin believed that art in the best sense had to body forth a moral message; the idea of art for art's sake was anathema to him. Carlyle believed the artist was an agent of God, expressing the promptings of the Divine Idea, and interpreting God to all of us. Fra Lippo Lippi expressed this same belief in Browning's poem by the same title.

- Ruskin closely associated beauty with godliness or goodness and ugliness with evil. Beauty he thought came from order, form, structure. Ugliness had no form, no shape, no unity, and no meaning. For Carlyle evil was rampant chaos and disorder. Goodness or blessedness came from control, from orderly and structured work or activity that brought one closer to God. Evil could be conquered, or at least held at bay, by means of hard work.

- In *Past and Present* Carlyle insisted that the twelfth century in many respects was better than the nineteenth, mainly because that century was characterized by a vital and unifying faith. Ruskin accepted that idea and preached that the Middle Ages were a better period in history than modern times. In *Modern Painters* he saw a principle of unity and obedience in the paintings of the Middle Ages, but in modern paintings that principle had been replaced by a false concept of liberty. In medieval paintings not a cloud lacked an angel, but too many modern paintings, produced in the confusion of a secular society, showed a total absence of faith.

- According to Carlyle's theory of history, periods of vital faith alternate with periods of denial and disunity. Periods of faith are splendid while periods of denial are barren. Ruskin applied that idea to the art and architecture of a people, and said that an age of living faith would produce great art while a period of unbelief would produce only facsimiles or fragments. In two major works, *Seven Lamps* and *Stones of Venice,* he held that a people's architecture expressed its ethical and moral standards.

- Carlyle's theory of history helped Ruskin formulate other ideas dealing with art and faith. In *Stones of Venice* Ruskin stressed the theme that vital art comes from vital faith. The Middle Ages had such faith and therefore produced the magnificent architecture of the great Gothic cathedrals. As that faith faded during the Renaissance, pride and infidelity began to show in the architecture. In the Victorian Era no great art is possible because no great faith exists to sustain it. He views the nineteenth century, therefore, as a dormant seedbed for a more vital era to emerge at a later date.

- Students of Ruskin are often surprised and perplexed to learn that he favored the Middle Ages above the bustling Renaissance. Yet his reasons for doing so are clear enough. He believed the revival of learning that took place during the Renaissance brought skepticism that undermined and ultimately destroyed the faith of the Middle Ages. Renaissance art reflected this loss of faith. Instead of painting the souls of men and women, the great artists of the Renaissance with wonderful skill painted mere bodies. Ruskin's view of the Renaissance is consistent with his idea of history, and yet not wholly convincing. The new artists believed that a beautiful body inevitably reflects a beautiful soul. Browning viewed the art of the Middle Ages as sterile in comparison to the passionate art of the Renaissance. Fra Lippo Lippi's great aim in life is to paint men and women as he sees them; he complains that he is tired of painting saints and more saints.

- Carlyle had praised Dante and Shakespeare as hero-figures in the guise of poets. Intensity was Dante's dominant quality while Shakespeare had a deep and penetrating "calmly seeing eye." Ruskin affirmed this evaluation and called Dante the most intense of poets. Shakespeare, he said, was able to "keep his eyes fixed firmly on the pure fact." That phrase, if not a verbatim repetition of the one used by Carlyle, echoes it. Ruskin also claimed both Shakespeare and Dante were great poets because they thought strongly, felt strongly, and saw truly. That placed them in the first rank of poets.

- Also in the lecture on Dante and Shakespeare as heroes, Carlyle asserted that all deep thought is musical. Ruskin interpreted this to mean that any literary style based on deep thought would show itself as lyrical and musical. Therefore, his own style is often so musical, so regular in its meter, that one is able to scan it as though it were poetry. In fact much of his writing is a kind of prose poetry. One example from *Sesame and Lilies* (note the poetic title) will suffice: "Let her loose in the library, I say, as a fawn in a field." Note the use of alliteration, a device usually reserved for poetry. Note also the pause or cæsura breaking the rhythmic progress of the line. Though prose, it is also a line of verse. One may find numerous such examples scattered through his writings. The style as well as the content of *Modern Painters* made him a celebrity at twenty-four.

- Carlyle's influence remained strong even when Ruskin had moved away from art criticism to focus on the social and economic problems of the day. Ruskin's economic theories reflect the presence of his master so thoroughly that perceptive Victorian readers saw them mainly as warmed-over Carlyle. Yet Ruskin wondered why his theories had not become popular, and gradually grew bitter when he thought no one was listening. In several important books that targeted cash payment and laissez-faire, Carlyle attacked the "classical economics" of Adam Smith and David Ricardo. He also attacked the law of supply and demand with its evil of "over production" when millions in the world had not even a shirt to call their own. In *Munera Pulveris* and *Unto This Last* Ruskin continued Carlyle's vigorous attack, citing the worst practices of the political economists and branding them as intolerable. He was against cash payment, laissez-faire, and buy-cheap-sell-dear profiteering. Many thought his position was admirable, but they were not able to acclaim Ruskin as a great thinker or leader. They liked his lucid, poetic style but the substance of his work, the ideas that propelled it, they had heard before from a stronger voice already established.

- In *Past and Present* Carlyle had denounced the jerry building that had grown to monstrous proportions after the Industrial Revolution. He claimed this shoddy practice required London to be rebuilt every seventy years, but if you build the city once in the right way with good materials, and it will last a thousand years. In the "Lamp of Sacrifice" of *Seven Lamps* Ruskin also attacked the practice of competitive building. When buildings are thrown up at the lowest bid, they lack the integrity of good materials and careful workmanship. They grow old and ugly fast and have to be rebuilt too soon. In spite of these cautionary remarks, the practice of building shoddy structures rapidly and cheaply continued for years and years. Economic forces stronger than the voices of protest were behind the practice.

- Carlyle lamented the ugly streets in the cities and the ugly villages in the country brought on by industrialism. He complained about the dirt and the pall of pollution (soot and grime) that cloaked the cities. He urged the Captains of Industry to clean up the mess or see their children suffer later. In the *Crown of Wild Olive* Ruskin spoke out fiercely against the ugly, filthy, soot-choked cities with reeking, unsanitary gutters and iron fences that collected rubbish in the wind. In 1872 he organized a street-sweeping campaign and wielded a broom himself. He made practical road repairs with the help of his Oxford students. He gave much of his precious time to the St. George's Company, established "to slay the dragon of Industrialism." Writing in protest was for him a prelude to action.

- In *Past and Present* Carlyle had said that employer-employee relations had to be founded on fraternalism, not mere cash payment. It had to be founded on a principle of love, not antagonism. In *Unto This Last* Ruskin also advocated love as a motive force in management-labor relations. He condemned as nonsense the notion that antagonism between the parties is natural, and insisted there should be a principle of cooperation to replace antagonism. The employer should be a benevolent man willing to look after his employees in the same way a good military officer looks after his men. For Carlyle's idea of fraternalism (brother working with brother) Ruskin substituted paternalism (a father-son relationship). To his credit, it was paternalism that later caught on and seemed to soften some employers who had listened earlier to Smith and Ricardo.

- The workhouse, as we know already, was an abomination that Carlyle despised. It was a quack remedy replete with gross insults to the dignity of human beings. He never tired of attacking the workhouse, nor did Ruskin. In *Sesame and Lilie,* Ruskin cried out against the infamous workhouse as fiercely as Carlyle ever did. To illustrate his points he gave a moving account of the poor refusing to enter the workhouse, preferring to die as free vagabonds in the streets. The unemployed of the working class had become victims of persecution by a legitimate institution supported by the government. The middle class, in a position to correct the sorry scheme of things, was too busy worshipping the Goddess of Getting-On to pay much attention. Dickens also hated the workhouse and spoke out fervently against it.

- In a world become increasingly noisy, Carlyle praised silence as noble and divine. A testy critic, hitting upon that theory, described his collected works as "thirty volumes in praise of silence." In *Sesame and Lilies* Ruskin advised his audience to follow and obey this doctrine of silence in the presence of great books. Throughout the century libraries and hospitals were devoted to silence. Oxford University and the British Museum were emblematic of peace and quiet. In our time the practice has become only a memory and the doctrine has been tossed upon the scrap heap of history as unworkable and old-fashioned. Hospitals in these times are often more noisy and more congested than Main Street. Libraries have become "media centers" and rival the hustle and bustle of department stores. What has come to be called "noise pollution" most Americans don't appear to notice, though recently a law was passed to reduce by a few decibels the blather of ever-increasing television commercials.

• Carlyle's doctrine of work was eagerly accepted as a religious creed by his disciples, and all of them labored prodigiously. Ruskin as a writer produced nine volumes more than the master. In the third essay of *Sesame and Lilies* he paid high praise to the doctrine of work and urged its application to women as well as to men. Children could also work but not the many hours required of them by factories and mines. In the 1870's young women welcomed such remarks, for many of them eagerly wanted to work. He was never their champion, however, because his view of woman's role, like Tennyson's, was based on inverse flattery, which put women on pedestals but not in the workplace. Woman was seen as man's helpmate, as the angel in the house, and her work was to be done in the home. Mill, as you remember, felt otherwise; but neither Carlyle nor Ruskin were in sympathy with Mill's liberal view of woman's place in the world.

• In the essay "Characteristics" and in *Sartor Resartus* Carlyle had said that human beings can never reach the perfection of the Divine Idea, but that should not deter them from trying. He urged his contemporaries to strive for perfection and struggle toward it. Through struggle all persons could improve themselves and achieve blessedness even while falling short of perfection. Ruskin's "philosophy of the imperfect" stems from that idea. Man is surely no god and will never be able to achieve perfection, but when he struggles toward that goal his talents improve, and he turns out work of high quality. The imperfections in the product of a good workman are desirable because they give proof of this struggle. Browning took this idea and applied it to art in the poem "Andrea del Sarto," a companion piece to "Fra Lippo Lippi." The idea of struggle, which became in time a master idea of the period, he treated more fully in "Rabbi ben Ezra." In several poems by Tennyson these same ideas are brought forward.

- In almost all his writings Carlyle had emphasized the principle of obedience. In the "Lamp of Obedience" of *Seven Lamps of Architecture* Ruskin expressed similar social and political ideas that recognized the power of this principle. During the Middle Ages, he asserted, such a principle helped to make for unity and security in dangerous times. Every person, even the king himself, had some other person above him and knew exactly his place in society. In the nineteenth century obedience to another (except in the case of wives) had almost disappeared, and so the architecture of the Middle Ages could never be surpassed by that of the nineteenth.

- A final similarity in the thought of these two Victorian thinkers is the belief that every country must have a strong central government run by the wisest men. We call this form of government an oligarchy, and we have tried to achieve its ideal through the democratic process. But as Carlyle feared, democracy doesn't seem to work toward that end. The democratic process tends to produce leaders not much better than the people who elect them. That is why Carlyle and Ruskin distrusted democracy. Both believed that leaders should not be of the people but well above them. Mill could not accept this idea because he believed that rule by the strong man could lead to a dictatorship that would ultimately suppress individual freedom. He believed, too, that in any country where freedom is suppressed the people will eventually rise up at high cost to demand their rights.

Modern Painters (1843-1860) — This work by Ruskin was published in five volumes over a period of almost twenty years. Volume I (1843) was a defense of J. M. W. Turner against those critics who had said that his pictures were not true to nature. Ruskin contended that the critics had formed their ideas concerning nature without looking at nature. Then he showed that the sea, sky, and mountains are really like those of Turner. The volume is not only a defense of Turner, but also a general examination of the whole subject of landscape painting. Ruskin's purpose was to place English landscape painters, especially Turner, on a plane above the Italian and French favorites. Yet much of the work praises the landscapes of Renaissance painters in Italy. He stated his thesis this way: "The picture which is looked to for an interpretation of nature is invaluable, but the picture which is taken as a substitute had better be burned." In Turner he found an interpretation of nature that revealed majesty, infinity, mystery, and divinity. Beauty and nobility, he declared, are the chief criteria for judging great art. The first comes from sensing the hidden perfection in the world and in man. The second is reflected in the execution of the painting itself and reflects a nobility of mind and heart. Ruskin preached that great art could come only from good persons with large souls seeing nature undistorted. That theory was questioned near the end of the century, even rejected as the "art for art's sake" movement gathered momentum. An evil man could write a good book, it was argued, and a man without soul could paint a good picture.

Volume II (1846) develops this idea further. All art by its very nature is moral, and a person without morality will never be capable of producing great or even significant art. In this volume he enters into an explanation of the principles of art with emphasis on the view that nature is from God, and art can only interpret nature. Then in a lengthy digression he discusses Tintoretto. These digressions seem to be part of his method. Some of his finest and most impressive passages are found at the end of avenues leading away from the main topic.

Latter-day psychologists have seen these digressions as mental flaws that hint of future derangement, but that is the kind of nonsense unimaginative little minds often produce. An eccentric young man's estimate of the popular painters of the day, the book was deliberately unorthodox in style, method, and substance. The unique style was verbal and poetic, moving and beautiful, and often quotable. Each section Ruskin slowly read aloud to his parents and to his cousin Mary. At times the doting listeners shed tears of joy.

The method was to bring forth an abundance of rich imagery: the mountains, lakes, and castles he had seen on his travels. And if by association of ideas he chose to take a little side trip, the reader was expected to come along for the ride and for some interesting discoveries. The essence of the book, Ruskin's considered opinion of one English artist, swiftly became a comprehensive treatise on the principles of great art.

Volume III (1856) is mainly a digression. In this volume he discusses the grand style in literature. He maintains that the grand style is not general and abstract, but given to the particular and the sensuous. The grand style is as deep and clear as a mountain stream and as pure. Idealism must dominate to impart meaning to the artistic experience. It must generate within the viewer or the reader a more lofty sense of virtue and a keener ethical standard. The artist is therefore the best preserver of moral standards. Also in this volume Ruskin discusses the changing attitudes toward landscape through the ages. Within the general digression is a more compact digression on the Crimean War, which was going on as Ruskin was writing. What did he think of war? No war is worth the cost in human lives. Reasonable people should learn to avoid going to war, though at times it may seem the only solution. Then comes the very important digression, "Of the Pathetic Fallacy." This is the part of Volume III that is most often printed in anthologies and discussed in classrooms today. The digression also received attention in the 1850's. Some of his contemporaries called its label deliberately vague, cryptic, and suggestive of a subject not to be aired in polite society. In a separate discussion later on I will try to explain what Ruskin really meant by the phrase.

Volume IV (1856) takes up the technical subject of color in lakes, clouds, mountains, open skies, broad expanses and so on. It is rather technical throughout and less easy to read than its companion volumes. He discusses color in relation to the various countries of Europe, saying travelers scientists already knew that the color in southern countries differs in range and intensity than that of northern climes. In many respects this volume is also a hymn of praise to mountains, and to the

Alps in particular. He attempts to trace in less detail than usual the influence of mountains upon the psyche of the artist, poet, and writer. He is one with the Romantic poets in his feeling for mountains. Nature, he exclaims, is truly a great artist as she creates elemental forms of superb beauty for the enjoyment of mankind. Mill, who loved mountains too, would have said nature is unconscious as it creates beauty and has no mind to know whether mankind enjoys the beauty. As he rejoices in the beauty and majesty of the mountains, Ruskin thinks of the hard lives of mountain people. This could be a clue that by now he has become interested in social reform.

Volume V (1860) attempts to round out the discussion with a series of classifications. Ruskin likes to classify and gains as much pleasure from that device as Macaulay got from comparison. He sets up classes of the heroic, classical, pastoral, and contemplative painters. Then minutely he examines how these artists have interpreted and depicted natural objects. In his "investigation of the beauty of the visible world" he travels down a few byways and then returns to Turner and the Pre-Raphaelites. The work concludes with a lament for Turner who had died in 1851 after a long and lucrative career. He had become a Royal Academician nearly twenty years before his champion was born. He was famous and wealthy long before *Modern Painters* appeared. Ruskin did not discover Turner, but in the attempt to defend the artist against a few detractors he discovered himself.

His original intention was to praise and defend Turner, but as he became immersed in the subject a stern moral intention gained control of his talent. Increasingly he felt it was his duty to reform moral and ethical attitudes as they related to art, nature, and life. Two elements of a picture, he said, have the power to make it great; these are the picture's subject and its message. Its subject can never be low and its message must always be noble. A staunch middle-class Victorian, Ruskin insisted that every piece of art worth its name must teach and elevate. You don't look at a work of art merely to be amused or entertained. Greatness in an artist does not depend on his technical skill (cf. Browning's Andrea del Sarto), but in what his art communicates to the people who view it. Art in all its forms is therefore a vehicle of moral teaching. These ideas spawned a controversy on the subject of art and morality that was still going on at the end of the century. The "art for art's sake" movement of the last two decades of the century proclaimed that art had no moral responsibility whatever. Art could not endure being yoked to such an intricate burden, for its purpose was merely to exist.

That was the concept that motivated artists in the next century. Once in California I attended an art fair hoping to buy a painting for my living room. The first one to catch my eye was a huge vertical canvas the size of a door. The artist had used only two colors and had divided them a little lower than halfway down. At the top was a faded robin's-egg blue. The other color was a dirty yellowish-brown. Attached to a corner was a bright orange price tag with $500 scrawled on it in magic-marker black. That was it. I have described to you everything I saw. This thing masquerading as art conveyed no meaning other than a fuzzy impression of earth and sky.

The painter could have been saying that the world we live in is a dull and dingy place with only two poorly defined colors. Or perhaps he intended to say nothing. In my view, at least at the time, only the price tag made a statement. If I had been able to speak to him, he probably would have said that art holds a mirror up to life. If life is empty and without meaning, if the world is ugly, the art that reflects it will be the same. If your vision of our world were to jibe with his, you might willingly plunk down $500 for something any house painter could do in a few minutes, and yet I doubt it. Ruskin would have dismissed this attempt to bamboozle the public as not worth the frame you would have to buy for it. The work of art to be truly a work of art, even today, must show talent struggling to bring into the light an inner vision. Every artist should strive mightily to paint a picture beyond his power, for only in that way does he prove his worth. If they were among us now, the Victorians would be incensed by what passes for art in our time. But of course we live in a different time and such speculation is fruitless.

"Of the Pathetic Fallacy" — This famous chapter in Volume III of Ruskin's *Modern Painters* has occasioned more discussion than any other chapter. It is the chapter that is always anthologized whenever you find selections from his work. Crammed with vivid examples, the essay sets out to examine in great detail the difference between "the ordinary, proper, and true appearances of things" and the extraordinary or false appearances created by strong emotion or the imagination. These false appearances do not belong to the object itself but are assigned to it by either our fancy or our emotion. It is a pathetic fallacy, therefore, to suppose that inanimate objects have human qualities because these qualities exist only in the mind of the observer. The fallacy is represented by two principal types: the one of willful fancy illustrated by lines from Oliver Wendell Holmes, and the one caused by excitement of the feelings illustrated by lines from Charles Kingsley. In the first example Holmes speaks of the sensitive "spendthrift crocus" as "naked and shivering." Ruskin responds: "This is very beautiful, and yet very untrue. The crocus is not a spendthrift, but a hardy plant." In the second example Kingsley speaks of the rolling foam of the sea as "the cruel, crawling foam." Ruskin again responds: "The foam is not cruel, neither does it crawl. The state of mind which attributes to it these characters of a living creature is one in which the reason is unhinged by grief." The strong emotion makes this second example of pathetic fallacy more excusable than the first.

Even so, the greatest poets seldom resort to this kind of false impression. Only the second-rank poets seem to take delight in it. Then Ruskin explains that he is able to discern only two orders of poets and never a third. The first order (Shakespeare, Homer, Dante) is creative. The second (Wordsworth, Keats, Tennyson) is reflective or perceptive. All persons falling into the third rank are not poets regardless of their talents. True poetry cannot be called third-rate, and even second-rate poetry should not be published to burden the libraries of the world. Already there is more of the best than any person can read in a lifetime. Yielding to his love of classification, he categorizes the first rank of poets as those who feel strongly, think strongly, and see truly. The second rank is made up of those who feel strongly, think weakly, and see untruly. A third rank could be those who feel nothing and therefore see truly, but they are not poets. Those who submit to influences much stronger than they and see untruly because what they see is far above them are classified as prophets. They may not be called poets, and yet some poets may be called prophets.

His illustrations are always more interesting, though not more exciting, than the principles or theories being expounded. He quotes at length from a popular French poet (citing the stanzas without translation) who wrote of a beautiful girl preparing for a fancy-dress ball at the house of the French ambassador. The poet seems to be in the same room lovingly observing the girl and sharing her excitement as she puts the finishing touches on her costume. So long as he can watch and calmly sympathize, he records what he sees with great accuracy. But when his feelings get the best of him he veers from truth. Fully dressed and ready to depart, Constance admires herself in a mirror near the fireplace. Then to the horror of the observer a spark ignites her skirt. As soon as that happens, the second-rank poet begins to feel too strongly to see truly. Just when the girl becomes intoxicated with hope and joy, the fire consumes her. The poet imparts animate qualities to the fire and sees it as a beast devouring the girl and the abstract qualities close to her. "The horrible fire gnaws with voluptuousness, and without pity consumes her beauty, her eighteen years, alas, and her sweet dream!" When the crisis is over and calm is restored, the poet returns to his "pale and crystalline atmosphere of truth." The pathetic fallacy is said to be pathetic because it depends for its power upon pathos. It is fallacious and feeble because pathos such as that illustrated often warps the truth.

The Seven Lamps of Architecture (1849) — This work, one of Ruskin's most important books, is a digression from *Modern Painters*. He wrote it during the winter of 1848-1849 and published it in the spring. It made as great a sensation with the reading public as the first volume of the work from which it sprang. The book bristled with contradictions, paradoxes, and unfounded hypotheses, but was received enthusiastically as "the first treatise in English" to teach the significance of architecture in a nation's life. In the seven lamps of the title he developed the thesis that a people's architecture is an expression of their ethical standards and national life. Behind the rhetoric was a new theme that would eventually transform Ruskin from art critic to social prophet. Since the book was written during one of the century's most tumultuous years (1848), he could not avoid thinking about reform. It was the year of the Chartist petition in England and revolution in France, Germany, Italy, and Austria. It was also the year the *Communist Manifesto* was published in London. Yet Ruskin's book is primarily an extended hymn of praise on the beauty and noble style of Gothic architecture.

He theorizes that the lamps of sacrifice, truth, power, beauty, life, memory, and obedience illuminate all true art. Specifically the lamps are the leading principles of architecture as he sees them. They may also be called luminous principles to guide the footsteps of builders who wish not merely to make money, but to enrich the nation's values. Each lamp is carefully presented for consideration in a separate chapter, and that makes the book one of Ruskin's briefest and best-organized works. The chapter most often anthologized is "The Lamp of Memory" because there Ruskin examined the problems of restoring old buildings, and eventually the essay exerted a main influence upon the Gothic Revival in architecture. The enduring strength of that movement may be seen as late as our own century as new churches and new university buildings are erected in imitation of the Gothic. Throughout the book Ruskin praised the beauty and excellence of Gothic architecture, stressing as he did so the religious nature of great art.

"The Lamp of Sacrifice" — The title is suggestive of that kind of self-denial necessary to serve and honor one's God, or if not religious in a time of unfaith one's sacrificial energy may improve the condition of mankind. Sacrifice is the moral quality in building that prompts us to use costly materials simply because they are costly and the best. The principle applies to people who live in hovels and never have enough to eat but give all they have to build a magnificent church or town hall. It applies also to the workman who puts his all into his work, who goes beyond the requirements of mere function to make the building beautiful even in places where the human eye may never look. What, you may ask, is the good of ornament when no one will see it? Is it necessary to finish the bottom of a chair, that part which no one will ever see? Ruskin would answer that in doing so the workman is taking pride in his work and is aware that he is doing his best. That in turn brings him great satisfaction and the respect of others. The great cathedrals of Europe, as photographers have revealed in recent years, are often beautifully finished in places cloaked by semidarkness. The artisan believed no one would ever see his work, but that didn't mater. He saw it as he did it and after it was finished and took pride in it.

"The Lamp of Truth" — In this chapter Ruskin hits sham, pretense, concealment, and conceit in building. Here he praises structures honestly designed for the best use and built of the best materials. A good example of what he means by sham and pretense are those phony columns that don't hold up the roof but are themselves held up by the walls. Another example is the painting of wood to make it look like marble. He would not have liked the coloring of plastic to make it look like wood or metal or porcelain. He would be amazed at the phony bricks and tiles and ceiling beams, even artificial flowers, used for interior decoration today. Ornament of this sort, he insisted, is no good because it tells a lie. Yet few of us today are bothered by such materials in our homes. Is it because in a plastic age we have come to see plastic as useful, good, and at times even beautiful? A plastic fig tree never has to be watered, does not require sunlight, and never loses its beauty. Plastic Christmas trees are often more shapely than real ones, more fire retardant, and last longer. Ruskin, however, did not like synthetic materials and particularly machine-made ornaments. He maintained there was no individuality in them, nothing there to excite the mind. The creative workman using a machine could not express himself. When that happened, workers became merely extensions of machines.

"The Lamp of Power" — This chapter praises the majesty and the impressive dignity of buildings carefully erected. It urges architects to design buildings so as to impart to them a massive appearance against a background that makes the best use of shadow. The surroundings of a building and the way it reflects light and casts shadow are therefore important. A pyramid, for example, must not be placed in mountains; a low, flat structure will lose its identity on a desert. He complains that most of the buildings of the nineteenth century are false and like boxes. They may be functional, but simple and stark boxes have nothing aesthetically to recommend them. That statement may seem puzzling to you, for today the buildings we associate with Ruskin's time, the structures we call "gingerbread Victorian," are anything but boxy. Ornate to an excessive degree because of the Gothic Revival, they were inspired by Ruskin's praise of Gothic architecture. They represent an attempt to replace the boxy structures with a Victorian image of the Gothic. They copy some aspects of Gothic architecture because in later years Ruskin was able to convince planners, architects, and builders that such architecture was true, impressive, and powerful.

"The Lamp of Beauty" — In this chapter Ruskin, ever the Romantic, offers instruction to his readers as to what should inspire man-made art. Its beauty must come from nature, and only from nature. Buildings in every detail must be modeled after nature. Abundant ornamentation with no relation to natural form is grotesque. All beautiful lines, angles, planes come from nature. The pointed arch is derived from the termination of a leaf, and the lines of any beautiful building are seen in nature. Architecture that does not imitate nature is ugly and untrue, for man cannot imagine or create beauty without the aid of nature. "All most lovely forms and thoughts are directly taken from natural objects." His writings directly influenced Frank Lloyd Wright, perhaps the greatest of American architects, who went to nature for inspiration. In many of Wright's buildings you can see architectural images that are very similar to those in this book. He read the book during his formative years as an architectural thinker, and it shaped his theories concerning "organic architecture." Too often in books about Wright the influence of John Ruskin is given minimum notice.

"The Lamp of Life" — Here Ruskin says buildings are noble in proportion to how well they reflect the energy of the mind or spirit that created them. The surest sign of vitality in architecture, he asserts, is imperfection. The surest sign of the dead or dying is slavish, mindless imitation. Imperfection, as he defined it in his "doctrine of the imperfect," is the visible effort to execute more. It is characterized by unceasing struggle toward the unattainable, and it is very much on the side of life. Bold ingenuity gives life to a building, and so does the hard work of vibrant men working freely to produce their best. The workman lives fullest when he is creating. The medieval workman could freely depart from the master plan to invent as he worked. In so doing he left behind a part of his life in the building he helped to erect. Ruskin objects to Greek architecture because it is too perfect and too slavish. The Gothic by contrast is imperfect and infinitely variable.

"The Lamp of Memory" — In this chapter Ruskin develops the thesis that human beings may live without knowing a thing about architecture, but they cannot remember without architecture. A building should be a memorial of the life of the people who built it. A building should also memorialize the people who were born, lived, and died in it. Old buildings express and preserve the history and personality of a people, and thus have tremendous value. They are, or should be, lasting memorials of the lives of our ancestors, and that is why they should be preserved through the years. If restoration should become necessary, it must be accurate in every detail. If it is not, it will surely destroy the meaning of an old building, will destroy its history and the story it has to tell. The cathedrals of the Middle Ages, with significant stories to tell, were built to last a thousand years. Nineteenth-century buildings, in stark contrast, have no character and no integrity, are thrown up like boxes, and are not intended to last. Builders of the present, who care little for past or future, have to be taught that a good building honors the people who built it and perpetuates their memory. We have no right even to touch an old and beautiful building erected in a bygone era. Those who wish to preserve the legacy of the past frequently argue this last idea today. Their opponents love parking lots and fast cars and progress.

"The Lamp of Obedience" — This is the seventh lamp and the one that concludes the book. The number seems to have had a symbolic or mystical significance in Ruskin's mind, and he struggled with his own prolixity to limit the book to seven lamps. As he declares the need for common obedience, he shows himself once again a disciple of Carlyle. The statement also echoes Arnold's call for a principle of authority. In this chapter he states more fully his social and political faith in relation to architecture. He attacks the idea of unrestrained liberty for adults, as presented in Mill's *On Liberty*, saying there is no such thing in the universe. Everything in nature follows law. Obedience to law, not liberty, is the vital principle of the universe. Obedience in architecture requires the cooperation of many working together, and without that principle no order would be possible. Workers should be free as individuals, but if their work is to have an essential unity they must obey and be guided by a master plan. The Gothic architecture of the Middle Ages consistently observed this principle of obedience. Yet what passes for architecture in the nineteenth century does not obey any one principle. That is why England in confused times has no distinctive architecture, no distinctive art, and no clear understanding of good or bad.

The Stones of Venice (1851-1853) — This massive work in three volumes, written while *Modern Painters* was still in progress, is another digression. It takes the central idea of *Seven Lamps* and applies it to an analysis of the architecture of Venice from its founding to modern times. Its purpose is to glorify the type of architecture that developed in Venice during the city's greatest period, namely the Middle Ages. All three volumes glorify the excellence of Gothic architecture in contrast to what Ruskin calls "the pestilential art of the Renaissance." Gothic to his mind stands for virtue and faith while the Renaissance with its liberal rebirth of learning represents corruption, hypocrisy, a lack of obedience, and loose morality. He tells us that moral and spiritual changes down through the years are exactly mirrored in the architecture of Venice. When faith was at its peak, the Gothic architecture of the city was splendid. As faith declined during the Renaissance, the architecture yielded to an inferior style.

Volume I, published in the year of the Great Exhibition in the Crystal Palace, met with considerable controversy. The people attending the exhibition were asked to admire the huge palace of glass, a symbol of progress, even though its architecture ran counter to Ruskin's beliefs. In the "battle of styles" his championship of old Gothic rather than forward-looking Modern found little favor. Seeing much of his own thought in the volume and secretly pleased that a man with a mind to comprehend had listened to his teachings, Carlyle called the work a "true and excellent Sermon in Stones." Coming into their own as painters and poets and aware that Ruskin's influential voice supported their cause, the Pre-Raphaelites also praised the volume, accepting parts of it as their gospel.

The vivid chapter on St. Mark's cathedral in Volume II is the result of patient and exhaustive study, exact drawings, precise measurements, and copious notes. Practicing meticulous, indefatigable research, Ruskin ferreted out dates, sources, and origins of all parts of the cathedral, literally paying attention to individual stones. He invites the reader to observe carefully with him this building that has stood for seven hundred years, growing more beautiful with each passing year. He takes the reader by the elbow and points to scores of lovely and arresting features of the cathedral. He is careful to emphasize that it was built in Venice during the Middle Ages and is one of the finest achievements of that time.

Then he asks the reader to observe with him present-day Venice while keeping in mind the city's past glory. He points to the filthy streets, the run-down buildings, the idle, dirty, ill-mannered people, the vagrant children, and the ugly confusion of the scene. With vivid and powerful imagery he throws into contrast the period of faith when the cathedral was built with the period of unfaith that is the present. When a people lose their vital faith, he is saying, and devote themselves only to secular pleasures, they sink into degradation and lose vitality of expression. The inclusive architecture of the Middle Ages, he insists, was distinctive for its vitality of style and for its uniformity, and it also reflected the vitality of the people themselves.

"The Nature of Gothic" — Students of Ruskin agree that the most famous chapter in the entire work is this one in Volume II. Without delay he states his purpose: "I shall endeavor to give the reader in this chapter an idea, at once broad and definite, of the nature of Gothic architecture, not that of Venice only but of universal Gothic." The essence of Gothic architecture, underscored for the reader to remember, is vitality. "Pointed arches do not constitute Gothic, nor vaulted roofs, nor flying buttresses, nor grotesque sculptures; but all or some of these things when they come together so as to have life." This came about mainly because medieval workmen were free to use their own minds, their own invention or creativeness, in their own way. Before pursuing this idea further, he lists in order of their importance some Gothic elements to be found in a beautiful building and the characteristics in the builder they suggest to one who observes carefully:

The Building —	The Builder —
• Savageness	• Strength, rudeness
• Changefulness	• Love of change
• Naturalism	• Love of nature
• Grotesqueness	• Disturbed imagination
• Rigidity	• Obstinacy
• Redundancy	• Generosity

After presenting the list he cautions his readers that removing one or two characteristics will not destroy the Gothic identity of a building, but removing several will change it into something that can't be called Gothic.

Later in the chapter Ruskin discusses three major types of ornamentation: servile, constitutional, and revolutionary. What would you say are their qualities and how do they differ? The first type, *servile ornament*, is characterized by the workman entirely subjected to the intellect of the master planner. The Greek architect, for example, made the design and trained inferior minds to execute it perfectly. This practice left no room for thinking on the part of the workers. They were slaves literally and figuratively because their bosses owned their minds as well as their bodies. The English workman, though he would certainly deny it, is also enslaved. The modern system of assembly lines and division of labor, which forces a person to work in a very limited and mindless way, has made him a slave. It has taken away all possibility for the use of the human faculties in performing the job.

The second, *constitutional ornament*, is that type in which the workman is free and independent. He has a will of his own and has no fear of exercising it. Yet he renders nevertheless obedience to those above him. This is the type of ornamentation that originated and developed in the late Middle Ages when the workman was free and had a common Christian faith with other workmen. Even though Christianity confesses human imperfection, it has always recognized the value of each person. Human imperfection was painful to the Greeks and the Assyrians, but the Christian of later times contemplates the fact without fear or chagrin.

The third, *revolutionary ornament*, is that type in which no inferiority on the part of the workman is ever admitted at all. Inferior detail therefore gains importance because the persons executing every minor portion are required to exhibit skill and knowledge as great as that possessed by the master. In the attempt to endow the workmen with such expertise the powers of the masters become overwhelmed, "and the whole building becomes a wearisome exhibition of well-educated imbecility." This third type is the dominant type of the Renaissance when religious strife and lack of faith brought into existence many styles of helter-skelter architecture. The type reflects the confusion and turmoil of the time.

In an important passage Ruskin insists that human beings were never intended to work with the accuracy of machines, were never meant to be perfect and precise in their work. Yet in the average English room – "look round this English room of yours" – one sees objects of perfection everywhere: perfect finishing, accurate moldings, unerring juxtaposition of wood and steel. These symbols of perfection are signs of slavery more degrading than the African slave or the Greek helot. Perfect work makes the workman with mind and imagination little more than a machine. Division of labor divides not the labor but the man. Workers in the nineteenth century have become mere hands (mill hands, factory hands), and their dull, repetitive work requires no use of mental faculties. The division has been carried so far, Ruskin complains, that a man is not considered capable of making even a pin or nail. He must exhaust his life making the head of a nail or the point of a pin. Here is what can be done about this sorry state of affairs:

- Never encourage the manufacture of articles where the workman is not allowed to employ some part of his own invention.

- Never demand perfection for its own sake, for that always involves mindless machine work and degrades the worker.

- Never encourage imitation or copying of any kind except to preserve old records, for that precludes creativeness.

- Never ignore creativeness or invention; look for it and then consider the execution and whether the workman is capable of it.

In subsequent paragraphs of *The Stones of Venice* we find the fullest statement in all his writings of his philosophy of the imperfect. His purpose is to apply the doctrine more broadly, not restricting it to architecture alone. His thesis he states in italics: *"No good work whatever can be perfect, and the demand for perfection is always a sign of a misunderstanding of the ends of art."* Not a thing that lives can be perfect for it is always in a state of change. Imperfection is essential to all that we know in life. Yet this should not deter us as we strive for perfection. We may never attain it, but at least we can try, and the struggle will make us grow. When a workman is given the freedom to work at the highest level he can achieve without pain, his quality of workmanship slowly but solidly improves. Through constant effort he develops into a better workman and a better person and produces in time superior work that marks a pious and moral society.

Unto This Last (1860) — This is the book that marks the change in Ruskin's career from art criticism to social, political, and economic criticism. As he observed the scene around him, it appeared that beauty was absent from the everyday life of his time. With so little beauty in the world surely the system that regulated modern life was at fault. Too much industrialism and the ugly grime of city slums seemed to be unmistakable symptoms not of progress and power, but of a world without joy. With this realization, his aesthetic philosophy gradually became a social theory that opposed laissez-faire economics, rationalistic theories in general, widespread materialism, and the empiricism of the new science. The inevitable consequence of this new mode of thinking was an intense desire to revamp society so that beauty and meaning would be available to all. The essays that make up *Unto This Last*, a treatise on wealth and its uses, were published first in *Cornhill Magazine* edited by Thackeray. They raised a firestorm of protest. Ruskin had planned eight altogether, but Thackeray was able to accept only four essays. Ruskin's former admirers were beginning to view his doctrines as explosive and dangerous. Yet when polled in 1906, the Labor Members of Parliament consistently replied that *Unto This Last* was one of the books that had influenced them most.

The title (Ruskin had a penchant for poetic titles) is taken from the biblical parable of the laborers in the vineyard: "I will give unto this last even as unto thee." When the book appeared serially in 1860, the life of the industrial worker was scarcely above the animal level of brute survival. Made angry by this fact, Ruskin attacked every principle cherished by the industrialists of the age. The initial uproar seems to have yielded to a conspiracy of silence. *Unto This Last* for more than a decade was deliberately ignored and virtually unread. Yet by 1910 one hundred thousand copies had been sold in England and several pirated editions had been printed in America. For the first book edition of 1862, he wrote a Preface in which he listed certain advancements that could be accomplished if the leadership of the nation would only listen. All that was needed was to apply the principles in the book to the economic system with a serious intent to change it. By so doing, the following improvements could revitalize the nation:

- Free government schools where children would learn habits of gentleness and justice and the calling by which to live. They would also learn habits of cleanliness and health, and would be trained to read and write.

- Government factories and workshops established in connection with the schools. These facilities would produce good articles but would not interfere with private enterprise except in the way of fair competition. Good work would be constantly maintained, and pure substances sold at all times. This would force private enterprise to raise the quality of its goods. It would also put pressure on private enterprise to offer fair wages and improved working conditions. Before the end of the century many experiments were conducted to test this theory. Ruskin himself opened a teashop in London that sold unadulterated products at low prices.

- Government factories would absorb all unemployed people and would eradicate low wage rates by giving the unemployed a fair and stable wage. If willing to work, they would be taught good jobs. If they should become sick, they would be cared for at government expense. But if they proved lazy and shiftless, they would be treated like prisoners and forced to work for no wages. This demand, particularly forcing people to work, was offensive to legislators and never adopted even though England passed into law a national health insurance to cover workers who became sick.

- The government would provide pensions for the old and destitute in such a way that no feeling of shame would be associated with the pension. It would be an "honorable provision" that would not erode human dignity. The elderly would be taken care of in special homes, and no stigma would be attached to those places. National insurance in England and social security in the United States are presently both in effect to supply pensions to those who earned them by working for years before retirement.

In this Preface Ruskin tells us that the central purpose of his book is to give an accurate and stable definition of wealth and show how the acquisition of wealth is entirely possible without breaking moral codes. Wealth can be obtained under conditions of honesty, justness, and fellowship. One does not have to trample others or deal in shady practices to acquire wealth. And the prize even greater than the wealth is to know you acquired it all without hurting a single person and without compromising moral standards.

"The Roots of Honor" — This first essay of *Unto This Last* is the one most often read today. It advocated righteousness over self-interest and ideals over materialism in matters dealing with labor. It also called for gentle paternalism to replace the conflict so often found between employer and employee. Ruskin asserts that social and economic reforms can be accomplished only when there is genuine fondness of feeling, love, as a motive force, not mere self-interest or making a profit. Modern political economy, he says, has founded "an osssifiant theory of progress" upon negation of a worker's soul. This is the source of managerial failure because if a man is an engine, his motive power is the soul. The largest quantity of work will be done by "this curious engine" not for pay and not under pressure, but by the affection of the person employing the engine. This is a forceful statement of Ruskin's idea of mutual respect as a motive force in relations between employer and employee. A genuine concern for the welfare of all workers will help reduce antagonism. Labor and management will prosper not through the old antagonism, but through a more natural affection for one another.

In a passage that incited considerable controversy Ruskin calls for equality of wages for good and bad workmen alike. He argues that the natural and right system is when the good worker is employed and the bad worker unemployed. The false and destructive system is when the bad worker is able to offer his work at half price, and thus take the good worker's job or force his wages downward. Workers should be induced to take wages in the form of a fixed salary, and so enjoy year-round work instead of high wages that could mean layoffs and seasonal work.

Then carefully he examines the roots of honor of the merchant, or manufacturer, by classifying him with the soldier, preacher, physician, and lawyer. His purpose is to show that the merchant can be equally as dedicated. The public honors these professionals because they are not driven by self-interest; they work for the good of the public at large. By contrast the merchant has been thought to work only for his own good, and for this reason has not been honored by society. If, however, the merchant can be brought to value profits less and take on the important duty of providing for society, all people will honor him. Commerce will then become a respectable vocation that will lure thousands of talented young men into its ranks, and they will produce excellent results.

Near the conclusion of "The Roots of Honor" Ruskin focuses upon four ways in which the merchant can live up to his responsibilities and thus establish for himself and his descendants an honorable reputation:

- Produce only good goods, the best he can at reasonable prices.

- Look after his men as he would a son (paternalism).

- Keep his contracts regardless of what happens from day to day.

- Blame only himself for any setbacks or failures.

- Balanced with these four goals are the four main points of the essay:

- Equal pay for equal work, good and bad workers alike.

- Affection, not antagonism, between employer and employee.

- Fixity of wages and steady work even during slack seasons.

- Roots of honor found in honesty, service, and hard work.

"The Veins of Wealth" — In this second essay of *Unto This Last*, Ruskin takes on the Benthamites as he draws a clear distinction between two kinds of economy. He places his own economic theories under the heading of "political economy," the phrase much used by his opponents. Their views he labels "mercantile economy" because in his opinion the economic system preferred by the Benthamites has never been a bona fide political economy. It has always been, he insists, a selfish mercantile economy concerned only with the accumulation of wealth in the hands of a few. But his brand of economics, contributing mainly to the wealth of the state rather than a handful of individuals, is a true political economy. Then he poses and answers several questions. Since the essence of wealth consists in power over people, will not wealth further increase when the number of people increases? Will not wealth increase as people learn to do their jobs better, come to love their jobs, and so produce more? Will not wealth also increase as people improve themselves and thus become more valuable? Possibly the citizens themselves will be found in the final judgment to be the most durable wealth of a nation. In fact it may be seen, if one is willing to look into the matter, that the true veins of wealth are purple. These veins are not to be sought after in rock, but in connection with the vital blood stream of the people.

"The Veins of Wealth" alarmed not a few people with its exposition of socialistic views. Ruskin would replace capitalism (which makes only a few rich) with socialism (which distributes the wealth to all). In the latter system the workers who produce get their fair share of the wealth. Those who do not produce find themselves earning nothing or very little. Even though he may be called a socialist, Ruskin's socialism differs extensively from that of Karl Marx. He is at heart a Christian while Marx discounted religion altogether. Marx's theories appealed to one's sense of logic, but did little to stir the imagination. Ruskin, always a dyed-in-the-wool Romantic, calls upon the reader's sense of vision. Marx argued that all workers to a person are motivated by self-interest, and the populace may be divided into the haves and the have-nots. Ruskin attacks and rejects the notion of self-interest and material gain as motive force, and he asserts that love and affection rather than confrontation and violence can bring more lasting change.

Sesame and Lilies (1865/1871) — If one can say *Unto This Last* is the best example of Ruskin's work as a social critic, this book with an equally poetic title rapidly became one of his most popular. The book was well received and eagerly read, especially by women. It is made up of two essays delivered as lectures in 1864 (the year his father died) and published in the first edition of 1865. A third essay was delivered in 1868 and included in the second edition in 1871. The three essays now comprise the standard edition of the book. The title is rhythmic and memorable but not very clear. The term "sesame" is taken from the well-known phrase "open sesame" in the *Arabian Nights*, and means "open your minds to the treasure to be found in books and libraries." Ruskin chose the word to indicate that his lecture would deal with the cultivation of the spirit that is possible to one who opens the door to the secrets of literature. The person who can read a good book rightly has an open sesame to all the utterance of the wise and great. As indicated by the motto from Lucian, he also had another thought in mind. The sesame-cake promised in *The Fishermen* is bait to lead one to a simpler and more rewarding life.

It seems obvious that Ruskin has a similar meaning in mind. His aim is to urge his listeners to forsake the restless pursuit of earning, spending, and gathering for the life of the mind. That he believes is ultimately more rewarding than anything materialism or commercialism can offer. The term "lilies" is synonymous with the flower-like beauty of womanhood. It refers to the second essay of the book, and that essay Ruskin wrote especially for women. This second one accounted in large part for the positive reception of the book. Women bought the book for the essay meant for them and read it from cover to cover. Though avid readers and general believers in Ruskin, they did not always agree with him. These first two essays address themselves to the value of reading books in a crass commercial society. The third, often said to be the best of the three, denounces materialism, selfishness, and mindless competition. But there is much more in the book than merely this. It is a sweeping censure of his times based on the theme that people seem to care little for the true values of human life. They do not seem to know how to work together in brotherhood to help improve their lives. They seem unwilling to struggle even to secure their own happiness.

Ruskin scorns the vulgarity of the times and the crassness of common life. He says books can do little for people who place money above everything else. In the rush to make money they tell themselves they don't have time to read, and when they do read it's simply for escape or entertainment. However, if libraries were state-supported and free for the use of anyone, more and more people would make their way to them and begin to read good books. The mere idea of having free access to books would encourage them, and the free public libraries would also release the printed word from the control of commercial enterprises. The lending libraries that supply books for profit would no longer have the power to shape public taste.

Clearly he has in mind Mudie's Select Library which could often make or break an author with the decision either to buy his books or not. In effect Mudie's wielded rights of censorship over authors and would-be authors. If they chose not to buy a new book, as was often the case with authors such as George Gissing, that often meant very low sales for a struggling publishing house and a hard time for the author. Some novelists therefore crafted all their books with Mudie's in mind, paying careful heed to the rumor that Mudie never condoned any book that brought a blush to a maiden's cheek. Any book that could not be read aloud by a father surrounded by nubile daughters in the comfort of the family setting was seen as suspect and usually turned down. Ruskin thought it ludicrous that businessmen should have the power, though not the expertise, to arbitrate the contents of books.

"Sesame: of Kings' Treasuries" — This is the first essay of *Sesame and Lilies,* a slender volume which restored his popular acclaim. Delivered as a lecture in the town hall at Rusholme on December 6, 1864, it is intended primarily for men. The introduction plainly states his purpose: "I want to speak to you about the treasures hidden in books; and about the way we find them, and the way we lose them." He will not attempt to treat the subject exhaustively. His intention is merely to bring before his listeners "a few simple thoughts about reading," ideas that press themselves upon him each day as he sees the expansion of public knowledge. He will pull no punches as he attacks the spread of shallow, blotching, blundering, infectious information frequently called public education. Most people, he declares, read not for the development of the mind or spirit, but for "advancement in life," but what does that mean? Does it not mean becoming conspicuous in life, attaining a position whereby others will notice you? Is that not really the gratification of vanity motivated by love of praise? The sailor, guided by self-interest as he does the scut work on his ship, wants to be made captain so as to be called "Captain" by all the other men on the ship. The clergyman's fond ambition as he studies to become a bishop is to be called "My Lord" by all the people in his village. Is that a proper stimulus for reading books far into the night? Ruskin answers No, saying the people in both examples are reading to vent ambition in most cases and losing themselves in self-delusion. Then as he quickly returns to books and reading, he says it's all right to dream.

Again yielding to his penchant for classifying, he tells his audience that all books are divisible into two classes. They are the books of the hour and those for all time. A book is written because the author has something to say which he perceives to be true and useful and even beautiful. He chooses his subject and writes because no one else has yet written about it as he will. He is bound to write clearly and melodiously if he can (note the influence of Carlyle). If he can't write with a musical rhythm, at the very least he must write clearly. He puts on paper the best that is within him, saying: "This is the best of me. For the rest, I ate and drank, slept, loved and hated. This, if anything of mine, is worth your memory."

That is what Ruskin calls a book, and books of that kind have been written in all ages by great leaders, great statesmen, and great thinkers. What is so remarkable is that they have been preserved and are available to anyone who wishes to apply the necessary effort to read them. But life is short (you have heard that before) and if you read this, you will not have time to read that. The choice in these free times is left to the individual. Will you go and gossip with your housemaid or stable boy when you could take the same time to visit with kings? Will you jostle with the common crowd on a grimy street when this high-minded court is open to you? Inside among those gifted with the best minds the world has ever produced, you will find companions who will lift you to their level. Your place in the society of the living, the here and now, will be measured by your place in the company of those who came and went before you, leaving their legacy behind.

In the opening paragraphs Ruskin discusses reading and how to benefit from the treasures found in books. In the closing paragraphs he enters upon a severe indictment of Victorian England. A great nation, he avers, does not work itself into a frenzy over the sordid details of a legal trial that involves the murder of one ruffian by another. A nation claiming a conscience does not stand by and watch a friendly nation destroy itself internally. The allusion is to the American Civil War (1861-1865). In general England sided with the South, but offered no aid to either side. A nation calling itself great does not send little boys to jail for stealing walnuts and yet allow bankrupts and bankers to steal hundreds of thousands and go free. It does not go to war to force another nation to import a deadly drug, an allusion to the "opium wars" between Britain and China (1840-1850). It does not allow the lives of its poor to be rotted out of them by untreated disease or by want of a crust of bread. It does not court the friendship of a butcher who kills young girls in their fathers' sight, a reference to sending a new ambassador to an oppressive Russian regime. And finally, a great nation does not pretend to believe money is the root of all evil while motivated in all that it does by the love of money and the pursuit of money and spending money.

Ruskin concludes his lecture/essay by saying that a nation cannot last as a money-making mob. It cannot go on despising literature, science, art, nature, and human compassion. It cannot endure if it continues to concentrate its soul on money and nothing else. "Do you think these are harsh or wild words? Have patience with me but a little longer. I will prove their truth to you, clause by clause." Then separately he argues each point. Literature? We care nothing about books. Even wise people are forgetting that if a book is worth reading, it is worth buying. Science? Advances have been made, but we have surrendered Arctic exploration to other nations. Art? We have art exhibitions and art schools, but a nation that would take every other nation's bread out of its mouth is not capable of great art. Nature? The most beautiful places in the world we scarcely notice, and we continue to exploit nature: putting railroad bridges over superb natural falls, tunneling through delicate cliffs, filling every quiet valley in England with foundries that belch fire, polluting the air and the ground with coal dust, and building ugly resort hotels in the midst of grand natural scenery. We despise compassion? To prove this point he quotes from a newspaper the stark account of a cobbler who died of starvation even though he and his son worked around the clock to make a living. Why did the man not go to the workhouse? Because he preferred to die rather than go there. The English despise simple human compassion, for they will not see that their poor have enough to eat. When a nation ignores all that is truly of value, how can it possibly survive?

"Lilies: of Queens' Gardens" — This is the second essay of *Sesame and Lilies*, delivered as a lecture in Manchester in 1864. Here Ruskin expresses his sincere views on women and offers advice to them. His intention is to explain as clearly as he can the sphere, education, and duties of those women lucky enough to belong to the privileged classes. What he says came to be taken as the classic statement on the subject. Yet some women, because they saw him as traditional and old-fashioned, were not at all pleased by his remarks. His position regarding woman's place in society was that of most men of the time, including Carlyle and Macaulay but not Mill. As we have seen, Mill's views concerning women and their cause were somewhat radical for the time and unorthodox. Ruskin by contrast declares in the first part of this essay that woman's sphere is the home. As the angel in the house her function without a doubt is to comfort, encourage, strengthen, and uplift with her own spirituality the partner with a coarser spirituality that she has taken for life. At all times she must exercise a true wifely subjection, realizing that the sexes are different and have different duties in the world. It is the man who goes forth every day to struggle in the arena of life. The duty of woman is to clean and dress his wounds when he returns home.

Ruskin's view of woman is much the same as Tennyson's. In *The Princess* (1847) Tennyson indicated that a woman must be careful not to compromise in any way her femininity, her "distinctive womanhood." Woman was made to serve as the helpmate of man and should perform the sacred duty of redeeming certain defects in man. If woman differs from man, and few will disagree with this assertion, so does her role and place in society:

> Man for the field and woman for the hearth,
> Man for the sword, and for the needle she;
> Man with the head, and woman with the heart,
> Man to command, and woman to obey;
> All else confusion.

Forty years later, as indicated in the poem "Locksley Hall Sixty Years After" (1886), Tennyson had not changed his opinions on this subject:

> Strong in will and rich in wisdom, Edith,
> yet so lowly-sweet,
> Woman to her inmost heart, and woman to
> her tender feet,
> Very woman of very woman, nurse of ailing
> body and mind,
> She that linked again the broken chain that
> bound me to my kind.

Ruskin's opinion of womankind, formed early in his career, didn't change either as time passed. This essay on woman presents "the chief truths I have endeavoured through all my past life to display." Rejecting the notion that woman owes her lord "a thoughtless and servile obedience," he declares that her true function is to guide and uplift: "His intellect is for speculation and invention; his energy for adventure, for war, and for conquest, wherever war is just, wherever conquest is necessary. But the woman's power is for rule, and her intellect is not for invention or creation, but for sweet ordering, arrangement, and decision." With woman's role defined, Ruskin now looks at the home and its importance.

The home is the source of virtues and emotions to be found nowhere else, certainly not in the soul-soiling pursuits of men. The home is different from the world at large. It should be a place apart, a walled garden, a sanctuary safe and comfortable, where the exhausted man may be restored by feminine qualities easily crushed by the commerce of life. "It is the place of Peace," writes Ruskin, "the shelter not only from all injury, but from all terror, doubt, and division." When the hostile society of the outer world crosses the threshold, bringing with it the anxieties of the outer life, this shelter ceases to be a home. It is necessary therefore to preserve the home at all costs, for it shelters those values that commercial and critical interests threaten to destroy. The home should be seen as a sacred place, a temple. Performing her duty in this sacred place is the angelic wife and mother, with virtues man depends upon for his moral support.

Now Ruskin turns to that type of education that will best prepare the woman to exert her influence in the home. Surprisingly, it does not differ a great deal from the education he advocates for men. Women should have access to the same studies but should not be required to go quite so deeply into them. Even young girls should be allowed to roam at will in a good library, reading whatever they choose. Their inherent goodness, he believes, will tell them whether the books they read are worth reading. "Let her loose in the library, I say, as you do a fawn in a field. It knows the bad weeds twenty times better than you; and the good ones too, and will eat some bitter and prickly ones good for it." Some mothers of the day were not in agreement. The lending libraries, such as Mudie's Select Library, also thought a rigorous censorship was not at all bad when it came to impressionable females. One particular subject Ruskin himself would not make available to young girls. Because of feminine fanaticism in matters of religion, theological studies should be forbidden. At this point the agonies of his personal life invade his work and affect the soundness of his thinking. The intrusion here is religious Rose La Touche and the obsessive love he had for her. As his fondness grew into an overwhelming passion, Rosie became more and more disturbed and eventually lapsed into a destructive religious fervor. Ruskin intellectualizes the experience and concludes irrationally that all girls who choose to study theological doctrine will end up the same way.

Near the end of the essay he asserts that women have the same instinct for power that men have. Whether women believe it or not, they ought to realize they have tremendous power and a duty to use it wisely. They must use their power in the highest and most noble way to influence men, not to compete with them. Women were never meant to fight wars, but indirectly they are to be held responsible for the wars men fight. And why? Because they have it within their power to persuade their men to follow avenues to insure the peace. Women also have a responsibility to the sufferers in Victorian society, particularly affluent women who have the means and the leisure. Ruskin offers his support to those philanthropists, often tireless women, who were trying to help the poor. He closes the essay with some attempt to inspire them: "Among the hills and happy greenwood of this land of yours, shall the foxes have holes, and the birds of the air have nests; and in your cities shall the stones cry out against you that they are the only pillows where the Son of Man can lay his head?" One can imagine how he might respond to present-day homelessness, a time when entire families live with their children on city streets, or in cars, trucks, or abandoned school buses.

"The Mystery of Life and Its Arts" — This is the third and final essay of *Sesame and Lilies*. It was delivered as a lecture in Dublin in 1868 and included in the 1871 edition. Generally viewed as the best and most personal of the three, the essay is an exhortation to English men and women to work out the good life that is possible for all people. The opening paragraphs reflect Ruskin's dismay and disbelief that an intelligent public could be so indifferent to the notable and moving canvasses of Turner and of art in general. It is a mystery that "the most splendid genius in the arts might be permitted to labour and perish uselessly." Then he moves on to examine in detail the baffling indifference of mankind regarding religion and the purpose of life and the world itself. It is a mystery that men and women will not conduct their lives to reap better rewards even after they have been told how to do it time and again. It is a mystery that so many people in the world can be so frozen in their narrow views of life and so totally apathetic. It is a mystery that the greatest force for good the world has ever seen, Christianity, has lost its power among the people who need it most and may be in danger of disappearing altogether. Even though he himself was veering away at this time from orthodox Christian beliefs, he saw a real need for a vital church in the life of the nation. He is clearly lamenting the decline of faith in his time, and he sees nothing on the horizon to replace it.

Another mystery, as he sees it, is the lamentable fact that the greatest poets have made up fables about heaven and hell and the hereafter instead of telling us the truth. Even the poets will not give the people the truth, and they are the only ones who can. We ask them, are you certain there is a heaven? Are you certain there is a hell? Are you sure that men and women are "dropping before your faces through the pavements of these streets into eternal life? Are you certain they are not?" By way of answer we get only silence or gibberish. The poets and the wise religious men who claim to know tell us nothing we can trust, offer nothing to give us peace.

In these iron times the poets and those aspiring to become poets chant only dirges and songs of despair. One hope remains, however, and it can be found in those who work. We must respect the hewers of wood and the drawers of water, those who produce our food, shelter, and clothing. They are people of few words, these workers, but their deeds are good and their lives are worthy. From them we can learn valuable lessons but only by joining them, not by thinking about them or by talking about them. "You sent for me to talk to you of art; and I have obeyed you in coming. But the main thing I have to tell you is that art must not be talked about. No true painter ever speaks, or ever has spoken much of his art. The greatest speak nothing." The influence of Carlyle appears again in this remark: "The moment a man can really do his work he becomes speechless about it."

The Crown of Wild Olive (1866) — The title refers to the prize awarded a victor in the ancient Olympic games. It alludes to the importance of not working for a false reward. The book was originally a series of lectures. The first on "Work" was delivered at Camberwell in January of 1865. The second on "Traffic" was given at Bradford in April of 1864. The third and fourth on "War" and "The Future of England" were both delivered in Woolwich early in 1866 and at the end of 1866. The lectures contain some of the most eloquent passages to be found anywhere in the writings of Ruskin. Also in memorable passages are remarks on trade, industry, education, the conduct of the English people, and work. His earlier books – *Modern Painters, Seven Lamps, Stones of Venice* – had all been expensive books because of the plates used for the illustrations, and were therefore limited in sale and recognition. *Unto This Last* was inexpensive but unpopular because its social criticism was too strong. But with the publication of *Sesame and Lilies* and *The Crown of Wild Olive* Ruskin came into his own as a popular writer. The following year (1867) the corpus of his work received general acclaim at the ceremony in which he was presented an honorary doctoral degree at Cambridge. He was now in more demand as a lecturer than ever before, and though his health was often a bother he went on writing.

"Traffic" — This second essay of *The Crown of Wild Olive* is the one most often anthologized in our time. The title refers to buying and selling as in "charge as much as the traffic will bear." Here Ruskin discusses architecture in relation to religion and goes on to examine some false ideals of wealth. His remarks echo a number of passages in *Seven Lamps* and *Stones of Venice*. All good architecture is the expression of a nation's life and conscience. Taste not only classifies people according to what they like, but also is an index of a people's morality. Art inevitably reflects a nation's vices and virtues. An abiding faith will make for uniformity of art and architecture, but England has no abiding faith. It is lost in a cloud of confusion or locked behind oaken doors, and no leader has arisen among us to reclaim it.

The new schools and churches are therefore Gothic while the mills and mansions are not. That clearly shows you have separated your religion from your life. "In all my past work, my endeavour has been to show that good architecture is essentially religious, the production of a faithful and virtuous people." Yet too many people in England now worship the Goddess of Getting-On. For every one family worshipping this deity a thousand others must contend with the Goddess of Not-Getting-On. The competitive system works only for a few who gain enormous wealth while the thousands go hungry. The entire system should be supplanted with one offering fair wages, pleasant working conditions, and fine craftsmanship that consumers can admire. All labor that degrades the worker in any way or in any capacity should be eliminated. The countryside should be restored to its former beauty, and the cities should be clean and compact. Strong and hardy men needing work would be glad to clean and make tidy every square foot of every city.

Time and Tide (1867) — This book was published in the same year as Carlyle's "Shooting Niagara" and for largely the same reason. As a vehement reply to the reform agitation of 1867 it can be profitably compared to Carlyle's essay. It is made up of twenty-five letters written between February and May to a Sunderland cork-cutter named Thomas Dixon. Though a laborer whose name was not even mentioned by class-conscious critics of the book, the man was intelligent and perceptive and impressed Ruskin with the clarity of his economic concepts. Dixon began the correspondence and Ruskin followed through with these twenty-five letters. They center on the reform agitation of the time, but the central idea is to urge workingmen to consider not merely the question of suffrage, but the reform of laws preventing "honesty of work and honesty of exchange." His comments rapidly expand to embrace many subjects and proposals. In spite of its unevenness, the work has often been called the best summary of Ruskin's social and economic theories. Instead of selfish competition for material gain, he calls for the joy of hard work and the satisfaction of service in a purely authoritarian society where kindly over-seers replace greedy commercial tyrants.

Fors Clavigera (1871-1884) — The subtitle of this work is *Letters to the Workmen and Labourers of Great Britain*, but the letters are comparable to a newspaper column and are not addressed specifically to the working class. Ruskin is writing for all the people who work, "masters, pastors, and princes," and also the rank and file. The criticism of the nineteenth century that runs through the book from the first page to the last is deeply influenced by Carlyle. Ruskin's "divine rage against falsity" and what Carlyle called his "fierce lightning bolts" give the work strength and relevance even in our time. The recurrent theme is human loss and deprivation in the midst of great wealth and plenty.

The Latin title Ruskin himself fully explained in the second letter. *Fors* is a symbolic word that stands for force, fortitude, and fortune. Force means the power of doing good work. Fortitude means the power of bearing necessary pain and trial even as one does good work. Fortune means the unchangeable fate of a person. The phrase "Fors Clavigera" was intended to call up three great powers that form human destiny. These were the club (clava) of Hercules, the key (clavis) of Ulysses, and the nail (clavus) of Lycurgus. Simplified they were the deed of Hercules, the patience of Ulysses, and the law of Lycurgus. The three powers together were viewed by Ruskin as the human talent and ability to choose the right moment to strike with energy. He believed he was striking at the right moment to bring about social change. However, in the ninety-six monthly letters he has little to add that has not already been said, though some are self-revealing and personal. The style is more impassioned than in previous writings and the growing instability of temper more easily recognized.

By the time John Ruskin began to write as a social critic the combined impact of science, democracy, and industry had damaged the human spirit. The humanistic tradition was rapidly losing ground to the forces that favored an industrial and democratic civilization and the advance of science. Like Carlyle, Ruskin saw religion as an active and positive principle in the world, and he expected a sense of brotherhood to pervade humanity. For years he attempted to show that his contemporaries, absorbed in a selfish pursuit of wealth, had lost sight of their goals. He quarreled with the tendencies of the age because they placed more importance upon things than on spirit. He taught that men and women could escape the damaging effects of the material life through faith in the beauty of nature as a revelation of God.

His books were read and sold in great numbers, but the public ignored his appeal to find divinity in themselves and his appeal to a society of happy people living under the guidance of a loving God. He changed their tastes in art and architecture to some extent but barely touched their day-to-day lives. That failure, as he saw it, helps to explain why his books became increasingly strident. He pleaded for trust in the great humanistic tradition handed down from the Renaissance, but his contemporaries, too busy making a living, were not inclined to listen. He viewed himself as a deep and abiding thinker if not a philosopher, and he worked prodigiously to be heard and heeded. At the end, however, he began to wonder if anything he had said or done had made any difference whatever. In 1878 he resigned his position at Oxford, suspended the serial publication of *Fors Clavigera* (after writing of storm cloud and plague), and sank into recurrent madness.

Matthew Arnold

Matthew Arnold (1822-1888) was the son of Dr. Thomas Arnold who became headmaster of Rugby, published works of his own, and knew many of the important people of the day. For half a century critics were not able to use just the last name for fear of confusing father with son. In our time the son has greater prominence than the father, and so we don't have to worry much about confusing the two. In the 1850's Arnold enjoyed a modest reputation as a poet and wrote poems that place him in retrospect among the best poets of the century. He is now viewed by students of Victorian literature as one of the ten major poets of the time. If circumstances had permitted, he would have given his time and talent exclusively to poetry. In 1858, in a letter to his sister he expressed a desire to work solely as a poet. However, he would have to free himself of other duties and the reading public would have to recognize his talent with the same enthusiasm extended to other literary figures. That was a large order even for Arnold.

To devote his days and nights to poetry seemed highly unlikely, for he had been since 1851 an inspector of schools. He labored at that demanding and often dull position until 1886, just two years before he died. His job required him to visit grammar schools, mainly in the eastern counties, to observe and report as a duly authorized official. England had assumed governmental charge of the secondary school system, and Arnold during these busy years was partly responsible for establishing a new curriculum. He sat in on classes to monitor teachers and students and to observe the work they were doing. These routine tasks he performed with energy and good will, and eventually he earned a reputation as an authority on educational matters. In private, however, he grumbled about growing old strapped to a job that didn't bring out the best in him. Even so, his deeply entrenched moral sense prompted him always to perform well. We are not here, he said, to do only the work that pleases us. In a less than perfect universe, we often do the job we are paid to do and then somehow find the time to work at what we enjoy doing. That explains his pursuit of poetry, even though at times he thought the effort and the labor would break his health. It may also explain his achievement in literary and social criticism.

Matthew Arnold was born at Laleham on the Thames December 24, 1822. His father was appointed headmaster at Rugby School in 1828 and soon after became famous in English education. He took it on himself to reform the rigidity, incompetence, and oppression of the boarding schools that were attended mainly by the sons of the affluent upper classes. An earnest historian and a liberal theologian, he was prominent also in the religious life of the early nineteenth century. As a father he was stern but not overly strict and had a good relationship with his son until his death in 1842. As headmaster of Rugby, staff and students respected him to a high degree. Thomas Hughes attended Rugby and later wrote a best-selling novel about the school and his experiences there called *Tom Brown's School Days* (1857). In that book Thomas Arnold, called the Doctor, is seen as a kind and gifted leader making the right decisions daily and dispensing justice wherever he turns.

After 1828 Matthew spent the early years of his life at Rugby and at Fox How, the house built by his father in Westmoreland that became a compound for the Arnold family. At Fox How the boy met many of the notables of the day, including William Wordsworth, Hartley Coleridge, and Robert Southey. At Rugby he came to know Arthur Clough and also Hughes, who would later establish a utopian community named Rugby in the hills of Tennessee. Even though the experiment ultimately failed, the village with its fine library lingered on for years and is today a tourist attraction. In 1841 Arnold entered Balliol College at Oxford and graduated with second-class honors in 1844. With Clough he accepted a fellowship at Oriel College where he fell under the personal influence of

Newman. For a time the Tractarians colored his thoughts, but at length he decided not to subscribe to their doctrines. He later paid ironical tribute to his peaceful, quiet, and stuffy university in these memorable words: "Oxford. So serene! So venerable, so lovely, so unravaged by the fierce intellectual life of our century!"

In 1847 he left Oriel to become a private secretary to Lord Lansdowne. The ten years that followed comprised the period of his greatest poetic activity. During this interval he went to France and visited George Sand and Frederic Chopin. In Switzerland he met a young woman named Marguerite and fell in love with her. The next year in 1849 he published his first volume of poems. In June of 1851 he married Frances Lucy Wightman, a proper young Englishwoman and the daughter of a judge. Their married life was happy but nomadic because of the inspectorship granted in this year by Lord Lansdowne. The next year he published his second volume of poetry, written mainly in his spare time, and a year later came a third volume.

On the important issues of his age, Arnold's poetry expressed regret for the loss of that serene faith which had motivated an earlier time. Yet mingled with regret was a kind of resolution probing beyond disillusionment to a sense of endurance and even hope. Though not widely known, on the strength of his published work he was appointed Professor of Poetry at Oxford in 1857 and held the chair for ten years. Since the position didn't require the performance of academic duties beyond delivering a few lectures annually, he didn't have to give up his inspectorship. When he decided, however, to compile his lectures for publication, he turned his attention to critical writing. For the next thirty years he devoted himself mainly to prose.

Arnold was the first layman to hold the poetry post, and he alarmed the old guard when he delivered his lectures in English rather than in Latin. Algernon Swinburne, who later became an outstanding poet in his own right and a friend, sat in the audience and took notes. Between 1861 and 1865, when America was tearing itself to pieces in a not-so-civil war, Arnold gave a series of lectures on translating Homer and on the study of Celtic literature. He also wrote many articles for the periodical press, gained attention as a literary man, and met Browning, Ruskin, and Spencer. With the publication of *Essays in Criticism* (1865), a collection of nine essays contributed to periodicals in 1863-1864,

Arnold seriously began his analysis of the nation's culture. He was convinced that criticism had a definite moral value and that poetry itself was a criticism of life.

In 1868 he lost two sons, Basil at the beginning of the year and Tom in November. He buried them at Laleham and was overcome by grief but went on working and publishing almost on a monthly basis. In 1869 came his greatest work, *Culture and Anarchy*, which had appeared earlier in magazine form. The book expressed in lucid prose his social views and was very popular. The years 1870 to 1878 were given to a series of books on religious and ethical questions. During the last ten years of his life he returned to literary criticism, but also wrote on social problems. In 1883 Gladstone gave him a pension of 250 pounds a year, and in 1885 after lecturing in the United States, he published *Discourses in America*. The next year he relinquished his job as inspector of schools. He died at sixty-six of a heart attack in Liverpool on April 15, 1888. He had gone there to meet his eldest daughter returning on a steamer from America to visit.

After he did his work as a poet Arnold became a literary critic and after that a critic of the social, economic, and political scene. His work in that arena placed him in the ranks of Victorian movers and shakers. His criticism of life grew out of his criticism of literature, and yet from the beginning he was aware of the need for reform and the need for clear-thinking, decisive leaders. He believed that reform would have to rest upon increase of intelligence in a new generation. One way to secure this greater power of mind was the study of literature. Later the new scientists, including Huxley, would argue that literature is good for the heart but not so much for the head. The study of science and mechanics and the secrets of nature was better.

A believer in Carlyle's cyclic view of history, Arnold was convinced that his world in the Victorian Era lay between one that was already dead and another that was struggling to be born. The old values seemed to be rapidly slipping away, but they were not being replaced by anything better. It was a time when standards seemed no longer to exist. So earnestly he attempted to provide his contemporaries with standards they could follow and trust, with values that would enrich their lives. He placed his faith in the best that had been thought and said in the world. Though not deeply religious as was Newman, along with the latter he emerged as a dedicated traditionalist. Both men sought guidance and truth in the traditions of the past, and both were meticulous literary stylists. Arnold rapidly became a master of English prose, writing calm and elegant sentences for a wide audience.

"Preface" to *Poems* (1853) — With this lengthy preface he began his work as an essayist in the area of literary criticism. He would not have wasted his time had he done all of his work in this field. But as a privileged Victorian, an enlightened member of the middle class writing for middle-class readers in troubled times, he was not able to close his mind to the issues that afflicted them. Like Sophocles, he aimed to see life steadily and to see it whole. That meant he would have to regard literature as a component of something larger, namely civilization itself. He believed with Ruskin that a nation's spiritual life had to be vital and strong before there could be excellent art. Yet the world he saw around him seemed to have little faith in anything and had become increasingly indifferent to all forms of art. For him the term, "criticism" implied an activity much larger and broader than its application to literary works. Indeed all literature, including poetry, was a criticism of life. He thought poetry ought to be objective, noble, dignified, and should strengthen rather than undermine the human spirit. He also paid attention to design and proportion. Steeped in the lofty utterances of Homer, Sophocles, and Virgil, he felt only disgust for the vapid poetry of the so-called "Spasmodic School." The nineteenth century would have to produce better poetry, or turn to prose.

In this preface to the 1853 edition of his poems, Arnold condemns the poetry of the late forties and early fifties on grounds that it is too subjective and lacks unity. He declares that what passes for poetry in mid-century is little more than an aimless dialogue of the mind with itself. It gets lost in parts and episodes and seems unable to comprehend or even detect the importance of the whole. The best-known poets of the Spasmodic School – Philip James Bailey, Sydney Thompson Dobell, and Alexander Smith – infuse in their poetry far too much pathos and too much action that is merely painful. They try hard to present the tragic but achieve only the pathetic.

So with his eye on Homer, Aeschylus, Sophocles, and Virgil, Arnold sets up a standard to measure subjects suitable for poetry. The best poetry should be concerned with human actions that are universal and belong to human beings in all times and places. It should treat actions that appeal to the primary emotions that in all ages are the same because they are unchanging and permanent. It is therefore important for the poet to select an excellent action for his subject. While the date of the action is unimportant, true and objective construction is all-important. Style, defined as the expression of the action, is less important than selection or construction and must remain subordinate. The great action should be calculated to affect what is powerful and permanent in the human soul. In the confusion of the times the aspiring poet should look intently to the ancients for guidance: "they knew what they wanted in art, and we do not."

On Translating Homer (1861-1862) — In 1860, as professor of poetry at Oxford, Arnold prepared and delivered three lectures to explain the principles on which any translation of Homer should rest. We are told the students who voluntarily attended received the lectures indifferently. Their curriculum required them to translate in some of their studies a few classical verses, both Latin and Greek, but little more. Few of them at that time in their lives were in a position even to think about a professional translation of Homer. Arnold had misjudged his audience, but when the lectures were published in two volumes in 1861 and 1862, the general public received them well, reading them mainly for his views on literary matters.

Arnold concerned himself with those timeless problems of translation faced by any person who accepts the challenge to bring one language into another. Accurate translation of prose is difficult enough, but when a translator works with poetry he accepts a task that frequently results in failure. Like a woman (the Italians are wont to say), if the translation is beautiful it may not be faithful, and if it is faithful it may not be beautiful. Arnold examined English translations of Homer from the sixteenth century to his own time, noting that some were unable to capture important Homeric qualities. The lectures included adverse criticism of a translation brought out in 1856 by Francis Newman, a professor of Latin and classical literature in London. Annoyed by Arnold's remarks, Professor Newman published an angry reply in 1861. Arnold responded with his "Last Words," a lecture which dealt incisively with Newman's main arguments. Its comments on the grand style, often called Homeric, set up a definition long remembered.

Although Homer was capable of the grand style, Arnold maintains, his chief virtue was the grand and noble action. The grand style is present in poetry "when a noble nature, poetically gifted, treats with simplicity or with severity a serious subject." Francis Newman, Arnold allows, has a zeal for learning that ennobles any man, but Newman doesn't have the poetical gift, the intense "divine faculty" found only in the best poets to see their poetry as they see it. Lacking that faculty, he is not able to bring the grand style into another language, not able to translate Homeric poetry with admirable fidelity into English. Homer has treated a serious subject with great simplicity, but he has used his poetical gift to do it. Any translator lacking that gift will not be able to render Homer effectively into English. While Pope did the job better than Francis Newman and Chapman even better than Pope, no translator has been able entirely to capture the grand style of Homer. The same applies also to Milton and Dante. But don't go to Shakespeare looking for the grand style; you won't find it there. While admittedly Shakespeare has great talent, his work is seldom pure and flawless.

"The Function of Criticism at the Present Time" (1864) — This essay is the basic statement of Matthew Arnold's position as a literary critic. It was published first in the *National Review* near the end of 1864 and was reprinted as the first essay of *Essays in Criticism, First Series* (1865). The title suggests that Arnold's plan is to find out what criticism can do for his generation and what its function ought to be in complex and difficult times. The essay touches on nearly all the ways he would later use criticism, applying it to social conditions, science, philosophy, and religion, as well as to literature. In the first paragraph he tells us that the main function of the critical effort is the same in all branches of knowledge, namely "to see the object as in itself it really is." This could be an echo of Carlyle who believed the hero had the power to see into the heart of things, to detect the essence of reality and communicate it clearly to others. It is the idea of the poet functioning as prophet, one of the master ideas of the Romantic Era. It is quite similar to Ruskin's belief that great poets and men of vision must see truly. Carlyle's theory of history seems to underlie much of Arnold's thinking in this essay. It is the concept that sees two great forces in the world shaping its progress, faith and skepticism. Epochs of faith are splendid and fruitful while those of skepticism are stagnant and barren.

It is possible also to find here the influence of Wordsworth, for Arnold declares he has for that poet "the profoundest respect." He is careful to refute, however, the statement by Wordsworth that composition of any kind whatever is relatively harmless and therefore better than malicious criticism. Surely any criticism that is false or malicious should remain unwritten, but positive and constructive criticism such as Wordsworth himself wrote is not without value. He was a talented critic, and the world regrets that he did not supply it with more criticism. Arnold agrees that the critical faculty is lower than the creative, but he goes on to say that exercise of the creative faculty is not possible in all epochs and under all conditions. Therefore labor spent attempting to produce creative writing, particularly poetry of the first rank, could be better spent in preparing the seedbed to render the great work possible. The elements with which the creative power works are ideas, the best ideas current at the time. The creative mind takes these ideas and forms a synthesis of them to produce great art. But if the ideas available are not worth the taking, no such art is possible. The function of criticism is to analyze, assort, test, and classify ideas so as to make the best of them current and available to the artist. In an uncreative or critical epoch (such as the nineteenth century) that procedure is of great importance because it helps to prepare for the coming or flowering of a creative epoch.

In other words, the critic in times that lie fallow must establish an order of ideas for the creative mind to work with in better times. It is the duty of the critic to prepare a stream of fresh and true ideas as raw material for the creative mind. He must serve as a kind of middleman between philosopher and poet, and he must at all times make the best ideas prevail. When this has been done, Arnold asserts, there is a stir and growth everywhere, and out of this new awareness come the creative epochs of all the arts, including literature. The present time (1864) is in dire need of criticism to serve such a function as he describes. And why? Because the age lacks unity, is given to vulgarity and superficiality, is afflicted by erroneous Romantic values, and lacks a genuine power for creativity.

To bring about a resurgence of creativity, criticism is needed to provide stimulating ideas that are sane, sound, and new. He has said that his own time has yielded too much to the influence of the Romantic

Era. Now he explains that movement in the arts was premature in its flowering because it did not have sufficient materials for ready use. Then comes a statement that generated controversy: it did not know enough. Though possessing an abundance of energy and creative force, the Romantics did not know enough. Byron was empty of valid substance, Shelley was mostly incoherent, and Wordsworth lacked variety and genuine insight. All three had plenty of talent and feeling but not enough thought. They would have been greater poets had they read more books. Arnold is perceptive in this judgment, but only half right. One could argue that Pindar and Sophocles had few books, and Shakespeare was no deep reader while Shelley and Coleridge had immense reading at their disposal.

All that is true, Arnold would answer, but in the Greece of Pindar and Sophocles and in the England of Shakespeare the poet was surrounded by fresh ideas that animated and nourished his creativeness. Society was permeated with new and vital thought; it was intelligent and alive. In this milieu the creative power found its data, its raw material, ready to be shaped into art. Even when this does not exist, books and reading may enable one to construct a semblance of it, a world of knowledge and intelligence in which one may live and work. A good example is Goethe in Germany. At the time he flourished there was a prevalent critical effort, but Germany's life and thought didn't glow as it did in the Athens of Pericles or the England of Elizabeth. That was Goethe's weakness. The vigorous thinking of a large body of Germans, drawing upon learning and criticism, was his strength. Because English Romanticism lacked fresh and new ideas and the supportive power of unfettered learning, it could not provide a view of the world based primarily on thought or mind. The talented poets of that era therefore resorted to feeling as the basis for their work. Readers had to admire the clarity and force of Arnold's reasoning whether they agreed or not.

Later in the essay Arnold enters into a discussion of the word "curiosity." The critic worth his salt, he asserts, will find ways to whet his curiosity and develop "a free play of the mind upon all subjects." In that way he will be able to determine the best that is known and thought in the world. To accomplish this goal, he must refrain from taking sides and must at all times keep aloof from "the practical view of things." He must not become involved in questions of practical consequences and their applications. He must ignore or minimize all practical considerations, for criticism must serve no cause other than its own. The critic is required to measure the worth of the actual and the practical with the ideal and without ulterior motives.

Doing that he will bring to his criticism the all-important quality of "disinterestedness," which means he has no practical ends to serve. It is his business simply to know the best that is known and thought so that he can provide a current of fresh and true ideas with complete honesty. That is the function of criticism at the present time. That is the function of criticism at any time when skepticism, or unfaith, is the prevailing and pervasive mood. The free play of the mind on all subjects is the attempt to see life steadily and to see it whole. Criticism, therefore, must not be confined or restricted to one subject or a few such as literature or the fine arts, for all of society falls within its purview and can reap benefits from it.

Moreover, the critic can't turn his back upon social conditions that cry out to be corrected. In some measure the critic with a calm voice is a reformer. It is necessary for the critic to restore balance in calm and calculated replies to excessive and exuberant expressions of self-satisfaction. A good example is John Roebuck. Blinded by too much optimism, he sees all of England as a Garden of Eden: "I look around me and ask what is the state of England? Is not property safe? Is not every man able to say what he likes? Can you not walk from one end of England to the other in perfect security? I ask you whether the world over or in past history there is anything like it? Nothing. I pray that our unrivaled happiness may last." There is peril in such words and thoughts as these, for they encourage smug complacency at a time when England can't afford to be complacent.

To stress his point, Arnold employs the same method as Ruskin in *Sesame and Lilies*. He quotes directly from a stark newspaper account: "A shocking child murder has just been committed at Nottingham. A girl named Wragg left the workhouse there on Saturday morning with her young illegitimate child. The child was soon afterwards found dead on Mapperly Hills, having been strangled. Wragg is in custody." Note the final touch – short, brutal, bleak – *Wragg is in custody*. Does all this reflect England's "unrivaled happiness?" Does it reflect a state reveling in perfect harmony and bulging with happy people? When delusion such as that of Roebuck becomes rampant and widespread, says Arnold, criticism must reveal the truth with stark contrasts.

In another passage he describes the British Constitution with its love of facts and horror of theory as "a colossal machine for the manufacture of Philistines." He uses the term to mean a middle-class person who clearly lacks culture and refinement, is indifferent and resistant to any form of self-improvement, and seems actually to prefer a mindless and vulgar way of life. His first commentary on philistinism appeared in the essay on Heine (1863), where he ends the tenth paragraph urging his readers to popularize the word "philistine." He is aware of the biblical Philistines, enemies of the children of Israel, and neatly equates them with Victorian philistines who oppose the children of light, those who would remodel the old order. Heine, he says, might have settled in England after his work was done if not for the air polluted with smoke and the *ächbrittische Beschränktheit* (genuine British narrowness), which is almost a synonym of philistinism.

The four lectures Arnold delivered in 1865 "On the Study of Celtic Literature" continue his attack on philistinism with one of his clearest definitions presented after a warning to readers: "We are imperiled by what I call the Philistinism of our middle class." And what are the characteristics of this phenomenon? For beauty and taste it offers vulgarity. For fineness of feeling and moral earnestness it gives us brutish coarseness. Opposite an alert mind and spirit one finds a coarse unintelligence. All of these characteristics and more constitute philistinism. In a famous chapter of *Culture and Anarchy* (1869) he added more detail to this definition, drawing a distinction between "Barbarians, Philistines, and Populace."

What does Arnold say about divorce in "The Function of Criticism at the Present Time"? He denounces the Divorce Court, calling it a hideous institution that makes divorce possible but seldom decent or truly acceptable. It allows a man and a woman to get rid of one another, but only after flaying them emotionally and forcing them to trudge through "a mire of unutterable infamy." It's an institution upon which "the gross unregenerate British Philistine has indeed stamped an image of himself." The Divorce Court is sadly in need of compassion and competence. It was in need of reform from the inside out, but as late as the end of the century those wanting a divorce shunned the English court, even going to America to be divorced if they could afford it. Many couples lived in separation without a formal divorce.

Near the end of the essay even the casual reader will not miss Arnold's definition of criticism. "I am bound by my own definition of criticism: *a disinterested endeavour to learn and propagate the best that is known and thought in the world.*" And what is the purpose of criticism so defined? Its purpose is to establish a current of fresh and true ideas that will lead England out of its present confusion. Its purpose is to make available this current of ideas to anyone disposed to write creatively, for only in that way will the efforts of the critical epoch bring about a stir of interest in creativity that will spawn a new and vital creative epoch. Again one sees in these remarks the influence of Carlyle's theory of history.

The kind of criticism advocated by Matthew Arnold combines the curiosity and objectivity of the French with the sagacity and moral earnestness of the English at their best. His objective is to show that literary criticism is an exercise in discovery deeper and wider, and ultimately more rewarding, than merely seeking and finding the beauty and power of a piece of literature. It involves collecting, analyzing, and synthesizing the best ideas advanced by literature and the sources of knowledge it touches upon. You may call it the preparation of a seedbed, carefully and with precision, for the creative garden that will later grow and flourish. His fundamental premise is that literature is a criticism of life and that literature and life go hand in hand. Criticism, however, should not lose itself in partisan issues. It should cultivate an enduring attitude of mind, defined as "disinterestedness." He calls upon his age to abandon insular, provincial, partisan thinking and replace it with "the best that is known and thought" not just in England but also everywhere in the world. If that can be accomplished, then British institutions and the English way of life will be improved tremendously. Moreover, a better and more fruitful time will inevitably follow.

"The Literary Influence of Academies" — In this second essay of *Essays in Criticism* (1865) Arnold examines whether a formal body should be established in England, as in France, to keep an eye on the language and oversee its proper use. Although he admires the French Academy with its standards and prescriptive rules, he believes that such a legislative group for language would not be effective in England.

It would go against the grain of the English spirit. People living in freedom believe they own the language and would resent any restraints upon it. An attempt to standardize language could also harm creative endeavor. The English people may not be known for their quick and flexible intelligence, but they do have energy and honesty. Genius may derive from energy, and poetry is certainly the product of genius. Thus a nation known for its energetic spirit may well be eminent in both poetry and science.

England is such a country and proud to claim as its own Shakespeare and Newton. Such energy would not submit readily to a fixed standard established by an academy. Historically, England has always been greater in poetry than in prose. In uncreative periods when poetry doesn't flourish, prose necessarily comes forward to take the place of poetry. Even though the poetry of the eighteenth century was second-rate, that period managed to produce some excellent prose. The supreme master of English prose, he tells us, is Edmund Burke who lived entirely in the eighteenth century. Arnold views the nineteenth century as another period of prose. That kind of thinking led him away from poetic endeavor to the writing of prose. When that happened, the world lost a poet in full development.

"The Study of Poetry" — This well-structured and thoughtful essay contains some of Arnold's best literary criticism. It is one of several outstanding critical pieces collected and published in the second series of *Essays in Criticism* (1888). After several excursions into social and religious criticism, Arnold turned once more to literary criticism because he thought literature best exemplifies flexibility, perceptiveness, and judgment – qualities most needed by the English mind. The supreme power of poetry, he declares in this important essay, is the consolation it offers to troubled times and the strength that may be gained from it. Eventually in an era of unfaith poetry may possibly replace religion. Growing more Platonic over the years, he singled out Wordsworth for high praise because of his power to evoke the transcendental. He called for the removal of personal idiosyncrasies in poetry so as to reveal its unchanging beauty and truth. He made spiritual agony a touchstone of poetic greatness, and dismissed Dryden and Pope because they lacked that quality. He had said earlier that the eighteenth century was an era capable only of good prose. Chaucer, Rabelais, Molière, and Voltaire he placed second in rank to Homer, Sophocles, Virgil, Dante, Shakespeare, and Milton. Critics would later rescue Chaucer from the second rank.

Some critics object to Arnold's touchstone method for judging poetry. They say it leads to such errors in judgment as he made in ranking Chaucer. Because Chaucer didn't have "high seriousness," because in effect he didn't have the accent of Dante or Milton, he is seen as not belonging to the first rank. Chaucer may be large, free, simple, clear, shrewd, and kindly, but in spite of those good qualities his criticism of life is not such that it places him in the first rank. Because he chose to tell comical and bawdy stories when he should have been teaching moral lessons, his poetry lacks that high seriousness found among the greatest poets. Burns also falls short of high seriousness because his poetry displays a kind of bad-boy bravado. It may be that Arnold, an earnest Victorian, doesn't mean seriousness at all. Perhaps he confuses seriousness with solemnity, grimness, sadness, melancholy, prudery, and resignation. Surely one is not required to be sad or grim or melancholy in order to be serious. Chaucer's position among the greatest of English poets, one may certainly argue, rests upon qualities other than excellent seriousness. This doctrine of "high poetic truth and seriousness" came mainly from Carlyle's repeated application of the term "sincerity" to any poetry claiming to be great. One is forced to conclude that Arnold's evaluation of Chaucer, seen through Victorian spectacles, misses the mark.

"The Study of Poetry" states that the future of poetry is immense, for poetry has the power to render a tremendous service. In an age when dogmas, creeds, and traditions seem to be passing away, it will become more than ever a criticism or interpretation of life. With poetry the idea is everything, and that is why the critics must work hard to place in front of the poets the best ideas available. While all literature should be considered a criticism of life, poetry does it better. This favorite principle, this famous definition often repeated by Arnold, first appeared in the essay on Joubert (1864), although certain phrases close to it had crept into his writings as early as 1861.

In his perceptive essay on Wordsworth (1879), he said "poetry is at bottom a criticism of life." What does he mean by that statement? He may be saying that when a work of art possesses organic unity, it is a criticism of an organic society. Literature traditionally holds the mirror up to life not as it is but as it should be, and in that sense is a criticism of life. Or perhaps as a good Victorian he is asserting that poetry has a moral intent to put the finger on various aspects of life so as to judge them. He insists that poetry is either good or bad as it has or has not the power to strengthen, sustain, delight, and raise its readers ethically, morally, and aesthetically. While Arnold believed in the moral purpose of literature, as did Carlyle and Ruskin, he urged also the study of poetry as an art form.

In the essay on the function of criticism he had said that criticism must keep aloof from "the practical view of things." Only through "disinterestedness" could the critic be of real service in his aim to provide his generation with a stream of fresh and true ideas. By that term he meant that working critics had to remain aloof in seeking the truth and not become involved in partisan issues. It was necessary for them to stay out of the region of immediate practice in the social and political spheres. So Arnold himself attempted to do that in the group of essays that comprised his masterwork, *Culture and Anarchy*. Yet despite his clarion call for disinterestedness and his claim of being disinterested, some of his critics assert that as soon as he left "mere literary criticism" he ceased to be disinterested and became an avid reformer. That may be true, and yet he frequently fell back upon the principles first enunciated in "The Function of Criticism at the Present Time." In that essay he called for "a free play of mind on all subjects," and in later writings, particularly in *Culture and Anarchy*, he put the principle into practice. He wanted his ideas to change the minds of people, and he believed that reform would have to rest upon increase of intelligence.

Culture and Anarchy (1869) —This famous work is the third most important book of the century after the *Origin of Species* and *Sartor Resartus*. It grew out of the debate over the Second Reform Bill. Carlyle had responded to this debate with his bitter "Shooting Niagara," and Ruskin's response was *Time and Tide*. All three had grave doubts as to whether extending the franchise was anything more than a quack remedy. They deeply distrusted democracy and were trying to find another principle that might guide the nation. Arnold recommended a strong state that would represent all social classes and rule with disinterested wisdom while looking out for the welfare of all citizens.

The way to achieve that end was through culture as he had carefully defined it, but only if citizens were to achieve that culture.

The state had the duty to promote opportunity for the development of the individual so that in time all persons might eventually gain culture. The propagation of culture would create more and more children of light who would act in the best interests of the state and without class interest. The encroachment of democracy might very well produce anarchy, but an alternative to anarchy was culture. His book was a plea for the inculcation of culture in the individual and for culture as the foundation of society. Arnold wanted as usual a standard of ideas, a national mind that could demonstrate unity but not uniformity. He was not advocating the totalitarian state, as some of his critics have said, but rather the authoritarian state.

His political views stand midway between Carlyle and Mill. Carlyle had said that the individual is accountable to the state in every way, and his first duty is obedience. Mill contended that the individual should be accountable only to himself so long as his actions do not harm others. The government has no business interfering with the life of any citizen. Carlyle had preached that growth and happiness are possible by finding one's work and doing it. Working hard the individual will not only improve himself, but also the entire state. Mill said the individual can find development through self-interest, and that in turn can improve the state. Arnold asserts that self-development is an admirable goal but should not be left entirely to the individual. The state with wise counselors should guide the individual and aid his development. That is why his vision of the ideal state is less stringent than Carlyle's and less flexible than Mill's. As he wanted to set up standards for judging literature, he wishes also to establish standards for human behavior in society. Mill's ideas on liberty were not acceptable to Arnold. Instead of doing as one pleases, he exclaims more than once, one should act responsibly and do as one ought. The right-minded citizen will always keep others in mind. Mill wanted sectarianism in religion, but Arnold favors a state church that would spread the "sweet reasonableness" of Christ.

Culture and Anarchy is made up of six articles published earlier in the *Cornhill Magazine*, plus a preface and a conclusion. The first article, "Culture and Its Enemies," was revised to make the brief Introduction and Chapter I, which he titled "Sweetness and Light." The other five articles had the title "Anarchy and Authority" and became chapters II through VI. The title of the book was based on a word from each of the two titles that appeared in *Cornhill*. Readers were somewhat puzzled by the title. Since the theme of the book dealt with culture as a viable alternative to anarchy, many of them thought the title should have been "Culture *or* Anarchy." Even though the book should be read entirely, the first four chapters are the ones usually anthologized. An overview will show how the parts relate to the whole.

In the Preface we find the author's statement of purpose: to recommend culture, defined in a very special sense, as a way out of England's present difficulties. His definition of culture echoes important remarks made earlier in "The Function of Criticism at the Present Time." Culture is the pursuit of total perfection, both individually and collectively. It is striving to know, individually and collectively, the best that has been thought and said anywhere in the world. Using the knowledge gained from the struggle, individuals and the nation may turn "a stream of fresh and free thought" upon old notions and habits for a new appraisal and new directions. The acquisition of culture is "an inward operation," for perfection can never be reached without seeing things as they really are.

The Introduction, shorter than the Preface, confused some readers who had been taught that the introduction to a book, intended to instruct, should always be longer than its preface. Here Arnold takes issue with Frederic Harrison, a literary gadfly who later befriended George Gissing after publicizing the positivism of Auguste Comte in Britain. Arnold claims that Harrison's definition of culture is severely limited. He had called it simply "a desirable quality in a critic of new books," but Arnold's definition includes a great deal more. He tells his readers that he will try in the chapters that follow to get at what culture really is, what good it can do, and what is the special need for it among the English people.

Chapter I, titled "Sweetness and Light," defines culture as "a study of perfection." It is an inward, general, and harmonious expansion of all the faculties of the mind and heart. Its aim is to render an intelligent being yet more intelligent and to make reason and the will of god prevail. The criterion for cultured judgment is the best that has been thought and said in the world. Developing that criterion will lead to the creation of beauty (sweetness) and intelligence (light) in a nation. Arnold's definition of culture is similar in some respects to Newman's idea of a university. Both were seeking the best that a nation's culture could provide.

Chapter II, "Doing As One Likes," argues that culture as disinterested right reason offers a principle of authority to guide the nation. Here is the specific place where Arnold opposes Mill's view of individual liberty, saying that such a view encourages "doing as one likes." He is concerned with doing as one ought to do, the best in society serving the idea rather than the ego. Doing as one likes is a principle of anarchy; doing as one ought is the principle of culture. So Arnold sets up two principles of behavior and says take your choice. Choose one or the other, culture (doing as one ought) or anarchy (doing as one likes). He concludes this chapter by arguing that the children of light ought to rule the nation because they are the servants of the idea, persons of culture from all classes. These children of light, competent and intelligent men and women, must have the authority to act upon their ideas. Without that principle of authority too many obstacles would negate their work in the world as leaders.

Chapter III, "Barbarians, Philistines, Populace," sets up three social classes indicated by the title and takes the position that the best of these should rule the state. Though Arnold has no particular love for the Philistines and frequently finds fault with them, his main hope lies with them. Why? Because they are the powerful middle class already posited to rule. The Barbarians, his name for Carlyle's do-nothing aristocracy, are blind to new ideas and have ceased to count because they have relinquished their right to rule. The Populace, his name for the lower classes, in a few years might be a force to reckon with, but at present they have not begun to assert their importance. Disenfranchised and lacking organization, they are ineffectual and will be for some years to come even if they get the vote. If the Philistines can be endowed with culture, perhaps they will be able to rule responsibly, energetically, and effectively. Once more we see the ideas of Carlyle who believed only the captains of industry from the middle class had the ability to rule. They could rule a nation effectively because despite limited intelligence they were the ones who got things done.

Chapter IV, "Hebraism and Hellenism," asserts that the two basic forces in Western civilization are Hebraism (the influence of the Jews) and Hellenism (the influence of the Greeks). Although the aim of these opposing forces is identical, trying to attain perfection, the two are very different and the method of each very different. Hebraism has always stood for "strictness of conscience," while Hellenism encourages "spontaneity of consciousness." For a long, long time Hebraism has governed the practical affairs of the English, but what is needed in tumultuous modern times is the more open Hellenistic view of life. Again, the Carlylean influence is unmistakable.

Chapter V, "Porro Unum Est Necessarium," the one thing necessary or needful in awkward Latin, continues the discussion begun in chapter four and affirms the one thing absolutely necessary is to cultivate the Hellenic spirit, which the Anglo-Saxon world has for so long neglected. The Reformation, beginning in 1517 when Martin Luther issued his ninety-five theses, sold England down a side stream of Hebraism. However, the main stream of thought at that time should have been a freer and broader Hellenism. Echoes of Carlyle also appear in this chapter. At the end of chapter five Arnold's thesis, the promotion of a clearly defined culture for a troubled society that could save it from anarchy, has reached full development.

Chapter VI, "Our Liberal Practitioners," takes up the task of applying the principles stated in the earlier chapters specifically to current political ideas and practices. This final chapter attempts to make applications without fully succeeding for many of the principles discussed in the book. A lover of peace, Arnold misinterpreted minor disorders of the period as clear signs of impending anarchy. In direct opposition to Mill's liberalism, he advocated a principle of authority for the governance of all individuals. He wanted officials to have the power to clamp down on any individual that got out of line.

The Conclusion tends to summarize the main points of the several chapters. Juggling the thoughts advanced in the preceding chapter, he argues that the attempt on the part of the liberals to gain greater individual liberty and other rights for the individual can lead to more harm than good. Instead of paying so much attention to the rights of the individual, England would do well to consider what is best for the state, for the entire nation. He is at this point speaking out against the

Second Reform Bill of 1867. He feared it would place power in the hands of people who would not be able to use that power in a positive way. We have already seen the reactions of Carlyle and Ruskin to the Second Reform Bill. They too feared encroaching democracy.

As a social critic Arnold was in the camp of Carlyle and tended to oppose Mill. He would have a welfare state that is at the same time democratic, but democratic in a limited way and veering toward the authoritarian state. In his ideal society all capable citizens would be educated to tap that inward power called culture and would respond to a standard of right reason. That would obviate any situation requiring the person to act solely for himself and would promote unity without uniformity. The ignorant would be controlled while guided toward right reason. The state for Arnold is a corporate body made up of diverse individuals. These people, however, are expected to work for the well being of the state, and in doing so follow a principle more noble than self-interest. Their purpose is not, as Mill would have it, to work only for individual improvement. The book taken as a whole is a recommendation for an authoritarian state, which would represent all citizens in all classes and would rule for their total welfare. The citizens in turn would work toward the improvement of the state by gradually bringing themselves toward right reason. The instrument to secure this goal of right reason, Arnold declares more than once, is the principle of culture presented in the memorable phrase, sweetness and light.

The concept of culture, he said repeatedly, is based on the principle of *becoming* something, not merely *having* something. It teaches us that wealth is not an end in itself any more than health is an end in itself. Yet the philistines seek material wealth as their one reason for living and dedicate their lives to that pursuit. The practice should not be encouraged, for the nation in the nineteenth century is ready for Hellenism. The Greeks combined the forces of religion and poetry to attain an ideal concept of culture, and the English may be able to do the same. To become children of light, the English people must have a deep religious sense and also an unswerving sense of beauty, but their religion suffers from erosion and their poetry cannot sustain beauty. The slow movement toward democracy suggests positive reform, but without culture the democratic system will become nothing more than materialistic philistinism, placing value on what one has rather than on what one might attain. Or to put it another way, placing value on the material things one might eventually obtain ("the American Dream" to own as much stuff as possible) rather than placing a premium on the spiritual and mental strength one might attain. A major force in English life is the assertion of personal liberty, but freedom held in high esteem as an end in itself may lead only to anarchy. A principle of authority resting upon right reason must resist and eventually nullify this tendency to drift toward anarchy.

Arnold was deeply aware of the impermanence of all material things. Carlyle had taught him that history moves in great cycles with the material products of one period falling into decay to make way for a new period. In line with this he believed that great art receives its impetus in a period of faith and unity but declines in a period of denial. Because his own time lacked the structural unity that stems from a vital faith, Arnold felt it was incapable of producing great art. Contemporary poetry gets lost in parts and episodes, he complained, and contemporary architecture is a hodge-podge of conflicting themes. His period in history is a critical rather than a creative period and should therefore focus on the need to establish standards for guidance. A principle of authority is needed for English letters as well as for English society. The statement echoes Carlyle.

In a sense *Culture and Anarchy* is a piece of utopian writing. It is highly theoretical in places, but at the same time it tries to see conditions as they really existed at the time Arnold was writing in the late 1860's. Some of his critics, sensing the utopian character of the book, have attempted to show that his theory of the authoritarian state does not hold up either as a logical structure or as a practical one. At least one critic has compared Arnold's theoretical state to Plato's republic, saying he never intended practical implementation of his ideas any more than Plato did. That, of course, is nonsense that comes from ineffectual reading of the book. Arnold's effort may be seen as an experiment of light, but it is also an experiment expected to bear fruit. Arnold is allowing a free play of mind on the subject so that something of lasting value may be discovered. He wishes to stimulate thinking that may in time bring reform. The book rests on a close analysis of the state, its strengths and weaknesses, and in that sense is practical.

If you want a good grasp of Arnold's thought, you will read with close attention the first four chapters of *Culture and Anarchy*. These are the four that you will find in just about any anthology. The first chapter, "Sweetness and Light," perhaps the one most often read, takes its poetic title from Jonathan Swift's *Battle of the Books* (1704). Swift has the bees, representing the ancient writers, filling their hives with honey and wax and thus providing mankind with "the two noblest of things, which are sweetness and light." In the days of wax candles the figure of speech was apt and meaningful, but we should note that Arnold gives it a new application. He tells us that sweetness stands for beauty, and light is the term for wisdom and/or intelligence. The term "sweetness and light" is almost synonymous in meaning with the phrase "sweet reasonableness," which Arnold used to describe Christ in *Literature and Dogma* (1873). Both phrases eventually came into the language of everyday use and are now famous. He made it easy for his readers to absorb his ideas and retain them because, like Carlyle, he was a nimble and creative phrasemaker. Another famous phrase to look for in this volume is "children of light," his term for cultured persons of both sexes.

Most of these memorable terms appear in the first chapter of *Culture and Anarchy*. If we define them and remember their meanings, we can read the book with greater understanding. Then perhaps we can test its ideas for durability and determine whether any of them are relevant to our own time. Begin the exercise with the book's title:

"Culture" — The term is not used by Arnold as you would find it in your dictionary, or as Frederic Harrison and other writers were using it. He applies to the word his own definition, which can be found in several places throughout the book. In its simplest sense culture is the pursuit of perfection in a reality that is far from perfect. It is an inward process of individual development, a general and harmonious expansion of mind and heart, which improves not only the person but also the state. Culture has two aims, a private one and a public one. The private aim is summed up in a phrase from Montesquieu, "to render an intelligent being yet more intelligent." The public aim is illustrated by a phrase from Bishop Wilson, "to make reason and the will of God prevail." Culture is not a static condition, for it is concerned with advancing, with growing and becoming, a master idea of the period. The term "harmonious expansion" refers to individual development and is largely an internal condition. Arnold admits that his concept of culture has a difficult task to achieve. The idea of inward improvement is at variance with materialism and the lack of flexibility among the English. Yet if the aim to make culture prevail should be defeated, the alternative is anarchy – every person for himself – and that no one wants.

"Machinery" — While certain attitudes stand in the way to hinder the advancement of culture, its greatest enemy is the British faith in machinery. By resorting to a series of questions he carefully explains what he means by the term. What is freedom but machinery? What is population but machinery? What is coal but machinery? What are railroads but machinery? What are religious organizations but machinery? What is wealth but machinery? In a mechanistic age people feel that all problems can be solved by machinery, but that facile hope is nothing more than what Carlyle called "quack remedies." Culture seeks to establish standards so that intelligent people can see through the machinery of an industrial society (see things as in themselves they really are) to discover what is truly of worth. Close scrutiny, he tells his readers, will reveal that machinery is merely a·means to an end and not the end itself. The end ought to be greater and nobler than the means, and so it's important not to place too much importance on machinery.

"Philistine" — Arnold's first discussion of this term appeared in the essay on Heine in 1863. The next year in "The Function of Criticism at the Present Time" he gave it fuller scope, and now in *Culture and Anarchy*, five years later, the term is examined even more thoroughly and acquires large importance. Also in this book one can find Arnold's clearest definition of the term. In Chapter I he writes, "The people who believe most that our greatness and welfare are proved by our being very rich, and who most give their lives and thoughts to becoming rich, are just the very people whom we call Philistines." They are the middle-class merchants and their complacent families who worship an ideal of philistinism instead of the sweet reasonablness of Jesus Christ. This philistinism is similar in many ways to Carlyle's Mammonism and Dickens' Podsnappery. All three have adherents who come mainly from the middle class and celebrate materialism, machinery, and wealth. Philistines emphasize the rule of laissez-faire in business, pursue a warped ideal of freedom to do as they like, and look to the future with high optimism. Macaulay and Roebuck are excellent examples of upper middle-class philistines, and America is rampant with philistinism.

"Curiosity" — Arnold had used this term to describe an aspect of the competent critic in the essay on the function of criticism. It is a quality, he tells us, that any critic would do well to nurture and use, for it has to do with living the life of the mind for its own sake. It places value upon mental development and fairness of mind and is similar to Newman's education of a gentleman. Curiosity of mind is also a disinterested attempt to see things as they are rather than from a partisan point of view. Curiosity is a function of the disinterested intelligence, which does not lose itself in parts but attempts always to see and understand the whole. The purpose of such intelligence is to see the thing as in itself it really is. Curiosity guides one in that endeavor.

Concluding Chapter I, Arnold tells us "the pursuit of perfection is the pursuit of sweetness and light." The individual who labors to bring about the pervasive influence of sweetness and light is working "to make reason and the will of God prevail." The person who works only for machinery contributes to the general coarseness and confusion of the nation. Culture looks beyond machinery and has a passion for sweetness and light. It has an even stronger passion to see them both prevail. It cannot be satisfied with halfway measures, with seeing only a few subscribing to its standards. The raw masses of humanity and not a chosen few must also be touched by sweetness and light. Culture seeks to do away with classes and strives to make the best that has been thought and known in the world available to everybody. The people of culture are those who have a passion for broadcasting and disseminating the best knowledge and the best ideas of their time. They are able to use ideas freely and are nourished by them, not hindered by them. They believe in propagation but decry propaganda. Men and women of culture, living in an atmosphere of sweetness and light, are the nation's potential leaders. They are also children of light and apostles of equality.

In Chapter II, "Doing as One Likes," Arnold denies (as some of his critics insisted) that culture is only a perfumed ointment intended to heal superficial wounds. Culture, he tells them calmly and patiently, is a principle of authority established to oppose the assertion of personal liberty, "or doing as one likes." Roebuck had said that every man in

England should have the right to say what he likes. Arnold replies that if saying what anyone likes were not worth saying, it would be better not to say it. The London *Times*, responding to foreign criticism of the dress and behavior of English tourists abroad, had said: "every person in England should be free to do and look just as one likes." That comment seen in a newspaper may have provided Arnold with the title for this chapter. He insists that doing as one likes, the mindless exercise of personal liberty, is leading the country toward anarchy. But if individual liberty is subordinated to a principle of right reason, universal order will prevail. The principle of authority as a defense against anarchy embraces right reason, ideas, and light. Instead of doing as one likes, one should accept the standard ordained and authorized by right reason. One should have the intelligence to recognize acceptable behavior and do as one ought. Right reason, or culture, is therefore the proper and only defense against anarchy. His own best self should guide the individual because it serves the idea instead of the ego.

In Chapter III, "Barbarians, Philistines, and Populace," Arnold examines the three dominant classes in England and argues that a fourth class could emerge from these three and become the ruling class. The first of the three classes, those aristocratic Barbarians, have many of the merits of the barbarians of old. They are individualistic and have a driving passion for doing as they please. They love sports, exercise, and good looks. They have manners and a smattering of higher education that make them polite and chivalrous. Yet they lack a true source of light and are not truly accessible to ideas. They are barbarians because when it comes to ideas they live in darkness.

The Philistines, members of the larger middle class, work diligently by the best light they have. They have built cities, great ships, railroads, and mighty mercantile establishments. In them there is some hope for the future, but they act in accordance with the ordinary self and place altogether too much faith in machinery and the act of making money. If a leader is to come from this class, he must renounce the materialism by which it stands, the love of things and the aim to acquire things to make him happy.

The third class, the Populace, represents the noisy, under-privileged masses pushing aggressively to become Philistines and becoming more numerous each day. They live without standards or traditions and have no well-defined class-consciousness. As yet they have contributed little to society. They enjoy brawling and bawling, hustling, smashing, and beer. For years half-hidden, they are emerging from obscurity and squalor "to assert an Englishman's heaven-born privilege of doing as he likes." Their unrestrained behavior could lead to anarchy if ignored, but under supervision many of this class could become productive citizens, even children of light.

When he speaks of the middle class as building cities and ships, one might ask what role in this enterprise did the working class play? Did the middle-class tycoons build the railroads with their own hands, their own hard muscle? Are the stones of the cities baptized in their sweat, or that of the workingman? Arnold confesses that he himself came from a philistine background, but has broken with that way of life. Rejecting the philistines, he could not accept either the barbarians or the populace. He sees himself as one of the children of light but as an alien in Victorian society. "Within each of these classes there are a certain number of *aliens*, if we may so call them, persons who are mainly led, not by their class spirit, but a general humane spirit, by the love of human perfection." Their number at present is very small, but the number in each class will eventually become much larger. These are the children of light, the servants of the idea, a fourth class to come from each of the other three classes. The aim of culture is to increase their number so that in time they may take their rightful position of rule. Even though the philistines have a stiff-necked and perverse resistance to light, this fourth class will come mainly from them, but only if they can be endowed with culture.

In Chapter IV, "Hebraism and Hellenism," Arnold enters upon his famous distinction between two main forces that have influenced western society over a period of many years. At the beginning of the chapter he quotes Bishop Wilson: "First, never go against the best light you have; secondly, take care that your light be not darkness." Then he takes up the question of Hebraism and Hellenism, asserting that "between these two points of influence moves our world." It ought to be evenly and happily balanced between the two forces, but it seldom is. The aim of both forces is one and the same, to seek mankind's perfection or salvation, but they differ in their method of achieving that aim.

Hebraism, which pervades England in every corner, places emphasis on conduct and doing. The English are concerned only with getting things done; nobody seems really to care for the world of ideas. Hellenism he defines as spontaneity of consciousness, flexibility of mind, with emphasis on seeing things as they really are. Hebraism is strictness of conscience with emphasis on action, rule, and obedience. Its concern is right acting, but Hellenism is concerned with right thinking. Hebraists are men of action who act according to their own best light, but they lack that free play of thought on all subjects that makes for distinct culture. Hellenists, on the other hand, are primarily thinkers and dreamers rather than doers. They keep at all times a flexible, curious, and open mind but tend to be wallflowers.

Hellenism values knowing while Hebraism values doing. Both of these systems of thought address themselves to satisfying human need, but Hellenism aims to get rid of one's ignorance. Moreover, as Arnold notes, Hellenism seeks "to see things as they are, and by seeing them as they are to see them in their beauty." Hebraism asserts that blessedness lies in the moral life, while Hellenism declares it lies in the intellectual life. Hebraism has an awful sense of sin afflicting human life, but Hellenism sees the world as beautiful, enjoyable, and attractive. Hebraism resolutely walks by its own best light, but Hellenism takes care that its best light be never darkness. Both forces are profound and admirable, but what England really needs in the nineteenth century is more Hellenism. For too long the nation has been solely under the influence of Hebraism. The result has been too much action and not enough thought. During the Renaissance with its rebirth of learning England should have yielded as did Italy to Hellenistic influences. But the Reformation placed new emphasis on the Hebraic influence. Therefore, for more than two hundred years England has endured Hebraism when its true course ought to have been that of Hellenism. But for the Reformation, Hellenism might have spread quite early across the land to bring lasting results.

Culture and Anarchy was read by thousands of people in England and abroad, but it didn't have the impact or the influence Arnold hoped it would have. As Carlyle and Ruskin had attempted too much and gradually sank into bitter disappointment, Arnold was finding himself in the same position. Carlyle had seen a decline of faith in his time and so attempted to replace the old religion with a new one. Ruskin wanted excellent art and therefore proceeded to demand changes that would produce a society capable of creating superlative art. Arnold in similar fashion wanted disinterested literature and so began to demand a society that could produce that kind of literature. Because the society he advocated is utopian in many ways and not truly attainable in the real world, his failure to achieve the visionary aims set forth in *Culture and Anarchy* is not surprising. Yet one should note that with the publication of the book Arnold reached the apogee of his career as a Victorian thinker and would-be reformer. He was famous in Britain and America as the apostle of culture and well known on the Continent. Much in demand as a lecturer, publishing houses were eager to print whatever he wrote.

Between 1870 and 1878 Arnold devoted himself to religious topics. Critics hostile to his ideas on religion sometimes unjustly call this fertile period "the years in the wilderness." He published *St. Paul and Protestantism* in book form in 1871, and about this time began to read his mother's Bible a great deal. He also began to teach himself Hebrew. In this year he published two essays in *Cornhill Magazine*. They were released as a book in 1873 titled *Literature and Dogma*. Seven long essays in the *Contemporary Review*, called "A Review of the Objections to Literature and Dogma," he brought together under the title *God and the Bible* in 1875. Two years later he collected his last group of religious essays and called them *Last Essays on Church and Religion*. In these works of religious criticism he pleaded for a blending of Hellenism and Hebraism to temper the somber Protestant creeds. Arnold was seeking a compromise between Christian belief and the new scientific thought. He defined religion as "not simply morality but morality touched by emotion." He insisted that Christianity must survive on a foundation of morality. In trying to save the religion of his father he would discard its trappings but not its ethics, asserting "the object of religion is conduct." His concept of God he described as "a stream of tendency, not ourselves, that makes for righteousness."

Literature and Dogma (1873) — This book examines the history of religious idea and reaches the conclusion that religion, as indeed all of history, is characterized by progressive change. He wrote the book to restore the Bible to people who were confused by theology, metaphysics, and science. He wanted to convince such persons that they could not do

163

without the Bible, for anyone who reads it rightly will find in its pages solace and support. The book went through three editions in the first month after publication and caused quite a stir. It firmly rejected the supernatural and the miraculous in religion. Yet in tone and purpose it was deeply religious and brought thousands of the skeptical laity back to the Bible. Denounced as "pure Atheism" by some, it was a light in the darkness to others. Chapter XII, titled "The True Greatness of Christianity," is the one most often found in anthologies. The chapter has often been called a wholesome criticism of those reasons as to why Christianity endures as a great religion. Its power comes from the one God in trinity and trinity in unity. The religion is called Christianity because of the splendid teachings in righteousness of Christ the son. Arnold firmly believed that a proper inculcation of righteousness through reading the Bible could restore the present anemic faith and allow people to taste the sweet reasonableness of Christ.

God and the Bible (1875) — Two years earlier *Literature and Dogma* had created uproar. Numerous critical articles attacked the work and even the author for writing it. Arnold therefore felt that it would be fitting to respond to these objections. So calmly and methodically he made reply in seven articles that were later published as *God and the Bible*. In this, as in the previous book, he placed great importance upon reading and using the Bible as a source of inspiration in one's everyday life. Repeating a main idea in the book under attack, he spoke of the need for pervasive righteousness in English life. "Nothing but righteousness will succeed, and nothing is righteousness but the method and secret and sweet reasonableness of Jesus Christ." In a letter to Charles Eliot Norton in America, he expressed satisfaction with this book: "I seem to find some chapters in it to be the best prose I have ever succeeded in writing." To neglect this and the other books of religious criticism, even though they are now deemed his least significant contribution, is to miss some of Arnold's most penetrating literary criticism and some of his best writing. Because the assaults of science and the higher criticism upon the supernatural had eroded the inherited faith of his father, he felt it was necessary to examine the worth of the Christian religion and to defend it by means of conservative and constructive criticism.

In 1883, after some ethical hesitation, Arnold accepted a pension of 250 pounds a year from Gladstone and set out immediately upon an American tour. He went to America hoping to return home with American dollars converted to pounds, but also because he felt Americans in particular needed his message. When the ship docked in New York in the afternoon of Monday, October 15, 1883, Andrew Carnegie was waiting to greet him and his wife and daughter. The man was a Scotsman with close ties to his homeland and a friend of Prime Minister Gladstone. He had become enormously wealthy in America and one of the country's most prominent philistines, an irony surely detected by his guest but judiciously ignored. Arnold was lionized in America but was also hounded by rude reporters who persisted in misquoting him. His first lecture, "Numbers: the Majority and the Remnant," was delivered in New York. He said his hope for the future lay not in the majority of the people but in the enlightened "remnant," who had it in their power to become children of light. He told his audience that America with its expanding population could produce a sizable remnant to improve a society lacking in grace.

It was a good piece of writing but not a very good lecture. The hall was too big, the acoustics were poor, and the audience had difficulty understanding his thick British accent. After some elocution lessons he had better luck in Boston. At Dartmouth he delivered the lecture on "Literature and Science," which he had carefully revised for an audience this country. The newspaper critics, nonetheless, claimed that he had insulted Americans with a warmed-over lecture already delivered and published in England. His lecture on Emerson was also sharply criticized, but on the whole the speeches he published later as *Discourses in America* were a success. From New England he went through the Middle Atlantic States and the upper South as far west as Chicago and St. Louis. Back in New York, he and his wife departed for England on Thursday, February 28, 1884. The leap-year day was gray, misty, and cold. His daughter remained in the United States and married an American, F. W. Whitridge. He became the president of the Third Avenue Railway Company, and for years they lived in Manhattan. He died at 64 of a botched operation on his appendix in 1916, and she died at 75 in 1934.

"Literature and Science" (1882) — This essay was originally delivered at Cambridge in 1882 as a rejoinder to Huxley's "Science and Culture." You will find out more about it when I discuss the controversy that arose between Arnold and Huxley. Students of Arnold see it as the classic defense of the humanistic tradition against the persistent and persuasive influence of science. He puts forward as fact what he calls four essential human powers: "the power of conduct, the power of intellect and knowledge, the power of beauty, and the power of social life and manners." The entire field of science serves only the power of intellect and knowledge. Men and women of education and intelligence have a duty to understand science and its importance in modern life, but to achieve balance in their lives they must also cultivate as fully as they can the other three powers.

Literature and the fine arts do not comprise the only fabric to make the complete person, but no person is complete without them. "I talk of knowing the best which has been thought and uttered in the world; Professor Huxley says this means knowing literature; but all the knowledge that reaches us through books is literature." Huxley is thinking only of *belles lettres* and would like to make Arnold say that knowing the polite literature of a nation is to know its culture. Because he knew that Huxley understood his theories better than that, Arnold was angered by the inference. Culture, he insists, means knowing what has been thought and said by the great imaginative writers both past and present, but it also means what has been thought and said by such men as Copernicus, Galileo, Newton, and Darwin.

"Civilization in the United States" (1888) — This essay was published in the *Nineteenth Century* for April of 1888, the very month and year of Arnold's death. It was the last of his social criticism, his last word on philistinism. The subject is America in the 1880's as seen by Arnold himself during his lecture tour in the fall of 1883 and early winter of 1884. Before he came to this country he had a preconceived notion of Americans. He generally thought of us as Burke and Macaulay had seen us, as displaced English people on the other side of the Atlantic. He had already said that the entire nation was filled to overflow with philistines of crude manners and a defective religion. Now with greater knowledge to draw upon, he is able to present a more detailed observation of American life.

It seemed to him that Americans were too much in love with themselves and with their vast, sprawling, raw, and new country. He believed their claims of manifest destiny (to become the strongest and largest nation of the future) were absurd. He poked fun at a California editor who was predicting that in time all roads would lead to that western state. The notion that California could become a leader of the nation and the cultural center of the world seemed ludicrous to Arnold. It was after all on the edge of the continent and more Mexican than American. It was 3,000 miles away from any city or location claiming a refined civilization and even less civilized than Chicago. Yet time has shown that the editor's estimate was closer to the truth than Arnold's. Today California has universities unquestionably equal in excellence to Arnold's beloved Oxford. At present the United States is arguably the strongest nation on earth, though China with a thriving economy and a population of more than a billion isn't far behind.

"Civilization in the United States" is of particular interest to American students and deserves a close reading. Arnold claims an admiration for Americans and our institutions. He likes our freedom and equality, our power, energy, and wealth. We have solved pressing political and social problems, he tells us, but have not solved "the human problem." We are singularly free of the stultifying class distinctions found in England, and the division between rich and poor is less profound. American society seems organized for the benefit of those with relatively small incomes, and the workers are better paid than in England. Also the workers in America live in more comfortable homes and eat better. While all luxuries save oysters and ice are expensive, plain food is generally cheaper and fresh fruit abundant. American women have unpleasant voices, but are naturally charming and not half so artificial and self-conscious as English women. The American woman doesn't have to worry about women of an upper class deriding her style and manner, and she is therefore at ease and sure of herself. And yet in spite of all this, American civilization is not "interesting" in the sense that it offers full satisfaction to those seeking the good life.

When Carlyle's brother spoke of emigrating, he was asked whether he was willing to give up all that is interesting in his life to eat a better dinner. The question was posed with tongue in cheek, but without knowing it Carlyle had used the word exactly as Arnold thought it should be used. The great sources of the interesting are grace and distinction and beauty, and they are not to be found in America. There is little to nourish the sense of beauty. It is a country inhabited by middle-class philistines who cannot comprehend the essence of beauty. The cities and towns are functional but not beautiful. Numerous place names are curiously ugly and assault the ear. Art and literature as yet have produced little that is really beautiful, and the grace that makes living an art is lacking in America. As to distinction the Americans have plenty of strong and shrewd men but few distinguished ones. Lincoln, according to Arnold, "is a man deserving the most sincere esteem and praise, but he has not distinction." In fact public opinion in America goes against distinction, for they glorify the average man and the funny man.

The newspapers, a national scandal, despise anything that even hints of elevation and often deliberately ignore the truth. Yet Americans love their press and brag about it. The "game of brag" goes on constantly, and no sane criticism has arisen to rebuke the endless self-glorification. Commonsense criticism is what the Americans need to put down this "hollow stuff," but it may be a long time in coming. The human problem remains as yet imperfectly solved because civilization in the United States lacks those two great elements of the interesting, elevation and beauty. Even so, the English people have much to learn from the Americans. As England becomes more and more democratic, the danger may no longer be a middle class vulgarized and a lower class brutalized, but a spreading predominance of the common and ignoble. The born lover of ideas and light, looking upward in America, sees a sky made of brass and iron. That rare person in England sees the same.

If Matthew Arnold had written all his prose in the field of literary criticism, he might have gained fame but not as a pundit. He had the rare gift of making his readers feel the significance and charm of great literature, and he was a poet who thoroughly understood his craft. But because he was a public official, a diligent Englishman in uncertain times, and the son of Thomas Arnold, he felt he had a duty to broaden his interests. Early he established the belief that without a fine civilization there could be no high and fine art. Criticism was needed to make available the best and to establish a new order of ideas so that thinking men and women could develop their full potential and promise. All his life Arnold fought against tendencies that threatened these aims. He lived in the center of the great movements of his time and viewed himself as a warrior in that fierce intellectual life which swirled around him. For him to prescribe culture as a cure for all that ailed England seemed very impractical to many, but the aim of culture was harmonious development of human nature so that humanity might reach its full stature in a true civilization. To implement this program, Arnold urged advancing the authority of the state as "the collective best self." He was a man of ideas and a worshipper of truth. Throughout his life he was a persistent seeker of light, and he worked with great energy to help others find the light. His voice, no longer quite so strong as in his own time but not entirely silenced by the din of science and technology that threatens to overwhelm us today, can still be heard throughout the English-speaking world. Even though modern society has moved far away from his ideal society, Arnold may possibly offer some degree of promise among those willing to listen.

8
Three Opponents of Democracy

Three outstanding prose writers – Carlyle, Ruskin, Arnold – were among the most vigorous opponents of democracy in England. Individualists in thought and manner, they attacked in their own way the liberal tradition that seemed to be running amok in their time. Middle-class democracy in particular had risen to its apogee and seemed unassailable, and yet this brand of democracy was primarily their target. When they first began to express their thoughts in some of the strongest prose of the era, the middle class had already established its claim to power. With the First Reform Bill of 1832 the aristocracy abdicated its rule and yielded to the men of industry and commerce. From that time onward the chief concern of the state was to maintain the laws and the regulations not of a feudal economy, but of a new and vigorous system that came to be called capitalism. In their rise to power middle-class captains of commerce had exploited the wage earner. Citing authoritative works of the eighteenth century as justification for their actions, and preaching the doctrine of laissez-faire, these industrialists were frequently ruthless in their treatment of their workers. The poverty, squalor, and suffering of the working class in the thirties and forties came gradually into the light of day and made a lasting impression upon responsible leaders. Something had to be done to meliorate the condition of the masses and done fast. Otherwise, England could fall headlong into a bloody revolution more deadly than the French Revolution had ever been. These writers prodded the lawmakers to reach a compromise in their squabbling and act.

Thomas Carlyle

Imaginative, compassionate, and angry, Thomas Carlyle was one of the first to denounce the ruling middle class. He could see for himself that it was creating and perpetuating intolerable conditions in the lives of people born into the working class. Under a brutal system driven by the profit motive the poor suffered unbelievable degradation and exploitation, and middle-class democracy seemed unable to solve the problem. So Carlyle rejected democracy as unworkable and sought to replace it with a benevolent dictatorship. Its leaders would be drawn from the best that England had to offer, and they would rule as effectively as high-ranking officers rule in the military. They would right the wrongs and put things straight with the same efficiency as military commanders. Carlyle's thought could not be identified with any one movement of the time. It was at once radical and reactionary and disturbing.

It was a puzzling and complicated potpourri of conservative Toryism, Scotch Calvinism, Romantic transcendentalism, and a type of socialism by no means liberal. He was influenced by the St. Simonians and looked forward with them to a new society to be built on the ashes of the old now being scattered by rationalism and liberalism. He was a Platonist and shares much in common with Plato. Both exalted the authoritarian state. Both believed the ordinary man could not be trusted with political power. Both saw the only suitable government as an aristocracy of gifted and well-educated men, the hero-kings of Carlyle and the philosopher-kings of Plato.

In 1839, at the time he was gathering material for *Cromwell*, Carlyle wrote his first important political pamphlet and titled it *Chartism*. It began a series of pamphlets that called attention to "the Condition of England Question." In ringing, passionate words it cried out against poverty and unemployment. Strong and able men who came into the world to work were without work and rotting in idleness. They were suffering and so were their wives and children. It was more than Carlyle could bear, and the pamphlet denounced the aristocracy, the middle class, and the liberals as impotent to face and solve the problem. He hinted that only a great leader could save a society so indifferent and depraved.

In *Past and Present* (1843) he let it be known he was vehemently against laissez-faire and more scornful than ever of encroaching democracy. He appealed to the captains of industry to act as heroes and establish a benevolent despotism. The aristocracy would not have to fade away in defeat. They could bravely acknowledge their loss of leadership and serve the new leaders in some useful capacity, as did the Titans of Greek legend. The *Latter-Day Pamphlets* (1850) focused once more on the social disorder in England. They were an impassioned plea for the reform of English government and contained scathing criticism of democracy and Parliament. The heated debate on the Second Reform Bill inspired *Shooting Niagara and After* (1867). It was a tirade against the bill and against democracy. His doctrine concerning the hero and his view of the common man, as well as his admiration for authority and obedience, made Carlyle an implacable foe of democracy.

When he looked more broadly at social life in all classes, he found a greater deterioration of human values than he expected. Industrialism with its worship of Mammon had created a materialistic society that ignored human values and focused solely on making money. Industrialism he called the parent of anarchy, for it threw men out of work and into pauperism, which could lead to rebellion. It disorganized the lives of working people and made them the victims of uncertainty. Nothing contributed so much to social anarchy as the policy of laissez-faire. The doctrine meant not mutual help but mutual hostility in the name of fair competition.

The leave-us-alone philosophy, intended for government officials who might try to dabble in the affairs of industry, set one man against another. This was the condition not only in the work place, but also in the general struggle for existence. It left the poor to perish from poverty and disease and the rich to die of gout and idleness. Democracy could do nothing to counter these conditions, for it had abrogated the old order to leave only vacuity in its place. History had taught Carlyle that self-government by the ignorant masses was impossible, for all attempts in the past had led to failure. The work of ruling men in former times had always been the work of the intelligent few. He was convinced until the latter part of his life that the hero-king would have to come from a source other than the aristocracy, from a source he despised in one sense but admired in another, from "the Captains of Industry" who belonged to the middle class.

Near the end of his life, confused and bitter because he believed nothing truly worthwhile had been done, he turned to the aristocracy for his hero-kings. He confessed his doubts as to their ability but asserted with a hint of flattery, "a body of brave men and beautiful, polite women ought to be good for something in a society fallen vulgar and chaotic like ours." He believed that the English nobleman had left in him, after considerable erosion, a vestige of chivalry and magnanimity. They were qualities no king or leader could do without, particularly when animated by strength of blood.

He continued to believe that the captains of industry could rule in some respects, and in time would seize the reins of rule, and yet he conceded the aristocracy by right of its ancestry should take the initiative. He warned the idle, foxhunting aristocrat that he could no longer hang by the bridle of the wild horse of Plebs (the common people) and expect to be safely deposited in his mansion. He reproached the do-nothing aristocrat for withdrawal from the fray to lead a life of docile submission. That was no existence for a man of honor, a man of an old and good family. His ancestors would not have hesitated to seize the opportunity by whatever means to rule and so should he. Carlyle was closer to the truth when he thought the middle class would have to supply the leadership of the nation. However, his love of the old traditions that for centuries had sustained the country, and his desperation when he saw nothing was being done, urged him to think again about who had the right and the ability to rule.

John Ruskin

Another influential writer/thinker speaking out against democracy was John Ruskin. He was convinced that middle-class liberalism had promoted and perpetuated economic, social, and political disorder. He insisted that capitalism be abandoned, that cooperation replace competition, and that all employers of working people be made honest, caring, and responsible. Like Carlyle, he wanted a decent standard of living for the workingman and security for him when he fell sick and couldn't work. As Carlyle had done, he placed his faith in an autocratic system and looked to English aristocrats to manage his ideal state. However, unlike Carlyle, he didn't urge the aristocracy to grab the reins of power, not even near the end of his career. Instead, he pleaded with them to usher in a new day by reforming themselves.

In spite of the reactionary political remedy that Carlyle and Ruskin advocated for the condition of England, they fathered the socialist movement that gained momentum later. Ruskin's ideal state was greatly influenced by Plato's *Republic* and by Carlyle's *Past and Present.* In this ideal or utopian community each person would perform to the best of his ability the function for which he was best fitted. Each person, like the medieval workmen who built the great cathedrals, would have the freedom to use his own mind as he worked but would be accountable to a master figure of authority above him. As Ruskin followed Carlyle in viewing the worker as a soldier, similarly he sought officers from the upper classes to command the soldiers. He believed the captains of industry, in spite of their worship of Mammon, would be able to do the job because they had the ability, the energy, and the tools.

Ruskin's remedy for a disordered society was authoritarianism. Like Plato and Carlyle, he thought a socialistic government of expansive authority could control the spread of anarchy from too much individualism, too much democracy. He believed the government should be granted power over the smallest details of the citizens' personal lives, instructing them how to use their leisure time and even telling them how to avoid problems in marriage and what to eat to stay healthy. The state would be a benevolent father figure (paternalism), dutifully caring for its citizens but also punishing them when they get out of line. He proposed a state that would be in a position to render all services to the citizens so as to make their lives better. The government should take it upon itself to build and operate factories, public utilities, free libraries, and retirement homes. To counteract the ravages of industrialism, it should have programs that constantly beautify the nation.

The state should also provide land for those willing and able to work it. Anyone not willing to work would not be supported by any state agency and would run the risk of falling into dire poverty. The bishops and clergymen would work with the government to care for the souls of the people and to guide them in their daily conduct. Obedience to duly appointed authorities would be valued by all as a leading principle of the state. That would make for a calm and ordered society. Democracy with its cry for liberty and equality was to his mind a system that would lead in time to the disintegration of society. He denounced individual liberty even in his writings on art and architecture and praised obedience in Carlylean fashion. He was deeply disturbed by the writings of the liberals who urged the advancement of what he saw as a rampant and unfettered democracy careening down a crowded and rocky road with no guidance.

In *Unto This Last*, the most powerful book he ever wrote on social matters, he attacked the current political economy and argued for a state that could become a model employer, manufacturing products of quality and providing fully for the physical welfare of the worker. Later works added little to what he had said in this book, for its ideas and principles remained with him to the end of his life. In his letters to workingmen, however, he added details to his scheme of social reconstruction and introduced the St. George's Guild. This guild was brought to reality in the 1870's to establish the Carlylean principle that in a sound society everybody works for a living. It pursued a practical policy of acquiring land for settlement, and into this scheme Ruskin poured a good deal of his own money. Laborers on the land would enjoy fixed rents, pleasant working conditions, a set amount of leisure, and a comfortable standard of living. Although he devoted extensive time and effort to the St. George's Company, an enterprise with the mission "to slay the dragon of Industrialism," the response was very disappointing. His ideal settlements, in reality often grim and grotesque, never amounted to much. The venture was too visionary to succeed in the workaday world, but Ruskin blamed its failure on apathy.

Almost in every detail Ruskin followed the teachings of Plato and Carlyle in the expression of his thoughts concerning the state. The mass of men, he said more than once, were not prepared to rule themselves either by virtue of intelligence or knowledge. If they were to improve their lot, it would be necessary to obey the wise and gifted few. It seemed fitting to Ruskin, as it did for Plato and Carlyle, that any state capable of controlling and directing the masses would have to be authoritarian. It would have to exercise great power tempered by great wisdom and would have to know with unerring judgment exactly when to do the right thing. The rulers would have to remember at all times that benevolence guided their actions, that a dictatorship without benevolence is never justifiable. Yet the authoritarian state would have to guard against the encroachment of democracy and be firm in its resistance to it. The state would not tolerate laissez-faire and private enterprise that could not compete with the government in making good goods to be sold at fair prices. The profit motive would become a thing of the past, and so would capitalism. For all of England's social, political, and economic problems Ruskin's solution was socialism but not the kind recommended by Karl Marx.

Matthew Arnold

Joining Carlyle and Ruskin in the assault on democracy and the defective civilization it supported was Matthew Arnold. In many ways his ideas were similar, but they also differ significantly. He called for more equality of the classes and frankly admired the greater equality he found in America. He said the English system was dedicated to inequality in property, distribution of wealth, and social life. So long as English society remained in the hands of the barbaric aristocracy, it would remain uncivilized. The upper class had yielded to the forces of materialism and the middle class to vulgarity. The lower class in its very numbers had the potential to make its will known and felt, but at present could not realize that power because it lacked leadership. Not one of the three classes, therefore, was capable of rule. A fourth class, the children of light, would have to emerge to assume the reins of power. Before that could happen a national system of public education would have to do its part to propagate sweetness and light. He believed in the value of firm authority and would expand the services of the state, but he didn't reject the democracy already in effect or expect it to disappear.

Potential leaders from the middle class would have to be educated by the state for service in government and the professions. He reasoned that if a plumber or pipe fitter had to go to school to learn his job, those destined to lead needed preparation too. They would not be degraded by the materialism surrounding them, and they would have no reason to practice laissez-faire, which threatened to bring the nation to anarchy.

Persons of ideas and light looking forward rather than backward, their actions would be guided by the Hellenistic view of the world. They would abandon the Hebraic or puritanical, and the result would be to improve and enlighten all of English society.

Though he criticized the middle class most severely of all – they were the vulgar philistines who dedicated their lives only to making money and acquiring things – the idle aristocracy to his way of thinking was the more formidable enemy of current civilization. They were a group of admittedly influential people who had withdrawn from active participation in the affairs of the nation and were therefore inaccessible to ideas. They were not willing to accept the consequences of change, and they promoted a rigorous social inequality that made other classes restive and resentful. The upper class had relinquished its right to rule, but continued to exert considerable pressure on public affairs by virtue of its wealth and social standing. Though Arnold held that the middle class was totally without culture, it was not so inflexible and closed-minded as the upper class. It was not unwilling to examine and perhaps adopt new ideas. For those reasons he looked to that class to promote his ideal of a kinder and gentler civilization.

Like Carlyle and Ruskin – one could also add Newman – Arnold denounced the rampant liberalism of the middle class as the main source of his country's confusion. He viewed society as an organism as opposed to the individualistic and mechanistic concept of the liberals. He urged the need for a strong state with the efficiency to act decisively in matters affecting the population. Rather than advocate an aristocracy that might govern in military fashion, as Carlyle was prone to do near the end of his career, Arnold looked for a remedy to make democracy itself more workable. Yet he too feared that the people would not be able to govern themselves and placed his confidence in the few. He hoped that eventually the children of light, the elite, would be able to make intelligence prevail within the democratic system. Drawn mainly from the educated middle class, these children of light would command the higher positions of government and would be able to insist on a pervasive equality throughout society. Arnold believed that democracy without equality would eventually curtail individual liberty to become essentially unworkable. It was clear to him that democracy could not fulfill itself in an uncaring society where there was great inequality in the conditions of life. Inequality split society into classes confronting one another.

In disagreement with Carlyle, Arnold saw promise in the common man and the possibility for genuine development. Carlyle emphasized the great superiority of the few, but Arnold stressed the humanity of all mankind and the capability of all classes to learn and improve. Carlyle saw the need for heroes to show the way, but Arnold believed that men and women could act for themselves to find the path that best suited them. It was easy for Carlyle to look with contempt upon democracy. It was just as easy for Arnold, concerned with the future possibilities, to look with favor upon it. Yet Arnold believed that English democracy was impaired by too much emphasis on individual freedom, which had little relevance to individual development. The liberal philosophy of individualism was promoting an extreme form of freedom, and that was leading the nation toward anarchy. It was rapidly trickling down to the lower classes and was causing them to march, hoot, threaten, and smash even as they insisted on their rights. The right to be disorderly in a public park would never lead to anything positive, for such behavior bordered on anarchy and had to be resisted. Firmness of rule had to be found to discourage it. Arnold's solution was culture based on a principle of authority that in turn was based on the right reason of intelligent leaders.

It may be seen that in varying degrees Carlyle, Ruskin, and Arnold opposed the capitalistic system and the system of laissez-faire that encouraged individualism and liberalism. Each in his own way opposed the democratic process and the form of democracy beginning to take shape at that time. All three opposed the concept of doing as one likes, which originated in the theories of Mill. They insisted that in an ordered society intended for the good of everyone, individuals must do not as they like but as they ought. All three sought a solution in a state that could exercise a strong authority upon its citizens governed by wise decisions. They thought that education could open doors for the implementation of changes in the present system. If education could improve enough individuals, the process would gradually improve society. The populace (the lower classes) also had to be educated, for increasingly they were assuming greater responsibility. In time some of the best leaders could emerge from the populace, for that class had energy.

Civilization, these opponents of democracy believed, had to rest upon a multitude of wise and well-educated men and women. That is why they sought better educational opportunities for anyone of any class willing to apply himself. Yet they all agreed that the best educated among the gifted would have to form the leadership of the nation. Somehow the candidate with the best credentials would have to be chosen, not the one with powerful backing from influential persons. Arnold differed from Carlyle and Ruskin in not wishing to install what he termed benevolent despotism, and yet he feared the masses were not ready for power. Carlyle and Ruskin were fearful that in time democracy would lead to anarchy. Arnold believed that it was a question of culture or anarchy. If the people could accept culture as he defined it, the nation would be able in the future to avoid anarchy. All three distrusted democracy with its tendency to allow the individual more and more freedom. Time has tended to nullify their fears, and yet the dark rumblings of rebellion we now hear in several parts of the world may stem from a misinterpretation of individual freedom.

Charles Darwin

In our time more people know Charles Darwin (1809-1882) than any other Victorian writer and thinker. After 1859 he was widely admired as one of the greatest scientists of his day. Fellow scientists in their writings and spoken comments sometimes displayed high respect by linking his name with Isaac Newton. Alfred Wallace, a noted scientist with similar evolutionary conclusions, called him "the Newton of natural history" and Thomas Henry Huxley, his competent supporter, compared the *Origin of Species* to Newton's *Principia*. The famous theory of evolution, which Darwin gave scientific credence to but certainly did not invent, rapidly entered the thought of educated people and touched practically every field of intellectual endeavor. Because of Darwin and other scientists of the nineteenth century, we no longer think of the universe as immutable and fixed. That was the eighteenth-century frame of mind, and to a large extent it was the thinking of the Victorian laity until Darwin came along. Today, because of Darwin's immense influence upon so many minds, it is commonplace to view the world as fluid, changing, becoming, or evolving. In any discussion of the intellectual currents of the Victorian Era the contribution of this one man must be carefully examined. His treatise on evolution was said to be the most important book of the nineteenth century, and over the years it has made him one of the most influential persons of modern times. To know Darwin is to be at the center of those events that shaped the new science and generated a controversy between science and religion not settled even today.

Born in the same year as Tennyson and Lincoln (on February 12, 1809 at Shrewsbury), Charles Robert Darwin grew up in a privileged and intellectual family. His paternal grandfather was Erasmus Darwin (1731-1803), who spent much of his life as a physician at Lichfield, the birthplace (in 1709) of Samuel Johnson. He established a botanical garden in the village and was well known as a naturalist, poet, and philosopher. He had proposed a theory of evolution in the 1790's, and as a boy Darwin heard the theory explained and discussed at dinner. The boy's maternal grandfather was Josiah Wedgwood (1730-1795), founder of the great pottery firm that bears his name. His son Thomas was the first photographer in England and a generous patron of Samuel Coleridge. Darwin's father was also a physician, locally distinguished with a thriving practice, and fondly remembered by his son as "the wisest man I ever knew." Enjoying good health, high spirits, a supportive family, and a liberal allowance to spend as he chose, Darwin was educated at the University of Edinburgh and Cambridge. For two years he studied medicine at Edinburgh and graduated without honors from Cambridge in 1831. In that same year he embarked as ship's naturalist on the H.M.S. *Beagle*, bound for South America and around the world on a five-year scientific expedition. "The voyage of the *Beagle*," he later wrote, "has been by far the most important event in my life, and has determined my whole career." He added that on that one voyage he became truly educated.

At the time he went to sea in December 1831 he was twenty-two. When he returned in October 1836, he was many years older in experience and had gained a passion for scientific research. In a letter written on board near Rio de Janeiro in May of 1832, he had this to say: "My mind has been, since leaving England, in a perfect hurricane of delight and astonishment, and to this very hour scarcely a minute has passed in idleness." The voyage, a rare opportunity for any young man fresh out of college, set the course he would take for the rest of his life. And yet it probably damaged his health. For the next forty years after returning, according to his son, Darwin's life was "one long struggle against the weariness and strain of sickness."

He married Emma Wedgwood after a brief courtship at the

beginning of 1839. Later in that same year he published the results of his biological observations in a book with a long but explanatory title, *Journal of Researches into the Geology and Natural History of the Various Countries Visited by H.M.S. Beagle.* In 1842 he and his wife set up their home just outside the village of Downe in Kent, where they remained independently comfortable for the rest of their lives. The house was soon filled with seven noisy children, but Darwin was shy and the house was a refuge for him. Scrutinizing his discoveries in the glare of Malthusian doctrine (increase in population is exponential while increase in the food supply is arithmetical), he came eventually to the theory of natural selection, which lies at the heart of his great book. After 1859 other books began to appear on a regular basis, but often they had to be simplified for a popular audience. His theories that seemed to rub religion the wrong way took the nation by storm and created something of an uproar. His name within a few years became a household word.

Though tucked away in the house at Downe, he was at the center of a fierce conflict affecting England and the whole intellectual world. All this attention did not change him. He remained as always a quiet, retiring, modest and simple person entirely free of arrogance or presumption. He came to know most of the great people of the day, and they all found him to be essentially pleasant. Carlyle said of him, "A more charming man I have never met in my life." Leslie Stephen recorded this curious reaction: "There is something almost pathetic in his simplicity and friendliness." People who knew him at the height of his fame found him "delightfully unconscious of his greatness." He was said to be perfectly natural and simple, "just like anyone else." But of course nothing could have been further from the truth. He was not at all like anyone else, for his mind was keen and fruitful and capable of the most rigorous scientific analysis. He was a born naturalist, but the authentic scientific impulse came to him on the *Beagle.* That awakening, as he moved in a little wooden world across the seas, carried him through forty years of intense scientific examination.

Also the publication of the great book in 1859 seems to have been entirely propitious, guided perhaps by a kind fate. Another naturalist, Alfred Wallace (1823-1913), reached the same conclusions at about the same time. As early as 1855 Darwin had perused a paper on species by

Wallace, and the ideas were alarmingly similar to his own. "I rather hate the idea of writing for priority," he wrote to his friend Charles Lyell, a famous geologist in his own right, "yet I certainly would be vexed if any one were to publish my doctrines before me." In May of 1857 Wallace sent him a letter containing materials again similar to his own, and Darwin admitted that to a certain extent they had come to similar conclusions. Late in the same year another letter came from Wallace. Darwin replied in a friendly tone but reminded him that while their theories were similar, he (Darwin) had been working on the species question for twenty years. The next mail from this man, arriving in 1858, contained a manuscript expressing a theory of the origin of species identical with his own. In no time at all Wallace, lying ill with malaria in the jungles of the Malay Peninsula, had caught up with Darwin's most advanced conclusions. In only three years he had reached the same unmistakable conclusions that Darwin had mulled over for twenty years, and the evidence seemed just as sound. His conclusions were not so elaborate and not so well documented, but they were plain and precise and certainly his own.

Perplexed, Darwin sought advice from Lyell, revealing a code of honor that in later years endeared him to millions. "Do you not think his having sent me this sketch ties my hands? I would far rather burn my whole book, than that he or any other man should think that I have behaved in a paltry spirit." At about this time scarlet fever invaded the Darwin household and killed his infant daughter. "I am quite prostrated and can do nothing," he confided to botanist Joseph Hooker. Lyell and Hooker later read before the Royal Society a joint paper containing the Wallace sketch and the sketch by Darwin. He was too shy to attend the meeting but urged them to acknowledge in detail the contributions made by Alfred Wallace. A short time later Wallace proved himself as much a gentleman as Darwin by stepping aside and allowing the better known and older man to claim the credit.

Honoring pure science above personal reputation in an uncertain world, Wallace refused to contest Darwin's work or to hinder him in any way. In another time and competing with a person other than Wallace, a gentleman such as Darwin might have renounced all claims to the theory. In fact he drafted such a letter to Wallace, as he tried to decide on the right thing to do, but never mailed it. So once more luck was on his side as he set about writing a brief exposition, an abstract of a larger work to come, which grew into a hefty volume and became his most important book. After the publication of the *Origin of Species* in 1859, though he did little himself to promote the book, his fame was assured. He died of heart failure in April of 1882 and was buried in Westminster Abbey near the graves of Newton and Herschel. Lyell had been buried there in 1875 at the bequest of Hooker. Emma and the children wanted their loved one interred at Downe, but the press and the pulpit decided otherwise.

Darwin was not a specialist in the present-day sense. He explored geology, biology, botany, zoology, and brought together huge masses of material. He formed a synthesis of these materials and drew conclusions that led to further investigation. His *Origin of Species* did not establish the reality of evolution, but marshaled impressive evidence in the form of scientific facts to substantiate a theory of evolution that was already old. It also brought forward in full detail the mechanism (natural selection) by which the theory could be explained. When he sailed on the *Beagle*, he believed (as did almost all people) in the immutability of species. But on that memorable voyage he observed abundant evidence that suggested otherwise. He returned convinced that all the life forms in nature were not fixed by special creation, but were the result of slow and steady change brought on by natural causes over long periods of time. Back in England he weighed and sifted evidence to reach the conclusion that species originate by means of natural selection, or the survival of the fittest, in the incessant struggle of life. "On the principle of natural selection," he asserted in the *Origin*, "it does not seem incredible that from one of the lower algae both animals and plants may have been developed." Natural selection working slowly as a process through long periods of time brings about evolutionary change.

Though technically a scientific theory to be argued by the geologists, biologists, botanists, and other scientists, the concept rapidly sifted down to laymen and came to be applied to all phases of life. It was a startling development that had its origin in rationalism and scientific investigation. But the book with the long and awkward title – *On the Origin of Species by Means of Natural Selection, or the Preservation of Favoured Races in the Struggle for Life* – did not come as a surprise among people whose reading habits extended beyond novelettes and illustrated magazines. Tennyson in 1850 had examined two different theories of evolution in the poem that became Queen Victoria's favorite, *In Memoriam*. Other persons before him, who were generally not members of the scientific community, had looked rather closely at the theory. In fact it was so well known to readers of serious books that when they heard Darwin planned to publish a long book on the subject, the entire first edition of 1,250 copies was sold out on the first day of publication. Not long afterwards a storm of controversy swept across the land and across the sea to other countries. To this day the controversy continues. Scarcely a year goes by that one doesn't see in the papers a squabble between opposing parties on the subject. The creationists who believe in the old-time religion and propose "intelligent design" sternly oppose the evolutionists, and the evolutionists shake their heads in resignation.

To appreciate the full importance of the theory we need to examine its development before it came under the scrutiny of Darwin. Any number of carefully written books on the subject will supply more detail. Most of them mention the several stages of development by which people were prepared for the theory. It began, so far as we know, with the Greeks. From Heraclitus and Anaximander came the vague suggestion that animal species are mutable. From Aristotle came the idea of a scalable series of organisms, the shading of one class into another, and the development of germ or seed into the plant. From the Stoics and Epicureans, and also from Lucretius, came the view that men and women are forms in nature closer to the animals than to the gods. Then came Plato who changed the direction of occidental thought with a complex of ideas later termed transcendentalism (the world of things transcended by a static world of ideas unified by Good or God). The Platonic theories halted mutability theories when they emphasized being rather than becoming. Not until the seventeenth century did thinkers overcome that tendency long enough to establish a concept called "the great chain of being." The chain extended in linear gradation from lowest to highest.

In the eighteenth century the subject of evolution was treated for the first time "in a scientific spirit" by the French scholar and botanist Georges Louis Leclerc, Comte de Buffon (1707-1788). He wrote the major work on natural history and made the Royal Garden in Paris a center for scientific research. Virtually all thinkers in his day viewed the world as fixed and stable, as unchanging since the time of the creation. But he theorized variation in animals according to environment and the ability to pass on the variation to offspring. His opponents saw the universe as a static creation regulated by set laws, and even the creation was not considered very old. In the seventeenth century Bishop James Ussher of Dublin calculated that God began the first day of creation at nightfall preceding Sunday, October 23, 4004 B.C. The job required exactly six days to complete, and on the seventh as the Bible affirms God rested. The work of other biblical scholars corresponded closely with that of Ussher because they used much the same methodology to calculate key events recorded in the Bible.

As early as the eighteenth century, however, the foundations were being laid for almost every branch of physical science, and the early scientists came upon facts that would not jibe with the idea of the world as stable and unchanging. At first they tried to fit the new ideas into the accepted pattern, but eventually Jean Baptiste Lamarck and others abandoned the effort to reconcile the new knowledge with the Book of Genesis. In 1809, the year of Darwin's birth, Lamarck postulated that species evolved by transmission of acquired characteristics and were plainly not the result of a few days' work by an almighty Creator. Contradicting the Bible, he stated that the creation was a process thousands or even millions of years old.

Learned men struggling with poverty were carefully and consistently doing scientific work, but not until 1830 did science arouse much popular interest. Not until the last decades of the century did it gain a sound place in the universities. Because academic instruction was mainly classical and in the hands of the clergy, higher education resisted the acceptance of scientific studies. But 1830 was the year that saw the publication of Charles Lyell's *Principles of Geology* and was therefore a year of triumph. At first Lyell attempted to show that his ideas could be reconciled with scripture and the Book of Genesis, but later he dismissed the biblical account of creation as lacking authority and unreliable. Lyell's biggest contribution was the uniformitarian theory, which held that the same laws now changing the universe have been working in the same way to change it for millions of years. From the study of geological strata he was able to say that many forms of life existed ages ago that do not exist in the present, and man has come late in the process of development. Nevertheless, mankind's existence on earth far exceeded the span that biblical chronology permitted. Even though most middle-class readers were dogmatic believers in the biblical version of creation, the sixteen-hundred-page treatise was received with high enthusiasm. Lyell himself was puzzled by that fact.

In 1844 the book by Robert Chambers, *Vestiges of the Natural History of Creation*, dismissed the concept of special creation and replaced it with a theory describing the development of various species. Anticipating Darwin by fifteen years, Chambers presented the theory that all life on earth gradually evolved over a period of many years, but under divine guidance. He implied that evolution was God's own plan for elevating the human race and was patently purposive. It was therefore a process more sublime than the mechanical operation of natural law. Tennyson eagerly accepted that theory as more optimistic than the one presented by Lyell. In later years Butler, Shaw, and Bergson also accepted the theory. Even so, the book was attacked by those scientists who still believed in the fixity of species and by the theologians who were shocked by the implication that man's ancestors were animals. The public was becoming accustomed to evolutionary theories and saw nothing scandalous in the book by Chambers. In 1852 Herbert Spencer published *The Development Hypothesis,* which set forth in turgid prose the theory of evolution and prepared the public even more for Darwin's book. The *Origin of Species*, as we have seen, was the culmination of a long line of thought about a theory that could not be demonstrated because of insufficient evidence. It was left to Darwin, who collected abundant evidence over a period of twenty years, to supply the necessary scientific credence.

3

The Origin of Species (1859) — With the publication of this "most important book of the century" a tantalizing theory that had been in the minds of thinkers and philosophers for many years was now given weighty scientific validity. The treatise begins slowly and gathers momentum as it goes along. It presents a dignified argument with the author convincing himself that evolution is indeed a fact, and the explanation behind the fact is natural selection. After a cautious Introduction in which he carefully outlines his basic plan, Darwin begins his discussion with horse breeding. Individual animals of a domestic variety differ from each other more noticeably than individuals of a wild species because of artificial selection. The farmer allows only his best stock to breed and plans the animal he wants with successive breeding. Natural selection is not unlike this artificial selection, for a species with many individuals coping with a diversity of conditions tends to produce individual differences. In nature as in all life one finds the Malthusian idea of struggle for existence. In nature there is constant conflict, an incessant struggle for survival against other life forms, against natural law, and against the physical environment established by natural law. Organic evolution is therefore the gradual accumulation of slight adaptations, "profitable variations" Darwin calls them, a process which helps one creature or one species to survive while others perish. This process the scientist termed natural selection. Herbert Spencer rather than Darwin is credited with calling the process "the survival of the fittest."

"Natural selection," Darwin explained, "is daily and hourly scrutinizing throughout the world the slightest variations; rejecting those that are bad, preserving and adding up all that are good." On a planet with limited resources a super abundance of life dictates an unceasing struggle for existence. To exist in nature is to accept an unrelenting contest between the hunter and the hunted, the smaller and weaker organism to be eaten by the larger. The slightest advantage somehow gained by a creature in this battle may insure its survival. It can then reproduce and pass on the peculiarity to its descendents and to the species. That means the strong will find adaptations to survive while those unchanged and weak will die. From this warfare new species of plants and animals emerge. As he observes this activity Darwin is more impressed by the progress that is made, as one species gives rise to another, than by the struggle. He assures us that death is generally painless and prompt, and "the vigorous, the healthy, the happy survive and multiply." He left unanswered the puzzling question of minute variations in a litter of puppies, or in a pod of seeds; that would concern the science of genetics in later years.

For many people his momentous work rendered the concept of evolution no longer a speculative and mind-teasing theory, but a scientific truth resting firmly on fact. The effect of the theory on Victorian religion was to create a bitter controversy. Conflict between science and theology was acerbic on both sides. The scientists were frequently arrogant, defensive, and belligerent; a similar attitude could be seen among the theologians. Pugnacity covered by a veneer of thin politeness prevailed. Several important questions were debated but never answered with satisfaction. Some of them I show here: In the light of scientific discovery is it now reasonable to believe in the story of Christian redemption? If natural law is at the root of all that goes on in nature, is miracle possible as a supernatural contravention? Is there any justification whatever for interference by God? Do the scientists actually have the presumption to suppose there is no God? The theologians who aired complaints genuinely believed that the scientists were hostile to religion. Science was robbing the world of its spirituality. God's beautiful world had become a cold mechanism ruled by natural law rather than transcendent goodness. Science questioned even the validity of sin and the human will. It wrested from man his importance in space and time. Physical cause and effect, the theologians argued, left no room for wonder, faith, dreams based on hope, or even religion. It undermined the traditional stories of the fall of man and the incarnation. It destroyed the view that nature was a marvelous system of purpose and design. Darwin's book presented only a theory and yet a theory that caused pain.

The book contained, in fact, not one but two theories. The first is the theory of organic evolution, which held that the first living molecule from the earliest time to the present has been a continuum through the process of speciation. The second is the theory of natural selection, which Darwin saw as the method of evolution. In his treatment of a vast amount of related evidence he did not bring man or mankind into the discussion. Yet he strongly implied mankind's descent from a lower bipedal animal resembling the apes. This implication immediately raised a hue and cry, which reverberated through the twentieth century and remains even now largely unsettled. It also caused many people to think about the so-called "missing link" and prompted scientists to go in quest of the first human being, the scientific equivalent of Adam. Not long ago a newspaper reported the findings of one such team: "The first human ancestor, the so-called 'mother of us all,' was a primitive woman who lived some 200,000 years ago in Africa." Clearly the search is continuing. While some people find both evolution and natural selection an insult to their beliefs and cherished values, Darwin said he saw no reason for his theory to upset religious people. Even so, the book seemed to attack the authority of the Bible and was also a tremendous deflator of mankind's ego. It was the second most important ego deflator after Copernicus. No longer a creature molded by God, man was only an animal in nature.

The Descent of Man (1871) — This is Darwin's second most important book and his second-best book even though excerpts from it are seldom anthologized. His daughter Henrietta is responsible for the vigorous style. The work is really two books in one. It deals with mankind for 206 of its pages and with sexual selection for the remaining 482. At the end of the book on evolution Darwin had predicted that his research would stimulate investigation in other directions. Twelve years later he applied his theories to human beings, taking the step he had cautiously avoided in the earlier book. Without beating around the bush, he proclaimed in this work that man was also the product of natural selection. Man, yielding to the same process as the other animals, had evolved from a creature similar to the great anthropoid apes. The position of man above the other animals came about not as the result of any one characteristic like acquisition of language, but because of upright stature, delicate and free hands (the opposable thumb), and the use of tools. The mental capacity of man walking erect, an advantage in the struggle for survival, made the use of tools and language possible.

Autobiography (1887) — This book was published under a longer and more descriptive title, "Recollections of the Development of My Mind and Character." It attempts to trace in a scientific spirit the evolution of Charles Darwin. Written between 1876 and 1881 and published posthumously, it was intended solely for his children. Because he knew and loved the audience he was writing for, his style is clear and charming and colored by family feeling. He combines the earnestness of Mill's autobiography with the warmth of a long and intimate family letter. He seems amazed that Darwin developed into Darwin, amazed that he evolved into himself. Once he had loved music and had enjoyed Milton and Wordsworth, but now he can only crunch scientific facts. He is astonished that he ever became an author, a member of the Royal Society, a thinker with ideas that once influenced others. He dwells upon the development of those ideas and the mind that thought them. He talks about himself in a tone of wholesome honesty and modesty, and even wonder, as he traces his religious attitudes from evangelicalism to agnosticism. Warm and human and humble, he is decent and appealing, and without the high moral tone of other eminent Victorians. Losing his faith as he became a scientist, he explains with disarming openness to those who loved him, he felt no distress.

As a scientist Darwin had no motive other than to seek and propagate the truth. Even though in time he lost his faith in organized religion, it was never his intention to attack religion or undermine the faith of others. In 1860, as the book of the century was stirring up a hurricane, he confided to Asa Gray, the foremost botanist in America and a long-time friend: "I had no intention to write atheistically. But I own that I cannot see as plainly as others do evidence of design and beneficence on all sides of us. There seems to me too much misery in the world. I cannot persuade myself that a beneficent and omnipotent God would have designedly created the Ichneumonidae to feed within the living bodies of caterpillars, or that a cat should play with mice. On the other hand, I cannot be content to view this wonderful universe, and especially the nature of man, and conclude that everything is the result of brute force." Though he couldn't see it, perhaps some sort of design apart from mechanics was inherent in life forms.

Thomas Henry Huxley

Less than a year after Darwin published the *Origin of Species* opposition to the book and its theories reached the point of vehement debate. In June of 1860 the British Association held its meeting in a cavernous room at Oxford packed with 700 people. Evolution was on the agenda. Huxley and other scientists were there, but Darwin himself was reportedly too ill to attend and was able to avoid the scene. The clergy hoped to nail the Darwinians at this meeting, embarrass them soundly, and put the monkey theory forever to rest. Bishop Samuel Wilberforce, called "Soapy Sam" by some of the debaters, was invited to speak. His strategy was to oversimplify evolution, stress its absurdity, and make it a joke to bring forth laughter. In a long harangue invoking good humor he attacked the theory with gusto but without knowing much about it. Then he turned to Thomas Huxley, who knew a lot about it, and politely begged to know whether the distinguished naturalist claimed descent from a monkey through his grandfather or from his grandmother?

For a moment there was silence, an awkward pause. Then Huxley was invited to answer the bishop. With calm dignity and quiet composure, not in the least ruffled by his opponent, he said he was there only in the interest of science and had heard nothing to shake his belief in Darwin's theory. It was in fact the best explanation of species yet advanced, and each day his belief in the theory became firmer. Quietly he corrected several mistakes made by the affable bishop. Then in grave tones, a deliberate contrast to the bishop's levity, he said he would rather have a monkey for his ancestor than "a man who used great gifts to obscure the truth." Huxley had carried the day. The hostile audience gave him nearly as much applause as accorded the bishop. After the meeting people on both sides of the issue, with frankness and fairness, complimented Huxley. Later he looked back on this experience as changing his opinions on public speaking.

In 1864, during a dramatic speech in the Sheldonian Theater at Oxford, no less a personage than Benjamin Disraeli took the opportunity to make his position clear regarding man's descent. "Is man descended from the apes or the angels?" he asked. He couldn't be absolutely certain at all times, he said with a chuckle, but he himself was on the side of the angels. Other speakers of more serious intent attempted to show that man occupied a favored and unique position between the apes and angels. Man had made great strides because unlike those two groups he was flexible and in movement and never static. He could move downward through reversion or upward through slow progression. Darwinism as carefully and plainly explained by Huxley left an impact upon the Victorians as profound as Mill's theory of individual freedom and human development. It inspired them with a vision of man almost godlike in his self-reliance and freedom of movement.

One result of all the talk about evolution was the conviction that progress is natural and inevitable and never accidental. "Progress," Herbert Spencer declared, "is surely not an accident but a necessity. What we call evil and immorality must disappear. It is certain that man must become perfect." The astronomer Herschel before his death in 1871 also expressed high hopes for the progress that would convey man toward a higher state. The Romantic doctrine of human perfectibility had taken on new meaning. The dim outline of a gigantic plan to make humankind perfect had been discovered by science. The belief offered infinite hope but was an over simplification and vastly naive. Huxley and others eventually disclaimed it. The cosmic process simply could not be viewed as a progressive design for good.

Thomas Henry Huxley (1825-1895) was born on May 4, 1825 in the village of Ealing near London. He was the seventh child of George Huxley, an underpaid senior master in a semi-public school. He received his early education in Ealing and a somewhat irregular education in Coventry, where his family moved in 1835 after his father accepted a position as manager of a savings bank. Before he went to London to study medicine, he had made good progress in a program of heavy reading and the study of French, Italian, and German. He matriculated at London University in 1842, graduated in 1845, and was appointed assistant surgeon aboard the H.M.S *Rattlesnake* in 1846. In December of that year the ship departed England on a four-year mission to chart the waters of northeastern Australia, a region unknown to science and even the Navy.

Huxley was just over twenty-one and eager for adventure. His medical duties would occupy only a part of his time aboard, and the remainder would be employed in scientific work. He would also have the leisure to read Carlyle whose writings would leave an indelible impression upon him. If the Renaissance could be called the age of geographic discovery, the nineteenth century with numerous voyages was the era of scientific discovery. Darwin, Hooker, Humbolt, Huxley, and Wallace – all of them promising young men – embarked on seas of opportunity as well as discovery. All returned with surefire plans and adequate means to make themselves famous. As Darwin on the *Beagle* had discovered his own Pacific, Huxley found a world of his own, a wife, and the drive he needed to become a renowned scientist.

The *Rattlesnake* was a slow and clumsy sailing vessel crammed with 180 men. It had not been equipped with adequate scientific instruments or reference books. It bristled with technicians but conditions were primitive. Huxley's bedroom, storeroom, and library were all a cabin no larger than a prison cell. A corner of the chartroom was his laboratory. This wooden and earthy world, smelly and stuffy, at first offended him. At length he adjusted and began to work industriously. On the voyage he made extensive studies of marine animals. His work on the variety of jellyfish indigenous to the coastal waters of eastern Australia established him as a leading zoologist by the time he returned home.

As another bonus, in Sydney he became engaged to Henrietta Heathorn, an intelligent and well-educated Australian girl. Ideally suited, they remained engaged for seven years before they were able to marry. His scientific studies went on day after day, and the ship eventually returned to England in November of 1850. On the strength of papers he had published, Huxley gained membership in the Royal Society in 1851 but could find no way to make a living. His mother died in 1852 and he became despondent, but went on working and writing. By his pen alone he earned 250 pounds a year. At last in 1854 he became a lecturer in the Royal School of Mines at 200 pounds a year. That allowed him to send for Henrietta, and they were able to marry in 1855. Tireless and always curious, he continued his incessant research even on his honeymoon.

In that same year, 1855, he delivered his first set of "Lectures to Working Men." They were so popular, once the word got around, that many people with smooth hands and clean fingernails dressed in working clothes to gain entrance. His first son was born in 1857, a year that found him in poor health and traveling in Switzerland to recuperate. In 1859 he was commissioned to review Darwin's *Origin of Species*, just published, for the London *Times*. Less than a year later he was defending Darwin in a speech before the Royal Institution. He had not planned to be drawn into the now-famous debate at the meeting of the British Association, but nonetheless proved himself a controversialist of first rank.

After that memorable encounter with the forces arrayed against Darwin, Huxley increasingly was called upon to champion the cause of evolution and soon came to be known as "Darwin's bulldog." In the years after 1860 he became the nation's most redoubtable defender of scientific truth and freedom of thought. He spoke in favor of higher education for women as early as 1860. In the essay "Emancipation – Black and White," occasioned by the end of the American Civil War, he called for educating both sexes of both colors. He vigorously opposed the exclusively classical education that dominated the schools and universities of the time, insisting that scientific studies were as important as literary studies in the pursuit of knowledge and culture.

In the autumn of 1876, fifty-one years old and at the height of his career, Huxley visited America to spread the doctrine of Darwinism. He intended at first simply to visit his sister Lizzie, who had settled with her husband in Tennessee. Then an American sent word through Frederic

Harrison that the whole nation was eagerly awaiting the arrival of the eminent scientist. Shortly after that Huxley was offered one hundred pounds to give an address at the opening of Johns Hopkins University. At length he accepted the invitation but refused the generous payment. He and his wife went first to New York and while Henrietta relaxed in Saratoga, he traveled to Yale to examine the fossil collection of Professor O. C. Marsh. He remained on the campus of Yale for several days and was interviewed by an enterprising reporter, who was surprised to find him not at all "highfalutin." With Henrietta he went to Boston and talked with the daughters of Longfellow and Hawthorne, attended a lengthy scientific meeting in Buffalo, and spent a week at Niagara on a "second honeymoon." From there they went to Nashville, where Huxley declared that no reconciliation was possible between the biblical view of creation and the scientific. Curiously, he received a standing ovation. Half a century later John Thomas Scopes, in the famous "monkey trial" of 1925, was found guilty of breaking the law by teaching evolution in the public schools of Tennessee. The close-minded climate that prevailed long after his visit and revealed during the trial would have appalled the scientist, and yet the irony of it all would not have escaped him.

From Nashville he and his wife traveled uncomfortably by train to Cincinnati and finally to Baltimore, where he gave his speech at Johns Hopkins after viewing the sights in Washington. Later a bible-thumping wag complained: "It was bad enough to invite Huxley. It were better to have asked God to be present. It would have been absurd to ask them both." Ignoring the theological response, Huxley went on to New York, where he gave three lectures on evolution and became a front-page sensation in the papers. The Connecticut sandstone, he declared, is a clear manuscript recording events many times older than any event preserved in the Bible.

Audiences received these lectures enthusiastically and so did most of the newspapers. Some attempted to mount an attack by claiming his material was too rudimentary and showed disrespect for American knowledge. But that was the customary attitude displayed by newspapers in regard to European visitors. When Matthew Arnold sailed to America a few years later, as we have seen, he received the same treatment. Huxley returned to England with pleasant memories of the United States and with a firm belief that the country would become a great power in the future. "I had a very pleasant trip in Yankee-land," he said to a friend, "and did not give utterance to a good deal that I am reported to have said there." In America both Englishmen had similar experiences with unreliable and inaccurate reporters who were eager to embellish facts to please their readers.

In 1877 Huxley published his lectures in this country under the title *American Addresses*. In the same year two other books from his pen also appeared. In 1878 two more books were published, and he also received the coveted LL.D. from Dublin University. Shortly after that he accepted another honorary LL.D. from Cambridge. He was fifty-three, in good health, working hard, and enjoying every minute of his career. He thrived on the accolades and the attention, and he loved the sound of applause. In 1881 when the School of Mines became part of a larger college to be known as the Imperial College of Science, he was made Dean of the College and Professor of Biology. He was much amused at being made a dean, admonishing a friend that a letter to a Dean (always capitalized) had to be addressed as "The Very Revd" or else. He did not stand much on etiquette, he said, but drew the line when it came to that sacred identity. In 1883 he was elected president of the Royal Society, and in 1885 another honorary degree came from Oxford University. In 1884 he went to Italy because of poor health and later resigned his professorship and inspectorship of fisheries to relieve the strain. In 1888 a second attack of pleurisy sent him to Switzerland to recover, and in 1889 he wrote his "Autobiography." In 1893 he delivered a famous lecture at Oxford and received the Darwin medal in 1894. In the early months of 1895 his health was shaken by influenza and bronchitis. An eminent scientist in his own right, he died on June 29, 1895 at the age of seventy. After 1860 Huxley gave much time and energy to the defense of Darwin and the theory of evolution. He attacked the attackers and did his job well.

3

Darwin's bulldog performed so exceptionally well that in less than a year he became famous. In all of his speeches he insisted that man is an animal in nature and related to all the other animals. He knew as well as Darwin himself all the details of the theory and could explain them better than Darwin. He popularized Darwinian doctrine, placed it in the minds of people everywhere, and got them talking about it. Some were fascinated by the theory; for others it tore down a necessary egotism and self-reverence. It also had the effect of undermining orthodox religious belief. The theory stimulated a controversy, which had at its core two conflicting views of life. The romantic or intuitive worldview of Carlyle and others became the adversary of the rationalistic or scientific view which Mill and his followers had advocated, and which Huxley was solidly behind. The basic questions were these: How does the seeker after truth find it? What tools does he use to find it? How does he recognize truth when he finds it? Huxley had little patience with romantic thinkers who argued that intuition and insight have the power to reveal the truth. He didn't deny the validity of that position but said it was unreliable because it couldn't be made to work all the time. The scientific method was far more efficient in probing the secrets of nature so as to use them for mankind. If civilization were to advance, the method would have to be taught in the new science courses in the schools.

Huxley distinguished himself in famous controversies with famous people, with Arnold, Gladstone, Spencer, Wilberforce, and others. He was able to win his battles because he was a man as morally earnest as Carlyle. For thirty years he preached the gospel of evolution wherever people gathered to listen. He wrote and spoke without end, always publishing his lectures to gain a wider audience. A collection of his speeches published under the title *Lay Sermons* (1870) covered both educational and scientific problems and extended his influence as one concerned with education on all levels. He wanted to see men and women of all classes attending the universities and preparing for the professions. Many of his best speeches were addressed to workingmen because, unlike Carlyle and Arnold, he soon lost faith in the power of the middle class to solve contemporary problems. He came to believe that classes like everything else evolved, and so he placed his hope for the future in the lower classes.

Before he died he was able to see definite signs of strength and solidarity in the working class. With full voting privileges, it was asserting itself in politics and was also taking advantage of the new education. When we talk of Huxley we tend to forget his influence on elementary and secondary education in England, but in some ways it was as strong as Arnold's. Also he labored in the cause of medical and technical education and expressed opinions concerning higher education in effect today. Although locked in dispute with Arnold and fundamentally opposing Newman, he shared with both a passionate love of truth and a superlative honesty. He had no wish whatever to destroy the humanism or the culture of Carlyle, Ruskin, Arnold, and Newman. He sought only a blending of modern science with the long humanistic tradition so as to produce results that worked. Though he died before his promise was entirely fulfilled, he succeeded in his aims more completely than most of the other thinkers, orators, and writers of his day. Future decades would prove that science was the key to open the mysteries of nature, and future centuries would owe a debt to his work.

"Method of Scientific Investigation" (1863) — In this essay Huxley demonstrates a remarkable ability to explain complex scientific concepts in terms the layman can understand. With patience and good humor he asserts that the scientific method has always been in the world and is used every day by the ordinary human mind. The main difference between the scientific method and plain commonsense is the fact that science tends to verify its conclusions by means of many examples. To show how the method works, he cites the now-famous example of the apples. Suppose you go into a grocery store to buy some apples. You select one and biting into it you find it sour. You look at it and find it hard and green. You select another and that too is hard and green and sour. The grocer offers you a third apple, but before biting it you see that it is hard and green. You reply there is no need to bite into the apple because like the others it will prove sour. Now if you examine the logic involved, you will find that inductive reasoning led you to the conclusion that hardness and greenness in apples go with sourness. Then you employ deductive reasoning to form a syllogism: "All hard and green apples are sour; this apple is hard and green; therefore this apple is sour." On the basis of this you make up your mind that you will not have that particular apple because you will not be able to eat it with enjoyment.

What you have done in this instance is to establish a law by induction, and upon that you have founded a deduction. Then you have reasonably concluded, using both induction and deduction, not to waste your money. Happily you live with that conclusion until some later time when you discuss the qualities of sour apples with a friend. You say, "It is a fact that all hard and green apples are sour!" Your skeptical friend asks, "But how do you know that?" You reply, "Because I have tried hard and green apples repeatedly, and have found them to be always sour." If this were science instead of commonsense, your experience with apples would be called experimental verification. If still opposed, you could go further to say that you have heard from people in many places who grow apples, and their conclusions, based on similar observation, agree with yours. In short, you have found it to be "the universal experience of mankind wherever attention has been directed to the subject." With more extensive verification brought before him, your friend is now willing (unless he is very unreasonable) to agree with you and is convinced that you are right. The scientific method is the same as the commonsense method. The only difference is that science requires every possible kind of verification.

"On a Piece of Chalk" (1868) — In this essay Huxley moves again from the commonplace to vistas of geological strata and fossil evidence. The essay is often cited as a masterpiece of inductive movement from the familiar and the close at hand to the strange and remote. Addressed to the working people of Norwich as well as to members of the British Association meeting there in 1868, he begins with reference to the ubiquitous English chalk. Once more he travels from the small to the large and discovers infinite riches along the way. As the French scientist Cuvier derived an entire theory from a single bone, Huxley moves from a piece of chalk to evolution and crocodiles. "Either each species of crocodile has been specially created," he maintains, "or it has arisen out of some preexisting form by the operation of natural causes. Choose your hypothesis; I have chosen mine." The essay was a sample lesson of sorts, an illustration on how to teach scientific principles in elementary and secondary schools. The explanation is clear and simple, and the speaker's tone is reflective of a teacher's patience. Huxley's informal style is plain, simple, direct, and economical.

4

"On the Physical Basis of Life" (1869) — This is another attempt
to illustrate complex ideas simply and plainly for a lay public to
understand. It presents some of Huxley's major ideas in easy-to-follow
fashion. Delivered in Edinburgh before a large audience that included
working people, he came on stage with a big bottle of smelling salts
and other commonplace articles. These, he said, contained the essential
ingredients of protoplasm, the physical basis of life. Vitality is not a
quality of spirit separate from nature, for all living things are made up
basically of one substance, protoplasm. Life comes from life, and living
protoplasm is created by living protoplasm. If there is no sharp distinction
between simple plants and animals, there is no real distinction between
protoplasm and inorganic matter except in structure.

The human mind itself is "the result of molecular forces in the
protoplasm which displays it." Man is a brother not only to the monkey,
but also to the molecule and the atom. Theologians scream that all this
is a threat to man's dignity: "they are alarmed lest man's moral nature
be debased by the increase of his wisdom." And yet as one thinks about
it, perhaps wisdom and moral cast are one and the same. With this he
pauses for a moment for his audience to absorb the idea. Then following
the empiricist method of David Hume, the eighteenth-century Scottish
philosopher and skeptic, he hits them with questions to make them
think. He asks whether matter is known or unknown and whether
natural law is only a probability. In a world full of uncertainty, do
we not need to know that our will counts for something? If indeed it
does, then man is brother to the molecule in a very restricted sense. As
he expands upon the importance of will in human life, Huxley shows
the influence of Carlyle. The lecture was well received in Edinburgh
and later became an influential essay. Its simplicity of style allowed for
easy understanding for anybody willing to take the time to explore the
subject.

English education tended to ignore the new science even after
Huxley came on the scene. It was not until the last three decades
of the century that reforms were made to introduce science into the
curriculum on all levels. The so-called public schools, which in fact
were private schools maintained for the sons of gentlemen, had become

by mid-century notoriously ineffective. Their funding was not large enough to offer teachers adequate salaries, and so many attempting to teach in these schools were not truly qualified. Also working conditions in the schools were often severe. It was not uncommon for teachers and students to suffer chills and frostbite in unheated classrooms, and the food that came from dirty kitchens provided few calories for warmth. In 1828 Thomas Arnold founded an authoritarian state at Rugby, where the boys were taught moral responsibility, the Bible, the classics, French, and German. Some other schools in England imitated his work, but general education for the most part remained in a sad state.

Too many exclusive and expensive schools, according to one faction making its voice heard in the controversy, offered a poor moral environment, taught subjects that had little to do with life, and taught just about every subject ineffectually. Instead of cramming the heads of pupils with dead languages and dead cultures (the argument went), the public schools as well as the universities had an obligation to offer science, mathematics, and modern languages. As might be expected, this liberal attack upon the impotence of the English educational system generated stubborn conservative resistance. Gladstone himself felt that a classical education, an exercise in the expansion of mind, was sound preparation for modern life. Nonetheless, a Royal Commission was duly appointed in 1861 to investigate conditions and later recommended sweeping, comprehensive reform. They mandated a curriculum that included the traditional subjects but also science. It was another memorable triumph for Huxley and one of the most satisfying.

"A Liberal Education And Where To Find It" (1868) — This essay was delivered as a lecture at the South London Workingmen's College after Huxley was made principal of that school. The address was given on the eve of the great educational experiment that began in 1870. At that time the lower classes were illiterate and yet pressing for power. They would eventually assume in just a few years more importance in English society. The big question was how to prepare them for the role they would play in the future. So in 1870 state-supported schools were established for any young person of any social class. Before this time the education of future leaders lay mostly in the hands of expensive and classically oriented institutions with haphazard curricula. Huxley called for a fast but orderly transition from the old to the new as soon as possible, and he wanted the nation to know exactly what the curriculum of the new education should be. The Education Act was meant to bring education to anyone who wanted it, but it would not be the type traditionally offered the sons of gentlemen. Newman had been concerned with educating the gentleman, but Huxley wanted a practical and workable curriculum for all the people. Modern history, modern languages, English literature, and the new science should be available for study by young persons of both sexes. Science was equal to literature in teaching moral and ethical values. Huxley would later argue this point with Arnold.

His criticism is aimed at the entire English system, but particularly he targets the primary and secondary schools. The classics are useless if the student afterwards can remember nothing of ancient life and thought. English universities bask in the glory of centuries, and all connected with them believe they are truly great institutions, and yet they have few if any distinguished scholars and produce nothing that can be called significant research. What is more, they offer little opportunity for advanced studies in modern science and culture. All that must change. England must accept a more realistic definition of liberal education. Many thoughtful people believe that education is the great panacea for human troubles, but they differ as to who should receive it and what it should accomplish. The politicians would educate the masses because eventually the masses will be the masters. The clergy would educate the masses because they are drifting into infidelity. The captains of industry would like to educate the masses because ignorance makes for inefficient workers. All three examples, however, express a narrow view of education. The masses should be educated because "they are men and women with unlimited capacities of being, doing, and suffering," and because "people perish for lack of knowledge." A liberal education should develop and discipline the total man or woman, making his or her body an efficient mechanism and the mind "a clear, cold, logic engine."

A liberal education should cultivate healthy and vigorous passions but a strong will to control them. It should cherish a sense of beauty and a tender conscience. It should offer the willing student a detailed outline of total human knowledge and should look to nature for its method. This point Huxley explains with amazing clarity in his extended metaphor comparing life to a game of chess. Readers were impressed and repeated the metaphor so often that it soon became famous. It endures today as a remarkable example of the clear, cold logic engine at work. The game of life, he tells us, is like a chess game but infinitely more difficult and complicated. Nature as an invisible opponent plays with each person a game of chess.

It goes without saying that a good education should teach the rules of the game, for "nature's pluck means extermination." If we play the game without skill, if we attempt to play and do it carelessly, we pay a high price. This doesn't mean that nature is cruel or malicious. Our hidden opponent is always fair, just, silent, and very patient. Our opponent is equally observant and never overlooks the smallest mistake, nor makes the slightest allowance for ignorance. As Mill had said, nature pardons no mistakes. Even so, nature has a way of rewarding the person who plays the game well. The one who does not play it well is checkmated. The defeat comes without haste but also without remorse. "What I mean by education is learning the rules of this mighty game. In other words, education is the instruction of the intellect in the laws of nature." To play any game well, one must know the rules.

"Scientific Education" (1869) — This essay, written and delivered shortly after the one on liberal education, attempted to bolster and strengthen the earlier points he had made. Huxley was speaking from his notes at a dinner of the Liverpool Philomathic Society and later published the lecture from these expanded notes. Scientific education doesn't contradict liberal education, since the goals of both are essentially the same. Scientific education, however, may be seen as more practical in its aims than liberal education. Since most people of the middle class are devoted to Ruskin's "Goddess of Getting On," science should be in their arsenal. A full grasp of scientific method will make their progress in the world less difficult and faster. As competition becomes keener, the person who can use science to his advantage is the one who will win "the struggle for existence which goes on as fiercely beneath the smooth surface of modern society, as among the wild inhabitants of the woods." A scientific education surpasses all others because it provides an abundance of useful facts to be used in the daily struggle. Scientific training in the secondary schools – he makes no distinction between education and training – should move from the most concrete science (physical geography) to the most abstract (physics). Always the inductive method, proceeding from facts to generalization, should be employed.

"On University Education" (1876) — This address was delivered *ex tempore* at the opening of Johns Hopkins University in Baltimore. Huxley had hired a stenographer to take down the speech and supply him with a fair copy, but when it came at the eleventh hour he couldn't read the man's handwriting. Americans were pleased to hear that Huxley's idea of a university was little different from their own. He favored the tendencies already dominant in American higher education. He disapproves of entrance requirements and suggests an open-door policy for the new university. He prefers individual course examinations at the end of the term to comprehensive examinations that are too broad in coverage.

He asserts that research is an integral and important part of university life, but should be done in combination with teaching. Medical training – Johns Hopkins was to become famous for its school of medicine – should be practical and professional without frills. Arnold and Newman would have insisted that a medical education, secured at great expense, be more than mere training. But Huxley argues that a physician should know what is best for his patients, not what is best for himself. He minimizes also the importance of architecture, perhaps causing Ruskin some distress, saying a university can do without fancy buildings, for brains and equipment are far more important than the structures that house them. He closes with a glimpse of America's future. In the cities "the gaunt spectre of pauperism" could stalk the streets (an idea from Malthus), but there is hope in "the moral worth and intellectual clearness of the individual citizen" in America.

5

"Lectures on Evolution" (1876) — The speeches assembled under this title, typical of Huxley as Darwin's bulldog, were delivered in New York to large audiences on three successive nights. In the first lecture Huxley examines adroitly and thoroughly three hypotheses concerning the earth's history:

- Present conditions have always existed and will eternally.

- Our world was created some 5,000 years ago as seen in Genesis.

- The organic world evolved naturally over eons of time.

In the two lectures that followed he demolished the first and second concepts by showing that only the third could accommodate the true facts of science. Drawing his illustrations from geological formations situated nearby (Niagara Falls and the Connecticut sandstone), he tears down the Pentateuch and builds an evolutionary edifice upon its ruins.

Loyalty to pure truth, or truth as we perceive it he insists, is more important than loyalty to any creed. He also appeals to their sense of national pride to help Americans put down erroneous concepts based on biblical teachings, saying American scenery by virtue of its beauty and grandeur and great age shames Old Testament cosmogony. The Connecticut sandstone tells a story not of creation but of slow development, and its record is much older than anything the Old Testament has to offer. All three lectures were written during the time he was on tour in the United States and were a subtle compliment to the people who came to hear them. He viewed the Americans as worthy receivers of Darwin's doctrine.

"Science and Culture" (1880) — This essay was delivered as an address at the opening of Sir Josiah Mason's Science College at Birmingham on October 1, 1880. Mason had pulled himself up by his own bootstraps. As a boy he sold hot food in the streets and fresh vegetables from door to door. In 1810 he taught himself shoemaking. Later he became a carpenter, a blacksmith, a house painter, and a carpet weaver. Then he rose to become a factory executive and soon after that made a fortune running his own factory. The crown of his life of hard work and achievement was the establishment of his college at a cost of 180,000 pounds and five years of incessant labor. Huxley quite plainly admired Mason and pays him tribute in this essay, saying Mason was "thrown into the thick of the struggle for existence" and not only survived but prospered. He was a practical man of business and wanted practical courses at his college, not "mere literary instruction."

Huxley saw in the occasion a chance to campaign for scientific education in the face of two opposing groups: the pragmatic men of business on the one hand, and the "Levites in charge of the ark of culture" on the other. The first group had resolutely maintained that on-the-job training for industrial careers was far better than a college education. The second group, according to Huxley, held that the Greek and Latin classics were the best preparation for the competitive life of modern times. A science college founded by a self-taught man to offer only the most important courses seemed the perfect refutation of both groups. Huxley turned his guns mainly on the classicists by approving the exclusion of literary and classical studies at Mason's college. He argued that a scientific education without literature, though less liberal than one with literature, is just as liberal as one which contains nothing but literature, and it is far more liberal than one containing merely ancient writings in dead languages.

The best training for life, he asserts, is the scientific study of nature. The best training for coping in modern times is the scientific study of society. It is better for a person to know his environment, its penalties and rewards, than merely to know himself. The student who applies himself can acquire satisfactory and useful knowledge through the study of science, and that knowledge will remain with him and serve him for a lifetime. The study of literature, on the other hand, will supply him only with soft and imaginative knowledge that he may not be able to use at all in the affairs of life. Humane subjects are not exclusively the property of the humanities. Almost in mockery of Arnold, he declares that scientific study of society and nature is a better preparation for citizenship and life than to know the best that has been thought and said in the world. The statement seemed to Arnold so extreme as to be irresponsible. Was the scientist deliberately attempting to provoke the humanist to create a controversy? Huxley had taken a bold stand against Arnold's vaunted humanism. The address tended to rupture their friendship.

The two intellectuals had become friends in 1868 when Huxley invited Arnold to the annual dinner of the Geological Society. Knowing that the world saw them as serious antagonists, they happily criticized one another as a long-running and largely private joke. Huxley, for example, insisted that Arnold had invented the wise, oracular Bishop Wilson, for no churchman ever spoke so eloquently. Their letters continued the banter even as they drew upon the expertise of each other for certain facts. At that time they had not fully realized how profound were their differences. In both was an uncompromising moral sense that made them both dogmatic. Both were essentially stoical, and neither had ever shown much sympathy for religion or its teachings. Both despised the narrow complacency of the puritan middle class and recognized the need for more intelligence in the national life. An important difference, however, cannot be overlooked: one was a scientist and a rationalist while the other was a poet and a humanist. In "Science and Culture" Huxley referred to his friend by name and took him to task for holding certain theories unacceptable to any sane person. Arnold's eloquent reply came in one of his American discourses, "Literature and Science" (1883). Scientists, he said, often get lost in the mysteries of nature while tending to ignore human nature. Men and women in their quest for a sense of conduct and beauty cannot live by scientific formula alone. The wisdom belonged to Arnold, but the future would fall to Huxley.

"Agnosticism and Christianity" (1889) — This essay was published first in the *Nineteenth Century* and then collected with other essays for publication in book form. Dr. Henry Wace, the chancellor of King's College in London, had attacked Huxley's agnosticism. An agnostic, he said, is one who pleads no scientific knowledge of the unseen world and therefore refuses to accept the authority of Jesus Christ. Those who call themselves agnostics are practicing evasion and deserve a stronger term – infidels – to describe them. Huxley replied that he failed to see how the two very different terms, agnostic and infidel, could be used as interchangeable words. Agnosticism, he explained, is not a creed but a method that employs a single principle. That principle, fundamental to modern science, urges one in matters of intellect to follow reason rather than emotion and accept no conclusion unless demonstrated or demonstrable. He is an agnostic because he is not willing to believe in God without proof. Newman had shown that he could believe in miracles on faith alone, could accept conclusions without proof, but Huxley can't do that. Taking a purely rational approach to the mysteries of religion, he can't be certain of God's existence until he has seen the proof.

Agnosticism is therefore a resigned position of not knowing. Huxley was more than well qualified to define the meaning of the word because he himself had invented it. He coined the term "agnostic" at a dinner held prior to the formation of the Metaphysical Society in 1869. Earlier he had complained that everybody in those iron times was some kind of -*ist* or -*ite*. Echoing Carlyle, he said that he alone was "a man without a rag of a label to cover himself with." And so he invented the term to clothe himself in a mantle of respectable denial of Christian belief, which could not be called infidelity. At the first meeting of the Society, founded to debate whether truth can be arrived at by the spirit as well as by the senses, he said agnostic was the opposite of Gnostic. That was the name of a philosophical sect dating from pre-Christian times and claiming to know all the mysteries of the universe. The Gnostic quite simply claims to know; the agnostic claims not to know. An agnostic is one who holds that the existence of anything beyond and behind material phenomena is unknown and perhaps unknowable. A First Cause or invisible worlds above or beyond the world we know through our senses are subjects of which we know nothing. Huxley carefully explained that "agnostic" differs considerably in meaning from "atheist," defined as one who denies or disbelieves the existence of any kind of God.

Almost immediately a controversy began which lasted twenty years and culminated in the series of charges and counter charges of which "Agnosticism and Christianity" was only a part. In 1871 the editor of *The Spectator*, in reference to Huxley and his followers, said this: "they themselves vehemently dispute the term 'atheism' and usually prefer to describe their state of mind as a sort of know-nothingism, or agnosticism." In 1876 an article in the same journal supported that definition: "Agnostic was the name demanded by Professor Huxley for those who disclaimed atheism and believed with him in an 'unknown and unknowable' god." In other words, if deity lies behind evolution, and if evolution is only a pattern in a great creative design, the cause is unknown and (so far as one can judge) unknowable.

In 1880 Huxley's agnosticism was attacked in the *Saturday Review* with the earlier and stale cry of atheism: "In nine cases out of ten agnosticism is but old atheism writ large." Then in 1882, J. A. Froude published Carlyle's trenchant opinion expressed as analogy: "The agnostic doctrines were to appearance like the finest flour from which you might expect the most excellent bread; but when you came to feed on it, you found it was powdered glass, and you had been eating the deadliest poison." It was an outrageous statement but typical of Carlyle in his later years. Huxley admired the author of *Past and Present* as a great man, but Carlyle (grown bitter and crusty by then) had no use for the younger man. Meeting him in the street one day (the story goes), Carlyle grumped: "So you're the fella who believes we all came from monkeys, eh?" Before Huxley could put down his surprise and make a thoughtful reply, Carlyle covered his ears and walked away.

As a young man Huxley was moved by Carlyle's writings and to his dying day was able to quote from his books. As a rationalist he rejected many of Carlyle's concepts, but the doctrine of work guided him throughout his life. He worked long and hard at what he did, and he did it well. It was said that he threw the full weight of thought, feeling, and will into everything he pursued. He was clear, logical, well informed, and brilliant, but as a warrior fighting for a cause he sometimes lacked an open mind. His attitude toward religion and other important questions was often one of bland dismissal. The older he became the harder he fought. The younger Huxley, who wrote engagingly on a piece of chalk and a liberal education, is surely more pleasant. Though we may admire him for the power and clarity of his thought, the controversial essays that made Huxley famous in his day have less interest for us today. Yet we still read him for his thoughts on evolution and education, the scientific method, and whether agnosticism is a valid position when one loses faith in organized religion.

Science and the Higher Criticism

After 1859 life among the Victorians could never be the same. The *Origin of Species* delivered the final blow to the hope that science somehow would find a way to support biblical text and its view of man. A close reading of Darwin's book and the numerous assertions of Huxley made it clear that evolution did not always promise progress. Hand in hand with evolutionary progression went reversion, or retrogression. Even if science could be interpreted as promising a rosy future, it had called into question the validity of the entire Christian story upon which religious faith rested. The cherished belief that a benevolent Providence had created man in pristine perfection as an act of love, and had made the universe especially for him, was no longer tenable. Science had shown that for the moment man was the most highly developed creature in nature, but was subject to the same laws that governed all other life forms and could in time lose his supremacy. The scientists called into question any evidence long presented that an eternal God loved man as a special and favored creature. Any "proof" had been quickly dismissed. Even man's intelligence did not set him apart. He had more intelligence simply because he occupied a more advanced stage of evolution than his fellow creatures lower on the scale. Moreover, he was motivated not so much by a unique intelligence as by the same physical drives which he shared with other animals in a common struggle to survive.

The theory of evolution effectively shattered man's view of himself as the crown of creation. Even harder to accept was the theory of natural selection. No creature, including man, could now be seen as acquiring at the moment of creation those distinctions that made it different. All creatures were nothing more than the present generation of a species that had managed to survive the bitter and ceaseless struggle for existence. They were dominant today, but they could be extinct tomorrow. The certain and divinely ordained great chain of being had yielded to change and chance. In the natural scheme of things projected by science, no creature was either stable or secure. Wordsworth's uplifting and beneficent nature, personified as a beautiful woman who never betrayed the heart that loved her, had become in Tennyson's time all "red in tooth and claw." Wordsworth's vernal wood filled with heart-warming impulses had become for Tennyson and the Victorians "a world of plunder and prey." The glorious human attributes so often praised by the poets were now merely refinements of traits shared with all other animals, and the nature created specifically for man and reflecting God himself was also a shared domain. However, a stern belief in the dogma of progress prompted people to believe these mindless processes might be leading to good. If indeed man shared traits with the animals, perhaps he could move upward and work out the beast and "let the ape and tiger die."

That, of course, is the idea of development so strongly implied by the theory. If the human species at one time had fins, is it not reasonable to suppose that in some other time it may have wings? In *Tancred* (1847), a novel by Disraeli, an intelligent and fashionable lady hit upon the same idea. She was talking about a bestseller that had just appeared. Even though it is given a fictitious name, the book she interprets is surely *Vestiges of the Natural History of Creation* (1844). "But what is most interesting," she explains, "is the way in which man has been developed. You know, all is development. The principle is perpetually going on. First, there was nothing, then there was something…then we came. We were fishes, and I believe we shall be crows…something with wings." Significantly, the lady was expressing ideas not fully explained until Huxley published *Man's Place in Nature* (1863), followed later by Darwin's *Descent of Man* (1871). Middle-class readers had seen that man was not exempt from that timeless process of change that affected all of animate nature. *We were apes*, she might have said, *and I believe we shall be angels.* But that in later years no one could say, for scientific inquiry had shunted aside the supernatural stories of heaven and hell, devils and angels, and the story of creation.

Evolutionism, or Darwinism as it came to be called, was another triumph of the secular tendencies that pervaded Victorian life. The theory was adaptable to the habit of compromise and enabled many people, such as the young woman we have just heard, to fabricate world views of their own. That often meant curious combinations of contradictory ideas, but some were able to fuse the clear results of science with liberal interpretations of God and the Bible that had come from "the Higher Criticism." This contribution to the Victorian religious crisis originated in German scholarship. Lower criticism of the Bible had dealt with linguistic and textual problems. The higher criticism, which grew out of basic studies, was the attempt to arrive at a correct historical and interpretative evaluation of the Bible. Its purpose was to establish the authenticity of the scriptures by relating them to the historical background. Before 1859 in England only a few books had appeared to shake the faith of the Victorians in eternal truth. But with the spread of the new science and the new historical spirit there occurred also a pervasive exposure to the new biblical criticism. The result of these forces combined was a rapid erosion of faith among the readers of the middle class.

While German thinkers were advancing biblical criticism, England had been insular and indifferent. Most Victorians of all classes believed in the Bible as divinely inspired from cover to cover. Each Sunday those who went to church – some in the lower classes did not – they heard that message from the pulpit. Few theologians were then approaching scriptural problems in a critical spirit. Herbert Marsh, Bishop of Llandaff who died in 1839, had made a tentative examination of the Bible as literature, and Henry Hart Milman's *History of the Jews* (1830) had disturbed readers by calling Abraham an Arab sheik. Thomas Arnold at Rugby had urged the study of history to throw light on biblical narrative, and slowly objective studies appeared.

More important than any of them was Coleridge's posthumously published *Confessions of an Inquiring Spirit* (1840). He placed emphasis on the spiritual authority of the Bible even though much of it, such as supernatural events and the miracles of Christ, could not endure historical and scientific scrutiny. He recommended, nonetheless, the new critical approach of the Germans in biblical studies. These were the pioneers in the historical method as applied to religion. Other works that stimulated a general interest in this direction were also in print, but the book that really shocked many Victorians was *Das Leben Jesu* by the German author David Strauss (1808-1874). Though Strauss published the book in 1835, it was not widely known in England until translated by George Eliot (Mary Ann Evans) in 1846.

Even though it was the negative side of the German critic's thesis, which claimed the most attention and caused the most distress, he concluded with Coleridge that the abiding value of the Bible was not its facts (which could be easily discredited), but its spiritual and ethical significance. His aim was to reconcile Christian theology with Hegelian philosophy. To accomplish this he wanted to destroy all belief in the supernatural and the miraculous. For him the Gospels were but a myth, and the supernatural impossible, because Hegelian theory viewed religion as a steady and gradual historical development. The sudden appearance of a perfect man in the timeless process of human development was unbelievable to Strauss because it rendered evolution meaningless. Perfection had to come at the end of the process, not in the middle or near the beginning. The story of Jesus as the perfect Son of God he saw as a myth reflecting the collective mind of the people. However, Strauss did not deny the existence of Jesus. There was such a prophet, he asserted, and the man gave his life for his ministry. However, the early Church fathers translated the human into the divine and supernatural Christ. Out of the natural tendency to construct myths came the perfect Christ of orthodox theology. *Das Leben Jesu* may have shocked many readers, but it provided the stimulus for sound literary criticism of the New Testament.

Strauss set out to write an accurate biography of Jesus that would employ the latest scientific and historical criticism. To a large extent he accomplished his aim, for he divested Jesus of divinity and presented him strictly as a man. His aim was to enlighten his readers, not to destroy their religious faith. He wanted only to chip away at faith in the supernatural and to urge a faith based on reason. He wanted to show that in essence Christian and philosophical truth need not be at variance. Moreover, he wished to point out as best he could the unity of the divine and the human. This aim had a strong appeal for some, but for others it was appalling. The book took some of their most cherished beliefs and placed them under a microscope. How could the delicate fabric of religious faith possibly withstand such examination? The supernatural was banished, the gospel story was reduced to myth, and the human took the place of the divine. What was even more shocking was Christ presented in full detail not as the son of the Almighty, but as the creation of the Church. The book spread consternation among the religious and faithful, not only in Germany but also in England. It had aroused some interest even before it was brought into English. In the translation by George Eliot, it became a bestseller and received much attention. The views of the translator were largely in harmony with those of Strauss, but Robert Browning had different opinions on this "higher criticism."

He vividly depicted this new element of religious crisis in his poem "Christmas-Eve" (1850). Its various scenes are enacted on a stormy Christmas Eve. It opens with a humorous description of a dissenting chapel somewhere in England filled to capacity with rough and squalid people. The pastor preaches emotional nonsense, but his adoring flock hangs on every word, taking comfort and satisfaction in all he says. Then the scene shifts to a richly baroque Christmas Eve mass at St. Peter's in Rome with emphasis on the contrast. The poem's third scene is a bare lecture room at a German university, where a pedant on Christmas Eve delivers unemotional tidings to bored and restless students. The three scenes depict the simplistic, ritualistic, and rationalistic points of view regarding the Christian story.

When all three are carefully considered, weighed and probed on the basis of effectiveness, Browning chooses the simplicity of the protestant Dissenters. The third and last scene, inspired by *Das Leben Jesu*, represents the third dimension of Christian thought in 1850. The "hawk-nosed professor" speaking of "the myth of Christ" is the image of David Strauss, and the doctrine the professor delivers is a composite of the German critic's main ideas. Strauss had reduced Christ from a divine being, the Son of God, to a man – the greatest of men, perhaps, but only a man. Browning was not shocked as some of his contemporaries were, and yet he objected to the dryness of this liberal religion which took its impetus from the higher criticism. He dismisses the professor's discourse, less pleased with German rationalism than with English Dissent or Italian Catholicism.

3

One of the most important books coming after the work by Strauss was another biography of Jesus. It was titled *La Vie de Jésus* and published in 1863 by the French scholar Ernest Renan (1823-1892). It too attempted to discredit the Bible's pretension to divine authority and was much influenced by Strauss. The turning point in Renan's career came in 1846 when he convinced himself that nowhere in the universe is there a higher intelligence than man's. His *Vie de Jésus* was plainly an expression of his conviction that intelligence and will lie not with the supernatural, but with man alone. The method he applied to biblical narrative was that of the historian. He did not attempt to reduce the stature of Jesus, and yet the inevitable result was a presentation of Jesus more as a man than divinity. His aim was to present a vivid picture of the biblical environment, its cults, creeds, and customs, and to show that Jesus was well adapted to that environment. Because of its literary skill, the book was well received and widely read.

In "The Function of Criticism at the Present Time" (1864), Matthew Arnold singled out Ernest Renan's recently published book for analysis and discussion. He said that while the French scholar's attempt to recapture the historical setting of the gospels was exemplary in some respects and certainly appeared to go in the right direction, it was not entirely successful. Even so, a fresh and new synthesis of difficult materials had been attempted if not achieved, and other work would surely follow. Additional work would have to look closely at biblical text to present a fuller picture, and that is what happened. In England, as well as on the Continent, researchers were carefully examining the Bible in the light of historical events.

In 1860, a few years before Renan published his book, a volume entitled *Essays and Reviews* was authored by a group of scholars that included Benjamin Jowett and Mark Pattison. Jowett was a very influential fixture at Oxford and Master of Balliol College. Pattison served as Rector of Lincoln College, Oxford and was a Church of England priest. Their book showed at a glance the pervasive influence among intellectuals of the German rationalists and the higher criticism. They discussed the problems of doctrine and hagiography in a polite and reverent tone but also in a critical spirit. Miracle, prophecy, divine inspiration for the scriptures were all challenged in the seven essays that made up the volume. Not one of the authors said anything shocking, and yet the book caused a spirited uproar of indignation.

Two years later John Colenso (1814-1883), Bishop of Natal in South Africa, published the first volume of *The Pentateuch Critically Examined*. It brought forth a storm of protest. The English bishops demanded his resignation, and the South African bishops tried to excommunicate him, but Colenso refused to accept the action. In England even Matthew Arnold attacked the book, claiming its author had done all he could to strengthen the current confusion and make it dangerous. Science should come from the men of science, he said, and religion from the men of religion; Colenso was crossing the line. Taking the scientific approach, Colenso questioned the literal inspiration of the Old Testament and its reliability as historical fact. He concluded that the first five books of the Hebrew scriptures (Genesis, Exodus, Leviticus, Numbers, and Deuteronomy), books traditionally ascribed to Moses and called the Torah, were not authentic. All five were forgeries. In particular, *Deuteronomy* was a pious and transparent fraud by the prophet Jeremiah. His views were not well received.

By 1862 other forces in addition to the higher criticism were assaulting biblical truth. In late November of 1859 Charles Darwin, who regretted using "the Pentateuchal term of creation," published the *Origin of Species*. By the early sixties the book was exerting enormous influence upon the minds of thinking people. There had been in earlier decades a good deal of speculation concerning the evolutionary idea, but the Victorians for the most part had remained steadily loyal to biblical teaching. Their view of history and the human race was fashioned mainly from what they had learned reading the Bible. In fact only a few months before Darwin's book appeared, a well-known clergyman had restated in a prestigious lecture the old confidence in the traditional faith. Also the new science of archaeology seemed to support with new discoveries the historical authority of the Bible. However, the evidence gathered by geology and paleontology had been mounting for a number of years and was indisputable. The newer "testimony of the rocks" challenged the older view that supported the biblical account. Fossil evidence found in rock strata suggested gradual change over thousands of centuries. That made the history recounted in Genesis suspect. The argument that one single day in Genesis could be viewed as an eon didn't stick.

Charles Lyell's uniformitarian theory, set forth in his *Principles of Geology* (1830), effectively discarded the premise of catastrophes. His theory maintained that the causes of geological change in the remote past were no different from those at present in operation. The gradual processes shaping the earth today, such as erosion, also formed the earth's features in the past. Such an assumption meant extending world history backward through eons of time. If the process is so slow that even the most advanced instruments cannot detect it, the argument went, vast spans of time are necessary to accomplish the effects revealed by geology. The miniature scale of history as seen in the Old Testament was accordingly rendered even more incredible. In the same years when the Oxford Movement was trying to revitalize faith, this book sowed seeds of grave religious doubt. But even before science and biblical criticism had made an impact, other forces were at work to challenge Christian faith. One was the personal loss of faith often recounted in full and moving detail, such as Carlyle's story of the "Everlasting No." Carlyle's faith had been shattered not by the teachings of science or by the higher criticism, but by eighteenth-century rationalism. The deism of that day denied the presence of a loving and protective god in the lives of men and women. It led Carlyle to ask a provocative question: "Is there no God, then, but an absentee God sitting idle outside his Universe?"

Three years after Colenso's book there appeared in England in 1865 an anonymous work entitled *Ecce Homo* (Behold the Man). Authored by Sir John Seeley, it was another book that placed emphasis on the humanity of Jesus rather than on his divinity. Seeley was a well-know historian and essayist who was made Regius Professor of Modern History at Cambridge in 1869. Reaction to his book was predictably sharp. Lord Shaftesbury extravagantly described its genesis as "vomited from the jaws of Hell." Again the treatment of Christ was not at all irreverent, but the audacity it took to see Christ as merely a man angered the orthodox. Throughout the sixties volume after volume was published to call into question one's faith. So the great period of mid-Victorian prosperity was tempered and tainted with doubt. The remarkable findings of the new science had emphasized evolutionary development, and that historical emphasis had expanded to stimulate a rigorous re-examination of the Bible. The faith in a beneficent anthropomorphic God gradually began to fade away so that even the belief in a guiding intelligence was severely tested. In a cold and mechanistic world the human race seemed alone and without succor.

Herbert Spencer

Herbert Spencer (1820-1903), who wanted to be known as a learned man as much as any person of his day, became the leading Victorian apostle of evolutionary progress. Among the philosophers who wrote in English, his books in spite of their difficult style were popular with general readers. He took his cue from Darwin and tended to interpret all subjects in terms of evolutionary theory. An evolutionist before Darwin, he had coined the notable phrase "survival of the fittest" as early as 1852. Unlike Darwin and other scientists, he had little difficulty equating evolution with progress. He is chiefly responsible for planting this idea, which many people take for granted, in the minds of his contemporaries who passed it on to the present day.

Progress, he insisted, was no accident of nature but part of the grand design and a necessity for the human race. It worked in harmony with the master plan to bring men and women closer to perfection. It operated through slow development by means of evolution to improve mankind. While his contemporaries honored him as an outspoken prophet, the skepticism of our time has diminished Spencer's stature even as we accept his ideas. Today, probably because of his irrepressible optimism as well as a ponderous polysyllabic style, his books are seldom read. However, a good prospector mining Spencer can find rare and unusual nuggets, for example his sesquipedalian definition of evolution given here word for word: "Evolution is an integration of matter and concomitant dissipation of motion, during which the matter passes from an indefinite and incoherent homogeneity to a definite and coherent heterogeneity, and during which the retained motion undergoes a parallel transformation." He is saying, as far as one can tell, that organic development represents a transition from a state of undifferentiated homogeneity to a state of differentiated heterogeneity. That ought to help, but to make the definition your own you may need to translate the translation.

You can see at this point why Spencer is not included in most modern anthologies. Yet to know something of his life and work will help you understand the tremendous impact of Darwinism upon Victorian thought. Herbert Spencer was born in Derby and largely educated by his schoolmaster father, who trained him to find causes for everything. From 1837 to 1846 he was articled to a civil engineer in the building of the new railroads. During that time he read widely in scientific works, and particularly the *Principles of Geology* by Charles Lyell. Through this work Spencer was introduced to the theory of evolution as expounded by the French biologist and botanist Jean Baptiste Lamarck (1744-1829). Subsequently, the theories of Lamarck and Darwin exerted a profound influence upon him. From 1848 to 1853 he was assistant editor of the London *Economist* and contributed during that time scientific and philosophical articles to the *Westminster Review.* While working at that job he met and became interested in the novelist George Eliot (Mary Ann Evans), author of *Middlemarch* (1871). She apparently returned his interest but waited for a decision from him. After drawing up lists of the advantages and disadvantages of a relationship that might lead to marriage, he decided to remain a bachelor.

At about this time Spencer also met Thomas Huxley who became a close friend. He urged the latter to read a paper he had written on the "Theory of Population." Huxley was impressed by the piece because its theory of social evolution was obviously based on something close to natural selection. Spencer's other friends saw him as a delightful eccentric who carried earplugs and used them when the conversation became boring. Huxley liked Spencer because he found the man a relentless theorizer with a probing if somewhat undisciplined intellect. Largely self-educated, he had learned all the details of the new science, had invented many gadgets, had planned and built railway bridges, and was now settling down to explain all the knowledge men and women had accumulated since exiting the caves.

By that time he had discovered his capacities through a process of elimination. The opera he discarded because to his mind it seemed irrational. Vegetarianism he gave up because it affected the vigor of his style. George Eliot asked him once why he had no lines in his forehead, considering all the thinking he did. "I suppose it is because I am never puzzled," he replied quite seriously. In 1852 he published *The Developmental Hypothesis* to explain his interpretation of Lamarck's theory of biological evolution. He frequently argued the question with Huxley, and they built a friendship on prolonged and profound disagreement. Huxley once said that Spencer's idea of tragedy was "a deduction killed by a fact." They made a good team because Huxley was full of facts and Spencer was full of ideas in need of facts.

In 1855 or thereabouts Spencer conceived an ambitious plan for a comprehensive system of philosophy embracing and integrating all existing departments of knowledge. In 1860 he wrote a prospectus of his system entitled *A System of Synthetic Philosophy*. Science in an age of specialization was suspicious of any person who took all knowledge to be his province, and yet he had the Baconian, or Renaissance man's energy, to construct the ambitious project in almost all its parts. For more than forty years (1855-1896), in spite of poverty and ill health he labored to complete his vast design, a synthesis of human knowledge under the universal law of evolution.

In 1859 Darwin provided him with another explanation of organic evolution. Without discarding altogether the Lamarckian theory of the inheritance of acquired characteristics, Spencer set to work at once to incorporate natural selection into his system. In *First Principles* (1862) he announced his plan to present a genetic history of the universe with emphasis on matter, motion, and force. His purpose would also include the ethical aim to provide "a basis for a right rule of life, individual and social." Successive installments included lengthy works on biology, psychology, sociology, and ethics. In addition to these heavy tomes came treatises on education, politics, and religion. Invariably his books assessed the impact of the evolutionary idea upon scientific, political, religious, and current philosophical thought.

In some of his volumes Spencer concerned himself with the individual and society. In the manner of Mill he insisted that the individual is not accountable for his actions in society so long as those actions do not harm others. State control he wanted reduced to a minimum, operating only to maintain internal order and to protect against external enemies. Individual liberty would be expanded in all areas of life, and competition would be encouraged on all levels of life. He proposed turning over to private enterprise the postal service and also public health from garbage collection to medical practice. He foresaw the day when there would be a balance between the desires of the individual and the needs of society. That would not only make the need to exercise moral choice obsolete, but would do away with the codes of morality – prudery we call it now – that hampered Victorian life.

He attempted a reconciliation of science and religion by positing God as inscrutable and unknowable and then proceeding to explain universal principles as governed by evolution. That brought some peace to religious readers, and while it was certainly no substitute for faith in a divine father, the seamless logic offered hope. Listen to a contemporary critic: "The strength of Mr. Spencer's writings lies in the absolute perfection of his logic. They are the outpourings of a perfect logical machine so adjusted as to work without error. Deduction, Induction, and Verification are so perfectly blended that in this nineteenth century it seems impossible to conceive their higher development." Spencer was surely pleased by the compliment, and it made him work even harder. The man seems comical at times (in the light of current thought) but ought to be remembered as a serious thinker seeking light. He approached the complicated subject of evolution as a philosopher rather than scientist and was vastly influential in his time.

In his first book, *Social Statistics* (1850), he postulated that all natural phenomena as they now exist developed slowly from elementary origins. Two years later in *The Developmental Hypothesis* he discussed the difficulty of reconciling modern scientific data with the biblical story of a single act of creation. Then in *Progress, Its Law and Cause* (1857) he theorized that each natural form proceeds from a simple to a more complex structure. Although Spencer never secured a wide following among professional philosophers – the denizens of the universities scorned him – many thoughtful people admired his earnest endeavor to systematize all knowledge within the framework of modern science and with focus on the evolutionary idea. Said one critic, heaping effusive praise upon him: "His applications of the theory of evolution have more profoundly influenced contemporary thought than the work of any other modern thinker." Spencer earned for himself a place among the foremost thinkers of the latter half of the century. However, his work was so exact an expression of Victorian liberalism that it fell into obscurity with the passing of the age that produced it. Today his reputation is no longer that of a philosopher expounding deep and original ideas, and the dust lies thick upon the books that many thought would change the world.

Leslie Stephen

Leslie Stephen (1832-1904) was a Londoner by birth who became, like Spencer, a prolific writer on the issues of the day. He was the son of Sir James Stephen, who held a high position in the British Colonial Office and for a decade was Professor of Modern History at Cambridge. His mother belonged to the evangelical Clapham Sect, and his brother became famous as a barrister and judge in the legal system of England. He himself won fame as a biographer, critic, and philosopher. As an indefatigable editor and critic, he was one of the most influential men of letters in the last quarter of the nineteenth century. He was educated at Eton, at Kings College in London, and Cambridge. In 1859, the year of his father's death, he was ordained a priest in the Church of England but remained at Cambridge to become a university tutor. During the American Civil War he visited the North and became one of its main supporters in England while most people supported the South. In 1864 he settled in London to pursue a literary career and contributed critical studies to various periodicals. He was an intellectual but also a noted athlete and mountaineer, and edited the *Alpine Journal*. A liberal religious thinker, his studies colored his thought with skepticism and agnosticism.

In 1873 Stephen published *Essays on Free Thinking and Plain Speaking* in which he defined his agnostic position. This open declaration of his views caused him to relinquish holy orders in 1875. In the *Fortnightly* for June 1876 he published an essay in the manner of Newman, explaining the reasons for his conversion to agnosticism. It was later expanded and published as a book in 1893. From 1871 to 1882 he was editor of the *Cornhill Magazine*, and during that time came to know many of the authors and intellectuals of the day. His first wife was the younger daughter of William Thackeray, and by his second wife he became the father of Virginia Woolf. In 1876 he published the first volume of a massive work entitled *History of English Thought in the Eighteenth Century*. Another sizable volume, *The Science of Ethics*, appeared in 1882. All the time he was writing these larger works he was contributing short biographies to the "English Men of Letters" series. Some of them were Johnson (1878), Pope (1880), Swift (1882), George Eliot (1902), and Hobbes (1904). He published also a biography of his brother, Sir James Fitzjames Stephen, in 1895. Giving up the editorship of *Cornhill Magazine* in 1882, he accepted an offer to edit the *Dictionary of National Biography*. As the leading editor of that massive undertaking, he saw to completion the first twenty-six volumes of the project.

Stephen relinquished his post on the DNB in 1891 but continued to contribute biographies until 1901. Publication began in 1886 and continues to this day as the *Oxford Dictionary of National Biography* with more than 55,000 biographies in sixty volumes. Stephen's share of the project consists of 378 articles that total more than one thousand pages. The standards that he established resulted in one of those rare and monumental pieces of English scholarship. The DNB may not be as great a work as the King James Version of the Bible, but some consider it to be almost as important. It is unsurpassed by any comparable compendium in any other language, and it matches the scholarship of the *Oxford English Dictionary* (OED). Every deceased English man or woman known to history is included in the work. A standard of meticulous accuracy was always observed. Any material that could not be fully substantiated was left out. Legendary and anecdotal story, regardless how interesting it seemed, surrendered to hard facts. Stephen's critical judgments were free of prejudice and quietly deliberate. While some of the articles have more warmth and color than those by Stephen, invariably his pieces tend to shed more light on the life and work of the subject.

When Stephen began collecting the materials for his *History of English Thought in the Eighteenth Century*, very little work had been done in the history of ideas. His work established that genre and gave impetus to it in later years so that eventually it became a legitimate scholarly discipline. The book remains today the definitive survey of the subject because it is fair in its assessment of materials and exhaustive. It had the effect of making later generations appreciate the contribution the eighteenth century made to the English-speaking world. A commentator observed that every time a Victorian opened his mouth he spoke ideas that came from the preceding century. In our time we fashion current ideas upon those of the centuries that preceded us. Our ideas in the twenty-first century represent a blending of eighteenth and nineteenth-century thought with accretions from the twentieth. The idea of progress, for example, is so thoroughly a part of our thinking that many of us of assume it has always been in the world. However, one of the foremost historians of ideas, J. B. Bury, has shown that the idea of progress is a relatively modern idea, coming first into prevalence with the rationalists of the eighteenth century, gaining momentum with the liberals in the nineteenth, and perhaps reaching its peak in the twentieth.

Stephen applied the principles of rationalism to the interpretation of the history of ideas. Intellectually he was at home in the world of "the Enlightenment," as some have called the eighteenth century, and he understood its intricacies. He completed his study of the era in 1881 and immediately began work on *The English Utilitarians*, which came out in three volumes in 1900. It is recognized today as the second most important of all the books he wrote. As one might expect, the book is strongly influenced by Hume, Bentham, and Mill. As a philosopher Stephen was eclectic and somewhat preoccupied with the problem of ethics. His comprehensive work in this field, *Science and Ethics* (1882) was clearly written and widely used as a textbook. His freethinking had a sincerity and dignity that went a long way to gain public respect for his views.

Lighter fare you can find in the book that came out of random studies, *Hours in a Library* (1892). It is informal, autobiographical, and easy to read. The most personal and self-revelatory of his works, *An*

Agnostic's Apology (1893), is quite typical of Stephen and his time. It depicts an almost imperceptible ebbing of faith, as painless as Darwin's, as he became immersed in rationalistic writings. In the process of becoming an agnostic he scrutinized the Old and New Testaments as purely human documents, and he denied the divinity of Christ. Losing orthodox faith, he replaced it with enthusiasm for science, a religion of humanity, and secular idealism. For a man such as Stephen, knighted in 1902, losing faith did not mean losing hope.

Leslie Stephen's agnosticism in the nineteenth century ought to be compared to the skepticism of David Hume in the eighteenth century, or to the atheism of Charles Bradlaugh (1833-1891) in his own time. Bradlaugh suffered financially, physically, and legally because of his militant atheism. From 1860 he was unrelenting as editor of the *National Reformer*, which he founded as the first journal in English to expound atheism. He was elected to Parliament in 1880, but for six years was refused a seat because of his professed atheism. When Parliament finally allowed him to take his seat in 1886, he became its first member ever to admit openly atheistic beliefs. His atheism came ironically from the same source as Stephen's agnosticism, from the rationalistic thought of the eighteenth century. Also like Stephen and other Victorian agnostics, he was rigorously moral and didn't smoke or drink. His mistake was to call himself an atheist in blatant defiance of prevailing morality. The agnostics, taking no such stance, had it better.

As an active agnostic Leslie Stephen contended that a purely social ethic having nothing to do with religion could tell a person how to live and how to die. Moreover, the person as a social creature would know in his own mind how to live well and how to die well. No religion was necessary to teach him those basic skills. He followed his own beliefs throughout his life and found time to play hard as well as work hard. At the time of his death he was able to look back upon many productive years of high accomplishment, and he brought into the world a little girl who would become a literary genius. As a philosopher he is not in the same league with Mill and Carlyle, but as the end of his life drew near he had earned for himself a more secure place in literary history than Spencer. He is remembered as a Victorian thinker who began life at the beginning of the period and lived into the next century. He was the model for Vernon Whitford in Meredith's *The Egoist* (1879).

Samuel Butler

Although he wrote many books during his lifetime, Samuel Butler (1835-1902) achieved literary success with only one book. Then in the twentieth century, shortly after his death, he gained a reputation based on another and very different book that had remained unpublished for twenty years. Butler was born into a family of distinguished churchmen on December 4, 1835 at Langar rectory in Nottinghamshire, the son of the Reverend Thomas Butler and the grandson of a bishop. He was educated at Shrewsbury School, where his grandfather had formerly been headmaster, and at St. John's College, Cambridge. His future plan was to go into the church, and after graduation he did parish work among the poor in London. Then as religious doubt increased and became a burden, he refused holy orders. He wanted to become a painter, but his family discouraged that pursuit as unprofitable. In 1859 his father advanced the money for him to emigrate to New Zealand and purchase a sheep ranch. He was there five years and worked hard not merely to make a living but to amass a fortune.

In 1864 Butler sold the improved ranch for double the sum he had paid for it. With more than enough money to support himself for the rest of his life, he returned to England and lived quietly as a bachelor in London. There he developed and pursued intellectual interests, including scientific research, classical scholarship, painting, and musical composition. For a number of years he exhibited his paintings regularly at the Royal Academy, but he is best known for a wide variety of prose writings. His books, among the most original and provocative of the century, speak his thoughts as a very eccentric and independent Victorian who followed no path but his own. Like Ruskin, he wrote at great length on whatever subject he found interesting at the time. One of his early books, *Erewhon* (1872), was a utopian satire that attracted the attention of readers in all ranks of life. But subsequent books were so eccentric in their opinions and so unconventional in their attitudes that Butler had to pay to have them printed.

A friend of Charles Darwin, he was in constant disagreement with Darwin's theory of evolution by means of natural selection. He insisted that "unconscious memory" was closer to the truth. In a series of volumes, beginning with *Life and Habit* (1877), he asserted that evolution was not the result of mere chance variations as theorized by Darwin. The evolutionary process worked instead by means of unconscious memory transmitted from generation to generation as acquired habit became more pronounced with the growth of the species. This same idea he expounded in *Evolution Old and New*, in *Unconscious Memory*, and in *Luck or Cunning?* With each book the idea grew richer and more elaborate while remaining essentially unchanged at the core. In company with this idea was a note of protest against the Darwinian banishment of mind from the universe. His contemporaries ignored Butler's special view of evolution, but the concept is now being seriously considered by modern scientists and has gained favor among some. It may be that Butler's reputation as an evolutionist, out of the mainstream and almost ludicrous in his own time, will be vindicated in our time.

On the subject of religion he wrote *The Fair Haven* (1873) in satirical defense of the miraculous element in Christianity. He expected his readers to see the irony and attach the opposite meaning to everything he said. But some reviewers took the book literally and seriously, when it was published under a pseudonym, and expressed outrage. It masquerades as a spiritual autobiography by one John Pickard Owen. The alleged author had become a devout unbeliever after reading Strauss's *Das Leben Jesu* and other samplings of the higher criticism. Specific sights in real life also brought disillusionment, for Owen says in the preface: "I was beginning to understand that sheep and cows were hollow as far as good meat was concerned. What right had they to assert themselves as so big, and prove so empty? The world itself was hollow, made up of shams and delusions, full of sound and fury signifying nothing." The verbatim borrowing from Shakespeare goes unacknowledged. In the story that follows Owen purports to suffer an agonizing return to faith in Tennysonian fashion after having doubted, but the entire volume is a fragile edifice of irony. The harder Owen works at defending miracles, the more dubious and ridiculous they are made to appear. If Matthew Arnold had read this book, he would have found the satire too bitter for easy digestion, and yet he might have smiled at finding another writer in agreement with his views on miracles. Butler's serious position is that Christianity is more vital and more workable when shorn of the miraculous element.

Butler also composed music and wrote about accomplished

composers. His essays on music were devoted mainly to high praise of Handel as the greatest of all composers. Few readers could agree with that position and again had to reckon with Butler's eccentricity. In the last decade of the century he busied himself with classical scholarship and made extensive studies of the Homeric poems. He reached the conclusion that Homer's *Odyssey* was the work of a woman, and the author of the *Iliad* was a man in sympathy with the Trojans. Near the end of his life he published translations of both epics in colloquial prose to counter the biblical flavor of the Lang versions. Andrew Lang (1844-1912) was a Scotsman who for more than forty years produced an amazing variety of writings that included poetry, biography, Scottish history, fairy tales, novels, and essays. Some of his contemporaries, but not Matthew Arnold, praised his careful rendering of the *Odyssey* as the definitive translation of Homer. The *Iliad* that he brought into English was not so well received, but the two together have achieved the largest sales of any of the many Homeric translations. Arnold, you may remember, had delivered three lectures in 1860 on translating Homer, but the record does not show what he thought of Lang's translation, and he was dead by the time Butler revealed a talent for translation.

Samuel Butler died in June of 1902. His one true novel, *The Way of All Flesh*, on which he had worked from 1872 to 1884, was published in 1903. Its publication was deliberately withheld to avoid family embarrassment. Though he made it a vehicle to express his unique opinions on evolution, readers have regarded the work primarily as a devastating indictment of Victorian attitudes eroding family unity. Butler could never have foreseen the posthumous success of this novel, and the same is true of the respect accorded his evolutionary books in the first half of the twentieth century. It is sweetly ironical that Butler was an anti-Victorian about fifty years too soon. Had he lived a generation later, when the reaction against the Victorian Era was at its height, when a new generation was in revolt against Victorian orthodoxy and stuffiness (just before and after the first world war), he might have been a very popular writer. His only novel, a masterpiece of English fiction, elicited high praise from George Bernard Shaw. Its caustic style and cynical wit gave the book great power. Except for a few fictional departures it is faithfully autobiographical, even to including a personal letter written by Butler's own mother. Behind the façade of Victorian respectability Butler finds no human warmth and nothing to admire, only ignorance and tyranny. Like his namesake, the Samuel Butler who published *Hudibras* in 1663, he sees hypocrisy as one of the enduring evils of mankind.

Erewhon (1872) — The title of this book is *nowhere* spelled backwards. Of Butler's many books, it was the only one that won him any true recognition during his lifetime. It was received, according to a contemporary critic, as "a shrewd and biting satire on modern life and thought, the best of its kind since *Gulliver's Travels.*" Yet from its publication Butler earned only sixty-nine pounds. Still, earning even a little was better than losing many hundreds of pounds as he did on his other books. *Erewhon* is trenchant and effective satire. An inverted Utopia located beyond a mountain range in New Zealand, it's a scathing criticism of Victorian life and habit in England.

Crime among the Erewhonians is viewed as a sickness. Embezzlers receive condolences and are sent to the Straighteners (psychotherapists) for medical and moral therapy. Physical illness, such as tuberculosis, is seen as a terrible offense punishable by strict laws. In that way Butler satirizes as inhumane certain Victorian tendencies to ignore victims of ill fortune and "economic law." The total lack of parental authority in Erewhon contrasts with parental tyranny in the Victorian household. The Anglican Church is bitterly satirized as the incompetent Musical Banks patronized mainly by overly devout women. Ydgrunism (the ubiquitous Grundyism dictating Victorian standards of propriety) imposes a stifling conformity. The Colleges of Unreason (Oxford and Cambridge) place high value upon dead languages (Greek and Latin), which everyone knows are useless. The chapter on machines seems prophetic of worries in our time. Fearing that the machines will eventually take over, the Erewhonians dismantle them all except for a few relics preserved in museums. Higgs, the narrator, escapes the hellish place in a balloon with a woman whom he later marries.

Erewhon Revisited (1901) — This was Butler's sequel. After twenty years Higgs returns to Erewhon and finds to his horror that his balloon ascent has been proclaimed a miracle. A religious myth has originated from the incident, he himself has become a god worshipped by the people, and a great temple is now ready to be dedicated to him. The Musical Banks (Anglican Church) have shamelessly exploited the miracle to bring about a religious revival that has spawned a vast proliferation of dogma. Hanky and Panky, professors in the Colleges of Unreason, have erected monumental systems of murky exegesis to stimulate theological controversy. Horrified by the mischief he has done and goaded by Hanky's maudlin sermon, Higgs attempts to tell the Erewhonians the truth and barely escapes the country alive.

Butler was shocked when readers failed to see the target of his satire and protested that he was deriding Christ. He attempted to explain that the real butt of the satire was the Church of England obscuring noble teachings. He said also that Higgs experiences the tragedy of truth seekers everywhere who see at firsthand an ugly warping of their ideas and actions. During his lifetime Butler managed to isolate himself by antagonizing Darwin, the Anglican Church, and many of his readers. Yet in 1906, four years after his death, Shaw wrote in high praise that Butler was "in his own department the greatest English writer of the latter half of the nineteenth century."

Spencer, Stephen, and Butler — All three were much influenced by Darwin, Huxley, and the social Darwinism that came later. They were also influenced by the higher criticism that tended to undermine the Christian faith. Two of them, Spencer and Butler, were disciples of Lamarck even as they were motivated by the teachings of Darwin. At the turn of the century George Bernard Shaw observed that Butler had insisted that Lamarck's theory of evolution was more accurate than Darwin's. Butler disagreed with Darwin because he felt Darwin had taken away the belief that man's destiny is guided by mind. Spencer had no such quarrel with Darwin. He applied the theory of evolution to all areas of life and wrote many books on the subject. He was widely read in his time and admired as a true philosopher. Leslie Stephen, author of many well-written books, is not well known to us today. Even so, he's an excellent example of how many sensitive Victorians lost their religious faith and began to doubt but found themselves in work.

William Morris

William Morris (1834-1896) is remembered as a major Victorian author because of his accomplishments in both poetry and prose. His reputation as a poet came first, but as early as his undergraduate years he was writing interesting and readable prose. Near the end of his life after writing about social, political, and economic problems inherent in Victorian society, he returned to imaginative writing and published a succession of books that spoke of strange adventures in faraway places. Between this earlier and later writing, when he was the foremost craftsman of his time and a political agitator for a new social order, he produced a series of essays and lectures to explain his artistic and socialistic views. His style made use of everyday words and was consistently plain, honest, direct, and informal. When he was only twenty-four he published his first volume of poetry made up mainly of narrative poems. Then at forty-nine he became a radical propagandist, preaching socialism in the streets, distributing socialist literature in Hyde Park, and several times getting arrested. His friends knew him as a poet who had written poems suffused with the color and spirit of the distant past. Now he struggled in the present against gargantuan odds to restructure Victorian society. His life-long friend, Edward Burne-Jones, found it difficult to understand why Morris abandoned art and poetry to embrace the cause of the workingman. It was a radical change even for Morris but something he felt he had to do.

Morris was born on March 24, 1834 in the London suburb of

Walthamstow. His father was a wealthy London broker in Lombard Street. His mother, Emma Shelton Morris, was the daughter of a music teacher. In 1840 the family moved to a large country estate in Epping Forest. The boy dressed in toy armor, rode on a lively pony, and pretended to be an Arthurian knight. Quite early he fell in love with the Middle Ages, and like Newman he read eagerly the *Arabian Nights*. With an interest in medievalism and Anglo-Catholicism he entered Oxford in 1853, intending to become a clergyman. Although he felt strongly the influence of Newman and the Tractarians, before his first year was over his interests had moved from religion to Pre-Raphaelitism. When he came of age he had at his disposal an income of nine hundred pounds a year when thousands of working men were earning fewer than fifty pounds. Educated governesses of the middle class earned far less than fifty pounds per year but had their room and board.

With some of this annual income to be used as he wished, while still an undergraduate Morris financed and edited the *Oxford and Cambridge Magazine* and took his degree in 1856. After graduation he met Dante Gabriel Rossetti and decided to try painting as a career instead of architecture. In 1857 he painted several pictures in the Pre-Raphaelite mode. In 1858 he published with little success his first book, *The Defense of Guenevere and Other Poems*. He married Jane Burden, one of Rossetti's beautiful models, in 1859. In that year he began to construct near London the famous Red House, which he designed and decorated himself. This project caused him to establish in 1861 a firm devoted to the creation of household articles both useful and beautiful. He and his partners worked with textiles, ceramic tiles, furniture (Morris invented the Morris chair), stained glass, wallpaper of intricate design, draperies, tapestries, and carpets.

These activities blended with his work as a poet. Composing poetry as he worked on a chair, he came to be called "the poetic upholsterer." In 1871 he moved to Kelmscott Manor House, and Rossetti came along to share the house. In this same year he illuminated Fitzgerald's *Rubaiyat* and became interested in prints and dyes. In 1877 he declined a professorship of poetry offered him by Oxford, for he was too busy with other pursuits and didn't need the small income they offered him or the prestige of the position. In that year he became an active socialist with the publication of *Manifesto to the Working Men of England*. Also in 1877 he also delivered his first public lecture, "On the Decorative Arts."

In 1881 he moved Morris and Company to rural Merton Abbey and went on producing beautiful and durable household articles. Two years later he became a member of the Social Democratic Federation, and a year after that he founded the Socialist League (1884). In the 1880's he published a number of books that reflected his socialist views and attended the International Congress of Socialists that met in Paris in 1889. By now he had entered the printing business. In 1891 he founded the Kelmscott Press to produce some of the most beautiful books ever printed. Also in that year he published his best-known book, *News from Nowhere*, and began preparing a sumptuous Kelmscott edition of Caxton's *The Golden Legend*. At the same time he labored as the most vocal supporter of socialism before the rise of the Fabians.

In 1893 in collaboration with Belfort Bax he wrote and published *Socialism, Its Growth and Outcome*. In 1894 he finished his translation of *Beowulf* and published the edition at Kelmscott. In the same year he published *Letters of Socialism* and "Why I Am a Communist" in *Liberty*, the latter emphasizing the differences between his brand of socialism and that of the anarchists. He spent the year 1895 busily translating from the Icelandic, writing, printing, designing, and delivering lectures. Also in this year he began his designs for the Kelmscott *Chaucer*, a book as splendid in its illumination as any medieval manuscript. In 1896, as he eagerly awaited completion of the *Chaucer,* his health began to break.

His doctor suggested a sea voyage, but instead of traveling southward Morris went to Norway to pursue literary interests. He returned in less than a month much weaker than when he left. Even so, he was able to publish a beautiful prose romance, *The Well at the World's End*, and dictate the conclusion of another, *The Sundering Flood*. He died at Kelmscott House in October of 1896 at the age of sixty-two. He is remembered not only as a great poet and thoughtful prose writer, but also as a painter, printer, weaver, translator, decorator, designer, businessman, agitator, and socialist. Poetry was but one of his many abilities and came easily to him. His prose works, some of them in strangely archaic language, fell from his pen with amazing speed. Near the end of his life he had become a sage on the Victorian scene.

2

Few professionals have ever shown the proficiency of William Morris in so huge a variety of interests and talents. The difficult act of composing poetry he viewed primarily as an act of craftsmanship. "If a chap can't compose an epic poem while he's weaving a tapestry," he once said, "he had better shut up because he'll never do any good at all." The many characters that people his verse and prose tales, though living in distant times and places, are wholesome and believable Victorians breathing Victorian air and struggling as a way of life. They work hard and reap the rewards of their work, but on occasion they suffer in silence. They live their lives as fully as they can and they die as well as they can. Morris himself, though unusual in some respects, was representative of hard-working and productive people in an era that seemed to inspire that kind of activity. He was a happy and energetic person though not always in the best of health. He always had several fruitful projects going at once and looked eagerly to each tomorrow.

In many respects, except for dying too soon, he was a very lucky person. Born to affluence and receiving an inheritance that left him wealthy for the rest of his life, he never once had to worry about money. One wonders what kind of life Morris would have led if he had been forced by circumstance to earn a daily wage or live in poverty. That same question should be applied to the other Victorian writers we've seen in this discussion. While they gained fame and money by means of their work, to a person they began their careers with considerable advantage. They were young men of privilege propelled into productive lives by wealth, family influence, and the prestige of Oxford or Cambridge. Surely any number of men with equal talent but without the support of fortune and family fell by the wayside. The privileged ones were also lucky (such as Darwin), and yet all of them including Morris worked long and hard to secure fame and leave behind a legacy.

Even after his company became large and profitable Morris worked side by side with his workers as a craftsman. His belief that beautiful products come only from workers who take pride in their ability led him to promote individual craftsmanship. That in turn urged him to become involved in the social problems of his employees. Like Ruskin, he believed that work of high quality was dependent on the happiness and self-respect of the worker. To test his ideas, he took ordinary men from the street, carefully taught them their craft, paid them enough to live comfortable lives, and allowed them the freedom to think for themselves on the job. He raised the condition of life among his workers and later shared profits with them. The medievalists who had influenced him (Carlyle and Rossetti) had merely looked back to pre-industrial days with envy, but Morris (guided by Ruskin) was putting theory into practice and making it work. Because he himself was enormously interested in every project he undertook, his enthusiasm rubbed off on his workers. Practicing fraternalism and relative equality instead of Carlyle's paternalism, he proved that management and labor could work together in a spirit of companionship toward a common goal. Like Huxley, he saw more promise in the working class than in the middle or upper classes. He became the voice of those members of the working class who genuinely wanted to improve their lives. For them he willingly marched in clamorous demonstration in the streets and went off to jail when arrested.

His socialist views are to a large extent simplifications of Marxian doctrine for working men. Because they are basic to an understanding of Morris, I will present them in summary before closer analysis. He saw two classes of society, the wealth possessing and the wealth producing. The former control the instruments for the production of wealth. They own the land, machinery, and capital. The latter use these instruments with the permission of their owners. While the capitalists are seen to be dependent on the efforts of labor, those who labor strive to improve themselves at the expense of those who have the capital. The aim of all work is to secure a profit. The workers must sell their labor at prices controlled by the capitalists. From that comes the competition among workers for a share in wages. It also creates competition among employers for a division of profits. The result is a working class that suffers from hunger, poverty, and squalor. Morris's ideal program of correction was equally simple. All the mechanisms of production are to be held for the common good by the state. The motive for all work, for production and distribution, is to be a comfortable livelihood for all, not to bring wealth to a few. A person's private debt to the community will replace obedience to any system. Repulsive but entirely necessary work will be made honorable and shared by the able-bodied. In his own labor, in the knowledge that he has always done his best, the workingman will find a sense of worth.

Intellectual chatter among students at Oxford – frequent wine parties loosened tongues and encouraged talk – was not always centered on Malory and medievalism or Keats and Tennyson. It was sometimes on Carlyle and Ruskin, Mill and political economy, and how one might improve society. Morris was always in the thick of these discussions and growing more excited by the moment. He was an idealist and a dreamer and yearned to take the world as it is and make it as it ought to be, a pleasant and happy place for everyone. "Do you know," he said years later, "when I see a poor devil drunk and brutal I always feel, quite apart from my aesthetical perceptions, a sort of shame, as if I myself had some hand in it.... I claim not to be separated from those that are heavy-hearted only because I am well in health and full of pleasant work and eager about it." In the 1870's and 1880's he saw a world order that was "trampling out all the beauty of life and making us less than men." The rich were getting richer and frittering away their time in luxury and idleness while the poor lived in misery. Workers with mindless and repetitive tasks were being turned into machines or being enslaved by them. Away at work for many hours each day, their homes were dirty and disorderly, and many poverty-stricken workers lacked even the basic necessities of life. Half of England had become "a foul and greasy cinder-heap." Morris was incensed by the conditions he saw around him. On the dogma of progress he had this to say: "If our civilization is to carry us no further, to nothing better, I for one wish we had never gone so far."

One should remember that even though Morris was wealthy and privileged, an artist and a poet, he was also a democrat with a deep interest in the welfare of humanity. At times he was puzzled by a system that allowed so very much to persons such as himself and so little to so many others. "Over and over again have I asked myself why should not my lot be the common lot. My work is simple enough; much of it many of decent intelligence could do. Indeed I have been often ashamed when I have thought of the contrast between my happy working hours and the unpraised, unrewarded, monotonous drudgery which most men are condemned to. Nothing shall convince me that such labor as this is good or necessary to civilization."

He was not able to labor for improvement from the outside and from a distance, as some reformers attempted to do. For him the disinterestedness of Arnold meant indifference and aloofness. To do his part, he had to go among the people he was attempting to help and encourage them to endure. When he became a socialist he was willing to sacrifice his time, money, talents, reputation, and robust energy for the cause. He dreamed of an ideal civilization but was content to attack the conditions around him first. His aim was to replace capitalism with a special brand of communism so as to make everyone economically equal. Under the new system, according to the laws of nature, all people would work to survive, and work expressing the happiness of the worker would become an art.

3

One unhappy result of the socialist activity that took its impetus from Ruskin was for Morris to give up poetry to work mainly with prose. The essays and lectures on socialism, which comprise so large a part of the *Collected Works,* were part of a program of action. The author's intention was to instruct, convert, encourage, argue, and agitate. Today we place these writings under the heading of propaganda rather than literature. Yet two books reflecting his political doctrines have a lasting value. *A Dream of John Ball* (1888) expresses socialist views, but it is also an imaginative romance. It is mainly a reverie with the narrator returning in a dream to the fourteenth century. There he finds himself caught up in the Peasants' Revolt. He listens to an moving speech by John Ball and later talks with the peasant leader, informing him of what must come to pass before his ideals can be realized.

The dream endures until the screech of modern factory whistles causes the dreamer to awaken with a start. Looking around in drowsy recognition, he finds himself once more in his own time and comparing the present with the past. Ranging the two centuries side by side, he realizes that change even with advancement always brings with it new problems. He reaches the conclusion that if the ideal of John Ball in the fourteenth century was not to be realized, similar ideals in the nineteenth will not be quickly or easily attained. In fact, hard reality may prevent any of them coming about at all. The other book, more imaginative and far better known and yet charged with political doctrine, is *News from Nowhere* (1891).

Near the end of 1890 an obtuse anarchist faction seized control of the Socialist League. Morris, who had founded the group and whose personal funding had kept it going, was not at all in sympathy with the aims of the new leaders. Therefore, on principle he gracefully withdrew his leadership and membership. That gave him time to exercise his rich imagination and to write seven prose romances on medieval themes with such poetic titles as the ones that follow:

The House of the Wolfings	(1889)
The Roots of the Mountains	(1890)
The Story of the Glittering Plain	(1891)
The Wood Beyond the World	(1894)
The Well at the World's End	(1896)
The Water of the Wondrous Isles	(1897)
The Sundering Flood	(1897)

Into these prose romances he poured some of his best literary skill with no motive other than to entertain. Yet there are similarities between these writings and those on socialism, for the dream world of fairyland has much in common with the imagined world of the future. His story-telling ability and his unrivaled knowledge of the color and vitality of the Middle Ages are on full display in these books.

The style is rhythmic and old-fashioned and based on a small stock of Anglo-Saxon words. Some readers objected to Morris's style, but it seems well suited to the fairyland atmosphere that he wished to evoke and sustain. In places it can be as beautiful as one of his stained-glass windows, as subtle as a tapestry woven in his shop with thin golden thread. An idealist and a lover of beauty, he seems more influenced by literature than by life in these romances. He turns his back on the present to recapture the past he dreamed of as a boy pretending to be a knight on a prancing pony. Now we must look at some of his work that came before the romances of the 1890's.

Hopes and Fears For Art (1882) — This volume consists of a series of plain lectures published to raise funds to help the Society for the Protection of Ancient Buildings. Some of the newer anthologies of Victorian prose have reprinted several of these lectures because they represent the mature thought of William Morris on art and society. The book is a collection of lectures given near the end of the 1870's before Morris joined the Socialist Democratic Federation. The three that follow are important.

"The Lesser Arts" (1877), coming first in this volume, was the first lecture that Morris ever gave in public. Under the title "The Decorative Arts," it was delivered in London near the end of the year. It places blame upon a culture in which the lesser arts become trivial, mechanical, and incapable of resisting the change imposed upon them by fashion. When that happens the greater arts, unaided by the lesser, lose their dignity and their effectiveness and yield to meaningless pomp. Morris shows himself a disciple of Ruskin when he complains in a digression that science is too much in the pay of the counting house and the drill sergeant to help clean up the landscape. Yet it would be easy for science to teach Manchester how to reduce smoke pollution, or Leeds how to get rid of dyes without polluting rivers.

Under such conditions – he tells his audience – art cannot flourish, but the lesser arts in their vigor should be the foundation for all the arts. They are very important because they bring beauty into the lives of everyday people. Art is the essence of beauty made available to delight people in their homes, in the streets of their cities, and in their places of work and worship. This is how he expressed his position: "I do not want art for a few, any more than education for a few, or freedom for a few." At present the lesser arts languish, but an increase of leisure may permit a return to native and traditional art forms more vital than any of the affectations from the Continent.

"The Art of the People" (1879), the second essay in the book, was delivered at the School of Design in Birmingham and later published as a pamphlet. Morris examines history to show that too much attention has been given to the warrior class, and later to the trading classes, but not enough to the creative populace. However, as the long quotation from Defoe at the head of the lecture shows, if people spend their strength on labor for bread to give them strength to labor for more bread, they will have no leisure even to think about art. A society that is truly civilized will find a way to let its citizens create and enjoy their own art.

In a vital civilization popular art will rise and flourish. The best ages in history were influenced by folk art, and the decadent ages repressed and distorted the native art of the people. A thought that is stirring in the world and may soon grow into something is the correlation that exists between work and art. There should be no dividing line between the worker and the artist, for all work is art if it expresses the happiness of the worker, and all art is work. But labor that degrades will never be able to produce anything more than misery. Desperately needed in the nineteenth century, "if life is ever to become sweet," is to produce "an art made by the people and for the people as a happiness to the maker and the user."

"The Beauty of Life" (1880) was delivered in Birmingham under the title "Labour and Pleasure Versus Labour and Sorrow" and was published as such the same year. Morris derides the ugliness of contemporary life and declares that the development of the aesthetic impulse is important. But the aesthetic impulse cannot be satisfied if the leaders of the nation have no eye for beauty and care little for that which delights the eye. "The danger is that the present course of civilization will destroy the beauty of life. These are hard words, and I wish I could mend them, but I cannot while I speak what I believe to be the truth." When the brightness of the Renaissance faded, a deadly chill fell upon the arts, and from that time onward popular art has been in decline. The world quickly seemed to forget that there had ever been "an art made by the people for the people as a joy for the maker and the user." By then work was synonymous with drudgery.

The century of commerce, his name for his own time, will not find a way to revitalize art unless people are taught to create a living art of their own and use it in their work and daily lives. The twentieth century may become "the century of education," for it may find a way to educate all people in true arts and skills and thus restore the beauty of life. A golden rule to be observed at any time is this: "Have nothing in your houses that you do not know to be useful, or believe to be beautiful." Two other essays, numbers IV and V in the book, were titled "Making the Best of

It" and "The Prospects of Architecture in Civilisation." Both aired his views on the importance of architecture in ordinary structures.

4

News From Nowhere (1891) — By 1887 Morris knew that revolution was not the tool by which England would bring about social reform. It was not a practical means for establishing an ideal society, nor could it bring progress in that direction. Having reached that conviction, he was able to turn his vision from the present and dream of a distant future. This utopian narrative with the alliterative title, a pastoral romance set in the future rather than the past, was the result. It is a picture of England in some remote future under the socialist system. The archetype of the genre into which the book falls is Sir Thomas More's *Utopia* (1516). The subject of More's seminal book – the Greek title means "nowhere" – was the unending search for the best form of government, and that is partly the focus of Morris's book.

The communism of Nowhere Land brought a happier existence to all its citizens. It allowed for universal education and religious tolerance and seemed in all respects the best system. A book that appeared in 1888, and presented an American utopia of the future, was Edward Bellamy's *Looking Backward.* Immensely popular, it glorified the contributions of machinery, the large cities of the year 2000, and a mechanistic paradise under state socialism. Even though Bellamy wanted public capitalism to replace private capitalism and therefore recommended communism, Morris wrote *News from Nowhere* in speak against the book. He didn't like some of Bellamy's ideas, particularly those concerning work and leisure and the belief that capitalism would be absorbed by the state. Much that he read in Bellamy's book seemed unworkable and out of touch with reality. On the other hand, he sympathized greatly with Butler's *Erewhon.*

A brief summary of *News From Nowhere* will give you a quick look at what the book is about. After a Socialist Club meeting during which the members discussed at length the future of socialism, a young idealist (Morris himself) goes to sleep murmuring, "If I could but see it!" He wakes up to find himself in an England greatly changed after two hundred years. It is a land that goes beyond his fondest expectations. The place has no prisons, no paupers, and no distinct social classes. The citizens are healthy and happy and treat one another kindly as equals. There is pleasant work for all people, and they thoroughly enjoy their work. Hunger, disease, and debilitating labor are merely memories of times past.

Pollution of the water and air is also a memory. Good architecture may be seen everywhere, and factories do not belch smoke or pour poisons into rivers. His guide remarks, "Like the medievals, we like everything trim and clean, and orderly and bright." There are no quarrels concerning private property and no divorces. Population is about the same as it was at the end of the nineteenth century but spread out evenly, and emigration is encouraged. Almost no crime exists in this machineless and semi-rural place, and very little immorality. Violence of any sort is rare. The idea that woman is the property of man vanished with private property, and women easily enjoy full equality with men. Government is free of fraud and corruption and runs smoothly for the good of the people. As for politics, as Niels Horrebow said of snakes in Iceland, there are none. The chapter on politics is therefore only a few sentences, surprising and refreshing.

"How the Change Came" is a memorable chapter. Its contents bear a striking resemblance to social and political events in Russia during the twentieth century. A massacre of innocent people started the revolution in Nowhere, but unlike the uprising of 1917 in Russia, it was mainly a bloodless rebellion. Afterwards the right people in positions of power were able to build the ideal society by always keeping in mind the importance of the individual. Gradually individualism yielded to communism, and the citizens became social beings rather than selfish, acquisitive, and unsocial creatures. Men and women began to perform notable actions in the new society not for reward or recognition, but for the sake of doing what had to be done.

At the apogee of their society, people no longer work to earn money because money, political parties, and private property have all vanished. Machines, which in earlier days tended to enslave the worker, have also disappeared. The idea of progress is no longer a governing dogma in the lives of people, and with it has passed the fever and the fret so much a part of the nineteenth century. Life in the distant future is simple and no longer competitive. An abundance of leisure allows all citizens to pursue whatever creative interests they find enjoyable. The dream traveler discovers that England has become under advanced socialism a virtual paradise. And yet all is not perfect. An undercurrent of discontent hovers on the horizon. With few obstacles left to overcome, a challenging intellectual life is absent. In this ideal country of the future, there is little opportunity for expansion of the mind and for individual growth. Storm clouds are forming somewhere.

The career of William Morris falls into two well-defined periods. Until 1877 he was primarily concerned with poetry and the fine arts. After that year he devoted more and more of his time to the problems of modern society. A boyish love of everything medieval led him to the study of architecture, armor, heraldry, romance, and Chaucer. He composed romantic poems in college, and later with the encouragement of Rossetti, devoted himself to art. *The Defence of Guenevere and Other Poems* (1858), his first volume of verse, contained some of his best poems. He was the pioneer of a movement in poetry and painting called Pre-Raphaelitism, but he was also an apostle of medievalism and a believer in socialism. He worked hard to be heard in a world that seemed to be shutting out the sun and coming apart at the seams. He imagined a utopian England always bright and calm and orderly, but without intellectual challenge his perfect world was not free of problems.

In 1883 Morris announced that he had become a socialist. For the next seven years he devoted his time and energy and quite a bit of his money to the cause of socialism in England. He viewed the industrial civilization of his time as oppressive and ugly. Attempting to find a sweeter life for all people, he was attracted to the theories of the utopian socialists. This group believed that society could in time eliminate stark inequalities between the rich and poor, owners and earners, the life of leisure and that of incessant labor. He joined the Socialist League in 1884 and contributed to its magazine *The Commonweal*, working earnestly to spread its gospel. But six years later he left the organization when an aggressive group of speechifiers began to dominate its meetings, airing ideas he opposed.

He expressed his dream of a vastly improved society in *News From Nowhere* (1891) and more briefly in a poem of 1884 titled "The Day is Coming." In the opening stanza he speaks of the future to a weary group that has gathered to listen. With unabated optimism he paints a glowing picture of the future, insisting that in every respect it will be better than the present. In the future hope and comfort will flourish in all classes. There will be better and more comfortable lodgings for working people. All who wish to work will have work and will not live in fear of losing it. No person will be required to work to exhaustion. All persons will have time for rest and refreshment, but there will be no leisure class. Fair wages will be paid to all workers, and those who work hardest and produce more will be paid more. No worker will become rich, but only those who refuse to work will remain poor. Though more optimistic in tone than *News From Nowhere*, the poem is a good summary of Morris's thoughts in maturity.

Walter Horatio Pater

When Walter Horatio Pater (1839-1894) published *Studies in the History of the Renaissance* in 1873, he became an Oxford celebrity overnight. He had entered the university in 1858 on a scholarship when Swinburne was an undergraduate and when Rossetti, Morris, and Burne-Jones were painting murals in the Oxford library. The year before that Matthew Arnold had become Professor of Poetry, and Pater would in time attend some of his lectures. The quiet university town, resisting modernity and heavy with the flavor of past centuries, enchanted Pater. He had already lived for several years in the shadow of the great cathedral at Canterbury, and the ambiance of Oxford was more exciting for him than even for Arnold. As a student and later a cloistered scholar, he became in some ways the person Arnold as an undergraduate had dreamed of becoming.

The outside world had no allurements for Pater. He never married and from the time he entered the university as an undergraduate, he lived there simply and quietly for the rest of his life. In one of the colleges he taught for his livelihood but found the time to bury himself in history, philosophy, and literature. Although he eventually became an agnostic, he had no difficulty whatever breathing the heavy religious atmosphere of the university. Encouraged by Benjamin Jowett, for many years an Oxford personage and Professor of Greek, Pater developed a love of Plato. Although he graduated with only second-class honors in 1862, Jowett had once said to him: "You have a mind that will attain eminence." That generous compliment, delivered by a man he honored as a mentor and supporter, would later haunt him.

Walter Pater was born on August 4, 1839 at Shadwell in East London, the son of a physician. The father, who died when the boy was quite young, had broken away from the Catholic Church before marriage. His son enjoyed the beauty of Anglican ceremony and planned to become a clergyman. He didn't care for the activities of other boys in school and suffered an illness after being kicked by one of them. His early reading tastes included Dickens and Tennyson, but at the university he read Plato, Goethe, Wordsworth, Keats, Carlyle, and Ruskin. By the time he received his degree he had become a religious skeptic, and instead of being ordained he accepted instead a teaching fellowship at Brasenose College.

From 1864 until his death in 1894 he was a faculty member at Oxford, leaving campus only occasionally when not on duty. In 1865 he made a tour of Italy, which greatly increased his interest in the life and art of the Renaissance. From that time onward humanistic sympathies took the place of earlier inclinations towards the church and religion. In 1866 he came under the influence of the art-for-art's-sake movement and seems to have strengthened it in some of his essays, including one on the poetry of Morris. The essays on subjects other than the Renaissance precisely were collected and published in 1873 as *Studies in the History of the Renaissance*. This was the first of several books, which established Pater as the most important critical writer of his day. His flair for critical writing may have come indirectly from Matthew Arnold, but because his eye roamed over many works by many writers no one person can be credited as an influence.

In 1874 Pater expected to receive a highly coveted academic post but was opposed by Benjamin Jowett, who found the *Renaissance* volume not to his liking. The man who had paid him a high compliment as an undergraduate now questioned his "pagan" and "hedonistic" views and stood in the way of his advancement. Pater grew frustrated, "failed to have the good sense to keep his tongue in his head," and doubts were raised regarding his moral sense and sexuality. For the next five years, his academic prospects damaged, he occupied himself with scholarship and publishing essays in periodicals. In 1880, deeply immersed in his writing and bothered by the academic scene, he gave serious thought to resigning his teaching position. Instead he took a leave of absence in 1882 to spend the winter in Rome.

In that city he worked on *Marius the Epicurean*, which appeared in two volumes in 1885. At about this time he began to live in London, when he was not teaching at Oxford, and he maintained that arrangement until his death. His chief critical work of 1886 was "Sir Thomas Browne," which was later incorporated in *Appreciations* (1889). In 1888 his volume on the *Renaissance* went into its third edition and won him renewed acclaim. In 1890 he lectured to a large audience and was surprised to find himself famous. In 1894 he traveled to Glasgow to receive an honorary LL.D. In that same year he suffered an attack of rheumatic fever and for a time was confined to bed. Resuming activity too soon, he was stricken by pleurisy but seemed fully recovered when on July 30, 1894 he died suddenly of a heart attack.

As he gave his time increasingly to publication, his prose grew in volume and depth. The one serious fault of his writing, as some of his critics were quick to point out, was a tendency to make his sentences too long. His style is highly wrought and baffles the casual reader. He believed that prose should be written as carefully as poetry, and he wanted each of his elaborate sentences to be tasted and savored. He revised his sentences over and over for the right word and the right effect, and he gained a surprising power over words. His aim was to write haunting sentences that suggest or drop hints rather than reveal or explain. Each sentence was the result of patient and unseen labor, and in some cases a unique procedure.

He put each of his sentences on slips of white paper. The sentence containing the central theme or dominant impression he placed on a slip of yellow paper. Then he sorted the slips of paper to arrive at the most pleasing arrangement of the sentences. Invariably it was an arrangement that appealed more to the senses than to the intellect. He achieved a style that may be described as cadenced, suggestive, seductive, musical, and at times complex and convoluted. His statements do not contain facts so much as impressions of facts. Instead of presenting ideas, his sentences suggest an idea, or the flavor of an idea. In his prose there is subtlety of thought, and yet he seems to view manner as more important than matter, covering or clothing as more important than substance. However, style and substance eventually made him the leader of a movement.

Shy, reticent, withdrawn, Walter Pater was by nature contemplative and scholarly. He was not concerned with contemporary social problems or political issues. Though he could feel compassion, there is nothing in his work to suggest sympathy with the plight of the masses. He became in time a major critic but not a social critic or even a negative critic. He never sounded a note of disgust or dismay, never expressed antipathy but only appreciation. He held himself aloof from personal quarrels (except for the academic incident of years past with Benjamin Jowett) and did not participate in the doctrinal controversies of his day.

Two dominant character traits helped to shape his work. One was a boundless sensitivity and the other a painful awareness of the brevity of human life. The latter directed him to embrace a philosophy of Epicureanism, or more precisely Cyrenaicism. Aristippus of Cyrene, a disciple of Socrates, had founded the Cyrenaic school of philosophy. Even though he regarded pleasure as the only absolute good in life, he was not a sensualist. His teachings asserted that pleasure is identical with good, but it has to be obtained through self-control and by seizing the moment. To fill each passing moment with intense experience, and to maintain the ecstasy of the moment day after day, is success in life though not happiness or joy. Happiness depends on chance, and life itself is only a moment. To expect undiluted joy for the entire moment is to ask too much.

Pater's writings, though perhaps not his life, were controlled by his ideal of beauty. The apprehension of beauty, defined as the essence of all art, came through the soul rather than through the mind. That explains the emphasis on sensation, especially those sensations evoked by great art. He places his faith in emotion rather than intellect, feeling rather than thought, the senses and sensitivity rather than brain. He reminded his readers that if beauty fades as fast as a rose in summer, so does human life itself. Our only responsibility is to ourselves, and we must enjoy fully "this short day of frost and sun" or lose it. We must savor each moment and "burn with a hard, gem-like flame" in the appreciation of beauty. After he published the volume on the *Renaissance*, the cry "art for art's sake" (heard as early as 1866) became more intense. He later professed surprise and even alarm when told that his books were exerting a strong impact upon younger readers. It is entirely possible that Oscar Wilde, George Moore, and others chose to see in Pater's work whatever they wanted to see. When Wilde matriculated at Oxford in 1874 and quickly gained notoriety explaining the new aestheticism, Pater's book was already his Bible. He dipped into the well of inspiration and called it "the golden book of spirit and sense, the holy writ of beauty." With characteristic exaggeration he announced: "I never travel anywhere without it. But it is the very flower of decadence; the last trumpet should have sounded the moment it was written."

Wilde proclaimed Pater the high priest of a cult whose members desired to burn with hard, steady, gem-like flames not merely in the appreciation of art, but in full-time pursuit of the exquisite moment. Externally Pater seemed unmoved by all the fuss he was creating, but inwardly he was troubled. When he was writing the "Conclusion" of *Studies in the History of the Renaissance*, it never occurred to him that a few paragraphs in summary of his views would become overnight the focal point of a new movement. He never suspected that these paragraphs would be distorted in meaning and taken as the manifesto of a new paganism that would lead ardent disciples in pursuit of dangerous delights. "I do wish they would not call me a hedonist," he complained to Edmund Gosse. "It produces such a bad effect on the minds of people who don't know Greek." He argued more than once that his book had little to do with hedonism, a philosophy that preaches a total surrender to pleasure. His book presented a philosophy of Epicureanism, not hedonism, and he explained the difference in terms of the ends sought by each. His followers as well as his critics, however, were not inclined to observe the fine distinctions of an academic mind.

His disciples tended to view him as a critic and leader who had no patience with the stuffy standards imposed upon art by the older Victorians. While his aestheticism was for the most part severely intellectual, they looked mainly at the sensuousness of expression and the importance placed upon form and color. They were moved by the injunction to live the moment granted them as fully as they could and with high intensity. To them his work seemed strikingly different from the dull writings of the moralists and seemed to mount a rebellion against traditional Victorianism.

As Carlyle had preached the gospel of work, Pater counters with an insistent Epicurean gospel. As Ruskin had proclaimed the inseparability of art and morality, Pater quietly observes that art should be appreciated for its own sake apart from ethical values. There is in Pater some of Arnold's fastidiousness, and he agrees with Arnold that the function of criticism is to see the object as in itself it really is. But he displays not one shred of Arnold's reforming spirit. Also he changes Arnold's famous dictum to the highly subjective question, "What is the object to me?" That question was seen as reflective of something approaching irresponsible impressionism. Yet all criticism poses and tries to answer the question: What is this work of art to me? It depends on the perception of the critic that stems from a state of mind.

Pater's mind was filled with *-isms*: with Platonism, stoicism, Epicureanism, Spinozaism, Romanticism, humanism, and religious thought (if such could be taken as an *-ism*). Some of the figures that peopled his academic head were Plato, Marcus Aurelius, Dante, Montaigne, da Vinci, Michelangelo, Bruno, Shakespeare, Coleridge, Shelley, Wordsworth, and Pascal. He was writing an essay on Pascal on the day of his death. The impressions that came from such a mind were of high quality and tinged with imaginative truth. In each of his essays he seeks to share with his readers that "unique impression of pleasure" garnered from the study of an artist or writer.

Of particular value to students of English literature are the detailed studies of Wordsworth, Coleridge, Lamb, Sir Thomas More, and William Morris. Oscar Wilde praised some of these essays in a review of 1890 as "absolutely modern in the true meaning of the term modernity." But the quality that Wilde really liked about Pater was his tendency to shock proper, church-going Victorians. He liked also the suggestion that a true lover of art with a special sensitivity could secure for himself extraordinary sensations not available to others. Wilde felt that Pater placed all standards in the taste of the individual, relied heavily on cultivating sensation rather than thought, and deliberately retreated into a fortress-like subjectivity.

The attitude that later came to be called Paterism was based largely on feeling and is therefore Romantic. But it is a new kind of romanticism colored by *carpe diem*, the new aestheticism, which bordered on decadence, and a philosophy of hedonism. The best example of Paterism is the one supplied by Oscar Wilde in *The Picture of Dorian Gray* (1891). In fact Wilde himself was a living example of Paterism, and by 1895 had become something of a national scandal. He quickly established himself as a spokesman for the movement known as "Art for Art's Sake." In 1882, one year before Matthew Arnold's visit to America, he traveled to this country and made a lengthy and lucrative lecture tour.

He dazzled the gullible Americans with his witty language, outrageous statements, flamboyant dress – his trademark green carnation quickly became famous – and other theatrics. He startled Americans with remarks on the new aestheticism and its philosophy, and hinted that Pater was the strong albeit reluctant leader of the new movement. If Pater had the reputation of being shy and reticent, there was nothing reticent about his disciple. He posed as a dandy and a rebel, a self-promoter and showman. He pandered his American audiences, telling them "to disagree with three fourths of all England on all points of view is one of the first elements of sanity." He attempted to put into practice many of Pater's theories, and traveled far and wide advocating the "new Hedonism" for the younger generation. To his great satisfaction he became a symbol of youthful iconoclasm.

Lord Henry Wotton in *The Picture of Dorian Gray* (1891) offers an explanation of the new hedonism. He advises young Dorian, just coming of age, to burn the candle brightly at both ends: "Live! Live the wonderful life that is in you! Let nothing be lost upon you. Be always searching for new sensations. Be afraid of nothing . . . a new Hedonism – that is what our century wants. You might be its visible symbol. With your personality there is nothing you could not do. The world belongs to you for a season." After this speech, an odd mixture of *carpe diem* and Victorian earnestness, the author himself comments: "Yes, there was to be, as Lord Henry had prophesied, a new Hedonism that was to recreate life and save it from that harsh, uncomely Puritanism that is having in our own day its curious revival. It was to have its service of the intellect, certainly. Yet it was never to accept any theory or system that would involve the sacrifice of any mode of passionate experience. Its aim, indeed, was to be experience itself. . . . It was to teach man to concentrate himself upon the moments of a life that is itself but a moment." The emphasis here is making the most of a life all too brief.

The touted new hedonism received its impetus mainly from the brief "Conclusion" of Pater's volume on the art of the Renaissance. The attitudes expressed there, and Wilde's flamboyant interpretation of them, suggest a genuine decline in Victorian vigor. Faith had gone out of the world, and a kind of paganism based on self-indulgence and rejection of the older generation was creeping into it. Wilde as harbinger was in his element.

Renaissance Studies (1873) — This is the book that established with its impressive prose Pater's reputation as the leader of the aesthetic cult. "It was from reading Pater's *Studies in the History of the Renaissance*, in its first edition on ribbed paper (I have the feel of it still in my fingers), that I realized that prose also could be a fine art," gushed one critic. In later editions the title of the volume became *The Renaissance: Studies in Art and Poetry*. The "Preface" and the "Conclusion" were important sections of the first edition. Some of the studies in between had already appeared as articles. It was a common procedure at that time for a well-known author to give a lecture, publish it as an article, place it in a book, and later revise it for a new edition. While some academics including Jowett didn't like the book, a number of discerning critics, in addition to Wilde, had high praise for it.

An early biographer of the author called it Pater's masterpiece and said its theme was this: "Imitate the men of the Renaissance and enjoy yourself. Like them, you will find your keenest delight in the attitude of the scholar, in the enthusiastic acquisition of knowledge for its own sake." That interpretation was more restrained than Wilde's impetuous reading and perhaps more accurate. Pater sees the Renaissance artists as working joyously for no other end than to create beauty. They find their joy not in a hedonistic surrender to sensual pleasure, but in the act of working and particularly the act of bringing beauty into the world. The pursuit of truth is a by-product of the pursuit of beauty, and the acquisition of knowledge has little to do with artistic endeavor. The section on Leonardo's "Mona Lisa" is the best example of Pater's impressionistic criticism. He veers away from dogmatic statements of fact and leaves the reader with warm and wavering impressions.

In the "Preface" to the volume Pater agrees with Arnold that the aim of all true criticism is "to see the object as in itself it really is." Then he adds that "in aesthetic criticism the first step towards seeing one's object as it really is, is to know one's own impression as it really is." It is necessary to ask, what is this work of art to me? What effect does it produce on me? Does it give me pleasure? If so, what sort and degree of pleasure? How is my nature modified in its presence? The answers to these questions provide the necessary tools for the aesthetic critic to form sound impressions. With such impressions he has no need to define beauty in the abstract or worry about its relation to truth or experience. The aesthetic critic regards all objects that he is called upon to judge as "forces producing pleasurable sensations," and this impression he seeks to explain.

The function of the aesthetic critic is to identify that particular virtue which produces a lasting impression of beauty or pleasure and determine its source. He must remember that beauty comes in many forms, and its degree depends on the genius of the person who makes it. He must ask, what is the virtue or the active principle in this work of art? The aesthetic function is to discover and analyze not merely the "active principle," but each particular manifestation of beauty as suggested by the mind of the artist. Near the end of the "Preface" we learn that Pater believes that the Renaissance, a revival of intellectual and imaginative enjoyment, really began in France near the end of the twelfth century. Most historians say the Renaissance began later than that and in Italy. They see the twelfth century as the Middle Ages.

The famous "Conclusion" to the *Renaissance*, only a few paragraphs in length, is that part of the volume which supposedly changed the lives of readers and gave its author the most cause for worry. Its regal sentences, along with those of the "Preface," set forth the following precepts that became the basis for the new aestheticism that flourished in the last two decades of the century:

- Epicureanism interpreted by his disciples as hedonism is the true end of life. It is natural for human beings to avoid pain and pursue pleasure. All of us want to live our lives fully and with intensity. Intellectual and emotional intensity can be gained in the presence of great art, and the experience can bring unity and direction to one's life.

- Total subjectivity, attacked as irresponsible impressionism, is the essence of aesthetic criticism. Art of any kind is primarily an expression of personality. The perceiver of great art benefits from understanding the life behind the art, the heartbeat of the personality that produced it.

- Rules that require obedience are not necessary, either for the artist or for the one inclined to appreciate what the artist has created. Each work of art has its own unique core of experience. Rules of form suggesting a special genre are therefore brushed aside, and the result is destruction of genre.

- Art for art's sake, though not expressed exactly in those words, is a main article of belief. Art has no duty to serve other ends. It need not be tied in with social problems, religious faith, or morality. This idea, clearly opposing Carlyle and Ruskin, generated much discussion on the subject of art and morality and the relationship one must recognize between the two. It was the idea that gave impetus to a movement already underway.

The Greek motto at the beginning of the "Conclusion" may be translated in these words: "All things give way to other things; nothing remains forever." So if all things are transient, life is valuable for the ecstasy of its moments. "While all melts under our feet," Pater writes, "we may well grasp at any exquisite passion, or any stirring of the senses, strange dyes, strange colours, and curious odours, or work of the artist's hands, or the face of one's friend." In this key passage, which exerted tremendous influence on Oscar Wilde and those prone to listen to him, Pater is saying that a life of the senses is the only life truly worth living. To live this life fully and completely, one must reach for and grasp "any exquisite passion" that arises, cherish the moment, and hold onto it as long as one can.

Success in life is to maintain the ecstasy of the moment because life itself is but a moment. In a passage frequently quoted Pater himself expresses the idea this way: "To burn always with this hard, gem-like flame, to maintain this ecstasy, is success in life." While emphasizing the brevity of life he does not consider the nagging question of human happiness, but does speak of the need to court new impressions and bring "as many pulsations as possible" into the moment that is granted us. We can know reality only through our senses, and so we should make one desperate effort to use all five of them effectively. Wilde and others interpreted this artistic credo, meant to offer inspiration rather than license, as an open invitation to taste all the pleasures of forbidden experience.

Alarmed by the misreading of Epicureanism as hedonism, Pater decided not to include the controversial "Conclusion" in the second edition of the *Renaissance* (1877). He hoped that suppression would defuse the uproar, but artistic integrity led him to replace it in the third edition of 1888. In a footnote he offered this explanation: "This brief 'Conclusion' was omitted in the second edition of this book, as I conceived it might possibly mislead some of those young men into whose hands it might fall. On the whole, I have thought it best to reprint it here, with some slight changes which bring it closer to my original meaning. I have dealt more fully in *Marius the Epicurean* with the thoughts suggested by it." Choosing to reinstate the "Conclusion," Pater believed that his novel of 1885 had clarified his views and corrected the misconceptions of his readers. That did not really happen, and yet this footnote seems to have taken him out of the harsh glare of controversy. His reputation as a Victorian intellectual with new and striking ideas that moved young readers to rebellion has since been one of ebb and flow. Today with a looser moral code directing our lives we wonder what all the fuss was about. Pater and Paterism must be viewed in the context of their time.

Robert Louis Stevenson

Equally versatile as novelist, poet, and essayist, Robert Louis Stevenson (1850-1894) is often omitted in anthologies that focus on Victorian prose and the people who wrote it. The best anthologies generally include some of his familiar essays, but seldom do they include excerpts from the travel books or the adventure books based on fact. Stevenson is surely not of the same rank as the great masters of Victorian thought, and yet he deserves to be included in any survey that pays attention to them. He belongs to the so-called Romantic Revival that took place in the last two decades of the century. He himself, as he lived his life in a ceaseless search for health, was the unequivocal personification of the Romantic wanderer.

His quest took him from his native Scotland to several European countries, the far west in this country, and to the South Seas. As with other world travelers at this time, when the planet we live on was huge and mysterious, he had a tremendous zest for adventure. Wherever he went, from every part of the world, he gathered material for essays that are filled with impressions of people, places, and things. He worked as an essayist and writer of short stories before he attempted longer forms, and the personal charm for which the man was famous comes through more surely in briefer pieces. His work as poet and novelist falls outside the boundaries of our discussion here, but the collection of essays published in 1881 reveals much of the man and his philosophy. He is remembered as a master of the personal essay.

Robert Lewis Balfour Stevenson was born near the end of 1850 in Edinburgh. He was the only child of a distinguished engineer who specialized in building lighthouses. An early attack of tuberculosis interrupted his schooling and caused him to travel for health, but all the time he was traveling he was reading a great deal and writing in notebooks. He entered Edinburgh University in 1867 to study the family profession of engineering, but gave it up to study law instead. While in college he alarmed his Calvinistic parents with his agnostic views and bohemian behavior. He passed his bar examination in 1875, but soon afterward abandoned the legal profession for literature. He contributed essays to *Cornhill Magazine*, which were published in book form in 1881 as *Virginibus Puerisque* (For Girls and Boys).

At about this time Stevenson also joined an influential club and made friends with prominent people. In 1876 he took a canoe trip through the canals and rivers of France, and on the basis of that adventure published *An Inland Voyage* (1878), his first book. This was followed the next year by a narrative detailing a trek through the southern French mountains, *Travels With a Donkey*. These early books reveal his mastery of an easy and familiar style, and his genuine love of an active life lived out of doors. As he was writing his travel books he felt he needed breaks so as not to tire himself, and so as a diversion he began to write critical essays. There were later published as *Familiar Studies of Men and Books* in 1882.

At Grez in 1876 he met Fanny Osborne, an American woman who was studying art in France. She was unhappily married, had a son and daughter in their teens, and was ten years his senior. They fell in love, and two years later she went home to California to get a divorce. In the summer of 1879, against his parents' stern advice, he traveled to America to be with her. He crossed the ocean in steerage (the cheapest way to travel) and went across America crammed into an immigrant train. He carefully recorded the experience and made use of it later in two books, *The Amateur Emigrant* and *Across the Plains*. At that time he had no job, no sustaining income, and was living from hand to mouth close to starvation.

In San Francisco still without a job he tried to live on one meatless meal a day, became dangerously ill, but went on writing. After several months of severe deprivation he became "a pitiable wreck," said his friend

Sidney Colvin, "ready for the hospital, ready almost for the undertaker." At this point his father came to his rescue with an allowance that pulled him out of poverty and allowed him to marry. He and Fanny married in 1880 and enjoyed full happiness together even as he sought to restore his declining health. For a time, in search of a place where he could breathe, they lived in a deserted mining camp. This experience later provided him with ample material for *The Silverado Squatters*, redolent of local color, which he published in 1883. In that year he published also *Treasure Island*, which became a classic among younger readers.

Plagued by his unpredictable health, yet hoping to grow stronger through travel and vigorous activity, he returned with his wife to England where they remained for seven years. During this time of peace and relative ease much of his best work was done. He wrote many hours each day, began to make money from his books, and quickly won fame and fortune. In these years he produced the enduring classic, his most famous work, *Dr. Jekyll and Mr. Hyde* (1886). Another book published in the same year and almost as famous was *Kidnapped* (1886). In 1887, after the death of his father and once more in search of health, he returned to America with his wife, widowed mother, stepson, and their servant, Valentine Roch.

On this voyage the group traveled by tramp steamer in bad weather with a cargo of apes and stallions for sixteen days. Stevenson found life at sea exciting, and he looked forward to each day: "I was so happy on board that ship," he confided to a friend in one of his many letters, "I could not have believed it possible. We had many discomforts, but the mere fact of its being a tramp-ship gave us many comforts; we could cut about with the men and the officers, stay in the wheel-house, discuss all manner of things, and really be a little at sea. And truly there is nothing else." To Henry James he wrote: "The voyage was a huge success, plenty of sailors to talk to, and the endless pleasures of the sea." He would never lose his love of the sea.

Stevenson went on to say that he would gladly give up his fame as an author "for a good seventy-ton schooner and the coins to keep her." He dreamed of owning a yacht that would take him across the Atlantic to Newport, Rhode Island. There he would hang around the docks and mingle with other yachtsmen and display the Union Jack to make it known he had come all the way from England. There he would spin sea yarns and brag about crossing the ocean in a small boat. "I know a little about fame now; it is no good compared to a yacht. That's fame to say you have crossed the Atlantic, and that's glory." The few yachtsmen who cross the ocean, even today with sophisticated electronic devices to guide them, indeed brag about it.

Stevenson was flattered by the unexpected appreciation he received in America, but he was willing to chuck it all for the sea. He had planned to go to a mountain health resort in Colorado, but to avoid the uncomfortable overland journey he spent the winter at Saranac Lake in the Adirondacks. That location had lately come into reputation as a place of cure, and there under the care of a well-known physician, he spent seven months from September of 1887 to April of 1888. He described the climate as brutal, but on the whole it seemed favorable to his health. During the winter he wrote twelve essays, including "Pulvis et Umbra" (Dust and Shadow).

All were written for *Scribner's Magazine* for the handsome sum of 700 pounds, more than $90,000 in present-day currency. In November of 1887 he informed a friend that he had been offered 1,600 pounds for the serial rights on his next book (nearly $200,000 today). He added that he felt a little guilty taking so much money from the Americans, but said he would certainly try to give them the very best he could do for that amount. Later, subsidized by an American publisher who was willing to buy anything he wrote and hoping that a sea voyage would cure his lung condition, he and his family traveled across the United States to charter in San Francisco a small but sea-worthy schooner christened *Casco*.

With a brusque but personable skipper and a small crew, including his servant Valentine Roch, they set sail for the Marquesas on June 28, 1888. This was the beginning of more than two happy years of cruising the South Seas. Stevenson disliked towns and cities and the press of civilization and had an insatiable thirst for adventure. This cruise was a chance to do what he had dreamt of doing since childhood. In just a few weeks good health and strength returned, and he grew bronze and hearty under the tropical sun. They dropped anchor in the harbor of Nukahiva, the largest of the islands in French Polynesia, exactly one month after departing. The magical effect of this first island landfall, after weeks of looking only at sea and sky, he described in the opening chapter of *The South Seas* and in letters to his friends. He had never been happier.

After spending six weeks in this group of islands and feeling remarkably strong in their delightful climate, the mariners sailed southeastward to Tahiti. In that place, legendary for its beauty, Stevenson fell sharply ill but was able to sail northward on a difficult and uncomfortable passage to Honolulu after the yacht was refitted with new masts. There in January of 1889 he paid Captain Otis his fee and settled down for a stay of six months, expecting eventually to return to the mainland and not go to sea again. But scarcely a month went by before he was writing to a friend, "I feel pretty sure I shall want to get to sea again ere long." Already he was planning to write a book about the cruise of the *Casco*. "The cruise itself, you are to know, will make a big volume. I believe the book when ready will have a fair measure of serious interest." His voyage had been a great success, accomplishing the aims he had set for it, but he was glad to be ashore. His wife had suffered seasickness from time to time, but he and other members of the party had thoroughly enjoyed themselves. "I am so well that I do not know myself – sea-bathing, if you please, and entertaining His Majesty [King Kalakaua]." The King could down a bottle of champagne in two gulps and could be heard on the other side of the island when he laughed.

The exhilaration Stevenson felt must have interfered with his writing, and yet he moved steadily along with several projects. He even found the time to answer a seven months' accumulation of correspondence. In most of his letters he praised the islands: "All the time our visits to the islands have been more like dreams than like realities. The people, the life, the beachcombers, the old stories and songs all so interesting. The climate, the scenery, and (in some places) the women, so beautiful. The women are handsomest in Tahiti." He liked being in port, and yet he was thrilled to be at sea with a sturdy little ship, alive and responsive, between him and the deep blue sea, "the perils of the deep" he called it.

Here is the way he described the day they sighted Hawaii: "It blew fair, but very strong; we carried jib, foresail, and mainsail, all single-reefed, and she carried her lee rail under water and flew. The swell, the heaviest I have ever been out in – at least fifteen feet – came tearing after us but never once caught us.... I never remember anything more delightful and exciting. Pretty soon we were lying becalmed under the lee of Hawaii, but the captain never confessed he had done it on purpose.... He did quite right, for to bring her to wind would have been a heart-sickening manœuvre." Stevenson died even as Joshua Slocum was preparing to sail single-handedly around the world in a clumsy and smaller yacht that he himself had rebuilt. The two sailors, loving boats and the sea, had much in common and would have been friends.

The first year of voyaging had been so rewarding that Stevenson decided to cruise again in more remote areas. He departed from Honolulu in June of 1889 on a trading schooner, the *Equator*, bound for the Gilbert Islands. Near the end of that year he found himself in Samoa, where he wrote his first Polynesian story, "The Bottle Imp." Enchanted with the scenery and the people, he stayed for six weeks and bought property on a mountainside that would later become his home. In 1890 he went to Sydney, Australia and decided while there to remain for the rest of his life in the tropics. To shake off an attack of illness, he left Sydney with his party on a trader steamboat, the *Janet Nicoll*, which took them to many remote islands from April to August 1890. In October he returned to his Samoan property of four hundred acres, made plans to build a spacious house, and by November had settled there. Vailima (Five Rivers) stood six hundred feet above the sea with a view in all directions of startling beauty. "The sea, islands, the islanders, the island life and climate, make and keep me truly happier," he wrote Henry James. "These last two years I have been much at sea, and I have never wearied." His daily life at Vailima was a respite from the harder life at sea.

"Here I am until I die," he announced in a letter, "and here will I be buried." One day after several hours of intense literary work, he came downstairs at sunset and played a game of cards with his wife. He talked of going to America on a lecture tour, said he was hungry, and the two began to prepare the evening meal. Then without warning he slumped to the floor and was placed in a large chair as a servant went for the doctor. He died of a cerebral hemorrhage on December 3, 1894 at the beginning of his forty-fifth year. The large Union Jack that flew over the house was hauled down and laid over the body. The Samoans passed in procession, honoring him as a fallen chief. The next day they buried his body on the shimmering mountaintop above his home. His epitaph was taken from the poem "Requiem" which he himself had written some years before:

> Here he lies where he longed to be;
> Home is the sailor, home from sea,
> And the hunter home from the hill.

On a mountaintop in Samoa those words, visible today, were placed above the grave of "Tusitala" (his Samoan name). His life was brief but he lived it well. During all his life he was a teller of tales, a sailor, and a seeker.

3

"Aes Triplex" (1878) — Stevenson's truest calling was that of the romantic essayist. One of his best essays has the awkward title you see here. For reasons never fully explained to anyone, he was fond of abstruse Latin titles, coined them frequently, and was unperturbed when readers did not understand the titles. This one means "triple bronze," a phrase comparable to "great courage." It comes from an ode by the Roman poet Horace. The essay was published in the *Cornhill Magazine*, edited by Leslie Stephen, for April of 1878. It was later one of the pieces that made up *Virginibus Puerisque* (another Latin title meaning For Girls and Boys). The volume was prized by some as "a layman's contribution to a philosophy of youth." This particular essay has been called "perhaps the most cherished of all philosophic essays in English" because of its theme. Everyone knew that the author himself had only a short time to live, and yet he was advocating an energetic and courageous life in spite of the brevity of his own existence.

A sickly person such as Stevenson proclaiming the joy of living touched sentimental chords among the late Victorians, and they loved him for it. Yet the utterance also satisfied a deep popular need. On the losses of growing old, for example, his attitude was cheerful and the opposite of Matthew Arnold's. "What is it to grow old?" Arnold had asked. "It is to spend long days without ever having known we were young." Every step we take in life, Stevenson countered, we find the ice growing thinner and more dangerous beneath our feet, but that's inevitable if one is lucky enough to grow old. It is not so painful as many suppose and no cause for worry. An old man about to die should drink his grog with gusto and tell racy stories and be glad he lived at all. He firmly believed we should live our lives as fully as we can until "God's pale Praetorian throws us over in the end."

Stevenson concludes "Aes Triplex" with a reference to Dr. Johnson and the great dictionary he produced: "Think of the heroism of Johnson, think of that superb indifference to mortal limitation that set him upon his dictionary, and carried him through triumphantly until the end!" In your life's work, he urges, don't be discouraged by Thackeray and Dickens who died leaving behind unfinished novels. It is better to do what has to be done and forget about the time you may need to do it. "By all means begin your folio, even if the doctor does not give you a year, even if he hesitates about a month. Make one brave push and see what can be accomplished in a week. It is not only in finished undertakings that we ought to honor useful labor." Then with reference to dying well he uses with imaginative changes a metaphor that Arnold made famous, life as a stream flowing to the sea: "Does not life go down with a better grace foaming in full body over a precipice than miserably straggling to an end in sandy deltas?" He insists that those who love life should face both life and death with strength, equanimity, and grace. "Heart of oak and triple brass must have girt the breast of him who first entrusted his frail bark to the angry sea."

"Pulvis et Umbra" (1888) is often cited as Stevenson's second philosophical essay that reaches the quality of a masterpiece. Its title means "dust and shadow" and comes also from an ode by Horace: "We when we have fallen are but dust and shadow." Written for *Scribner's Magazine* in America and published in 1888, it uses every device known to language to stress the theme of animal and human decency against a background of insensate evolution. The essay begins on a somber note:

"We look for some reward of our endeavours and are disappointed; not success, not happiness, not even peace of conscience, crowns our ineffectual efforts to do well."

Then he takes his cue from science to build a universe made of something called matter. "This stuff rots uncleanly into something we call life," and this "vital putrescence of the dust" we sometimes find disgusting. We can't escape it because it covers the earth in two main shapes, animal and vegetable. We know little about the plants – "doubtless they have their joys and sorrows" – but we surely share with one another a thousand miracles. We are animal, and all animals subject to the laws of nature "prey upon each other, lives tearing other lives in pieces." Our little rotating rock, not brown but green and blue, is loaded with predatory life. Drenched with the blood of victims, it "scuds through space with unimaginable speed," and that is the order of things. The image concludes the first part of the essay.

The second part opens with a view of that "monstrous spectre" we call man, surely an animal in nature and yet with surprising attributes. "Savagely surrounded, savagely descended, irremediably condemned to prey upon his fellow lives, who should have blamed him had he been merely barbarous?" Nonetheless he is often kind and valiant. This creature, strange to behold, harbors a sense of duty, "an ideal of decency," that may not be his exclusively but could run through all nature. "Doubtless some similar point of honour sways the elephant, the oyster, and the louse, for we can trace it in dogs and cats whom we know fairly well." Yet of all the creatures, though marked by failure in his efforts, man is the one most driven to do right. Wherever we see him, abundant examples of his ineffectual goodness convince us of his basic decency. Is it not strange that "this ennobled lemur, this hair-crowned bubble of the dust, this inheritor of a few years and sorrows" should live for an ideal? Do we share with all creatures our will to struggle and do well? In his brief span that man has been on earth he stands no longer apart, for the whole creation groans and strives with him. With the theory of evolution in mind, Stevenson shapes a philosophy of belonging and hope.

The tone of the essay is one of wry good humor but in asserting his theme he takes care to be serious. He gained as he lived his life a good supply of wisdom and sympathy that made him very tolerant of human failings. In a time of petulant and unforgiving class-consciousness among the British, and a stern prejudice against foreign women, he fell in love with and married a divorced American woman. Then he went off to live with brown-skinned people on a primitive island in the South Seas. He thoroughly enjoyed meeting and talking to people from all backgrounds on terms of equality. Later he filed away in memory all he had learned from them and wrote.

Though he proudly flew an oversized Union Jack over his house in Samoa, he had not even a suggestion of the jingoism demonstrated by Tennyson's Victorian youth in "Locksley Hall." While his style (at least in the essays) clearly shows the influence of Carlyle, he is the opposite of Carlyle in his love of freedom, democracy, equality. Yet like Carlyle he came to know firsthand "the pitiless cruelty of modern civilization" and shunned it whenever he could. Because he wrestled with a fatal disease all of his life, he knew also how unfair is the sorry scheme of things. To his credit he suffered severely most of his life without complaint and never grew bitter. Close to the end of his life he could say: "I believe in an ultimate decency of things; ay, and if I woke in hell, should still believe it!" He was echoing in those words the theme of the essay we have just examined.

4

In our time there has been a tendency to regard Stevenson primarily as a writer of children's books, probably because of the success of only two such works, *Treasure Island* (1883) and *A Child's Garden of Verses* (1885). Like Jonathan Swift, it pleased him greatly that he could meet the demanding tastes of children, but again like Swift he did not write exclusively for children. Much of his work was of a different nature, extending to masterpieces of horror and robust adult adventure. He chose to celebrate the vigorous joy of living when leading novelists such as Gissing and Hardy were penning grim and gloomy realistic works. He restored the familiar essay to a prominence it had not enjoyed since the time of Charles Lamb, and his letters are delightful to read. His poems, reflecting his love of life, influenced an entire generation of

English and American poets. Robert Bridges, poet laureate and friend of Gerard Manley Hopkins, wrote a sensitive appreciation of Stevenson. He observed that the writer placed more value on the things he learned in his travels than on what he gained from books and lectures. That comment Stevenson himself supported: "Books are good enough in their own way, but they are a bloodless substitute for life. It seems a pity to sit, like the Lady of Shalott [in his travels he had found the time to read Tennyson], peering into a mirror with your back turned on all the bustle and glamour of reality."

We know Stevenson best through his letters, many of them informal essays that invariably reveal the quality of the man. To George Meredith he wrote in 1893: "For fourteen years I have not had a single day's real health; I have wakened sick and gone to bed weary; and I have done my work unflinchingly. I have written in bed, and written out of it, written in hemorrhages, written in sickness, written torn by coughing, and written when my head swam for sickness." If he disagreed with Carlyle on other matters, when it came to work he was Carlyle's disciple. To his stepson, Lloyd Osborne, he insisted that he possessed no unusual talent: "I started out with very moderate abilities. What genius I had was for *work*." Probably no other writer ever worked harder to master his craft: "I sit here and smoke and write and rewrite from six in the morning till eight at night," he wrote to a friend a few months before his death. Stevenson believed it was his duty to give to his readers the very best of himself. That is why his books have a special appeal in our time and continue to be read.

Reading Victorian Literature

By now, at the end of our time together, we should have a good understanding of the representative prose written during the reign of Queen Victoria. Time and space wouldn't allow for discussion of all the prose but did include the best. The same rigorous selection was in effect for the writers who produced the prose. Other men and women were doing good work too, hoping to make a contribution to improve their world. As suggested by the title and motto of the book you have in your hands, most of these writer/thinkers were searching earnestly for light but often searching in shadow or confusion in troubled times. So what kind of man was seeking light in a shadowy, shifting, and murky world? He was a wise and well-informed man who wrote compelling prose as a teacher, preacher, and prophet. He wanted to lead his people out of the wilderness, and he believed he had the means by which to do it. In tumultuous and uncertain times (1832 to 1901) he worked hard to be heard by a sympathetic audience.

The result was a lasting contribution to the literature and social conscience of his day. At the end of his life he looked back to ask with some dismay whether anyone had heard him at all. At times he was gravely disappointed, even bitter, as he convinced himself that the people who needed him most had neither listened nor learned. At other times, in brighter moments, he was certain his work had value and was not done in vain. Performing as writers and thinkers in roughly chronological order were these ten: Macaulay, Carlyle, Newman, Mill,

Ruskin, Arnold, Darwin, Huxley, Morris, and Pater. Others of lesser note were Spencer, Stephen, Butler, and Stevenson. But one should also mention Dickens and other novelists as practical reformers even though their medium was the three-decker novel rather than expository prose. You will see more concerning them below.

I conclude this discussion with a list of titles to help the student of Victorian literature reach a fuller and richer understanding of the era. The list is not based on chronological selections as in the method already taken, but considers the important issues of the day. Not restricted to Victorian prose alone, it includes all types of literature prevalent during the period. Any person who reads these titles in the order presented, or in whatever order seems best, will eventually gain a sound knowledge of the Victorians.

I. Social and Political Issues

Carlyle:	*Sartor Resartus*
	On Heroes and Hero Worship
	Past and Present
	The French Revolution
	Chartism
	"Shooting Niagara, and After?"
Mayhew:	*London Labour and the London Poor*
Mill:	*On Liberty*
	The Subjection of Women
	"Nature"
	Autobiography
Macaulay:	"Southey's Colloquies"
	"Francis Bacon"
	The History of England (Chapter III)

Dickens: *A Christmas Carol*
                 Hard Times
                 Oliver Twist
                 Bleak House
                 Our Mutual Friend

Gaskell: *Mary Barton*
                 North and South

Kingsley: "Cheap Clothes and Nasty"
                 Alton Locke
                 Yeast

Disraeli: *Sybil, or The Two Nations*

C. Reade: *It Is Never Too Late to Mend*
                 A Terrible Temptation

Ruskin: *Unto This Last*
                 The Crown of Wild Olive
                 Sesame and Lilies
                 Fors Clavigera (selected letters)
                 Præterita

Butler: *Erewhon*

Gissing: *Workers in the Dawn*
                 Demos: A Story of English Socialism
                 The Nether World
                 The Emancipated
                 New Grub Street

Morris: *News from Nowhere*
                 "The Defense of Guenevere"

Clough:	*The Bothie of Tober-na-Vuolich*
Thackeray:	*The Book of Snobs*
Trollope:	*Phineas Finn* *The Prime Minister*
T. Hood:	"The Song of the Shirt"
E. Browning:	"The Cry of the Human" "The Cry of the Children"
Tennyson:	*The Princess* "Guinevere" from *Idylls of the King* "Lady Clara Vere de Vere" "You Ask Me Why" "Of Old Sat Freedom" "Love Thou Thy Land" "Maud"
Meredith:	*Modern Love* *Diana of the Crossways* *Beauchamp's Career*
Gilbert:	*Iolanthe* *Princess Ida*
Schreiner:	*The Story of an African Farm*

II. Scientific, Religious, and Educational Issues

Darwin: *The Origin of Species* (chapters 3, 4, 15)
                           The Descent of Man (chapter 21)

Lyell: *Principles of Geology*

Chambers: *Vestiges of the Natural History of Creation*

Wallace: *Darwinism*

Huxley: *Darwiniana*
                           "Improving Natural Knowledge"
                           "On the Physical Basis of Life"
                           "Struggle for Existence in Human Society"
                           "Liberal Education and Where to Find It"
                           "Science and Culture"
                           "Science and Art in Relation to Education"

Spencer: "What Knowledge is of Most Worth?"
                           The Principles of Ethics

Arnold: "Literature and Science"
                           "Numbers"

Newman: *The Idea of a University*
                           Apologia pro Vita Sua
                           Tract XC
                           "The Pillar of the Cloud"
                           "The Dream of Gerontius"

Butler: *The Way of All Flesh*

Trollope:	*Barchester Towers*
	The Warden
Pater:	*Marius the Epicurean*
Tennyson:	"The Two Voices"
	"Locksley Hall"
	In Memoriam
	"The Higher Pantheism"
	"Flower in the Crannied Wall"
	"Vastness"
	"By an Evolutionist"
	"Locksley Hall Sixty Years After"
	"Crossing the Bar"
Browning:	"Christmas Eve and Easter Day"
	"Saul"
	"The Epistle of Karshish"
	"Cleon"
	"Abt Vogler"
	"Rabbi ben Ezra"
	"A Death in the Desert"
	"Caliban upon Setebos"
	"Bishop Blougram's Apology"
	"Apparent Failure"
	"Epilogue to *Asolando*"
	"In a Gondola"
Fitzgerald:	*The Rubaiyat of Omar Khayyam*
Clough:	"Wen Gott Betrugt"
	"The Questioning Spirit"
	"Easter Day, I, II"

"Say Not the Struggle Naught Availeth"
"The Latest Decalogue"
"All Is Well"
Dipsychus

Arnold:

Empedocles on Etna
"Resignation"
"Self-Dependence"
"The Buried Life"
"Stanzas from the Grande Chartreuse"
"In Memory of the Author of Obermann"
"The Future"
"Thyrsis"
"Dover Beach"
"The Last Word"
"Rugby Chapel"

C. Rossetti:

"Goblin Market"
"Paradise"
"A Better Resurrection"
"Advent"
"Uphill"
"De Profundis"
"Sleeping at Last"

Thomson:

"For I Must Sing of All I Feel and Know"
"The City of Dreadful Night"

Selected poems:

Aubrey de Vere
Coventry Patmore
Lionel Johnson
Ernest Dowson
Francis Thompson

Meredith:	"The Woods of Westermain"
	"The Thrush in February"
	"Hard Weather"
	"Dirge in Woods"
	"The Lark Ascending"
	"Lucifer in Starlight"
	"Earth's Secret"
	"Song in the Songless"
	"Youth and Age"
Swinburne:	"Hymn to Proserpine"
	"The Garden of Proserpine"
	"Hertha"
Hopkins:	"The Wreck of the Deutschland"
	"God's Grandeur"
	"The Starlight Night"
	"The Windhover"
	"Pied Beauty"
	"Hurrahing in Harvest"
	"I Wake and Feel the Fell of Dark"
	"Carrion Comfort"
Henley:	"Invictus"
	"The Sands are Alive with Sunshine"
	"What Is to Come"
	"Space and Dread and the Dark"
Hardy:	"Shelley's Skylark"
	"The Impercipient"
	"Hap"
	"God-Forgotten"
	"The Darkling Thrush"

"The Convergence of the Twain"
"Ah, Are You Digging on My Grave?"

III. Cultural, Critical, and Aesthetic Issues

Macaulay: "Milton"
                "Samuel Johnson"

Ruskin: *Modern Painters*
                "Greatness in Art"
                The Stones of Venice
                "The Nature of Gothic"
                "Pre-Raphaelitism"
                "The Relation of Art to Morals"
                "Relating National Ethics to National Art"

Arnold: *Culture and Anarchy*
                Essays in Criticism (first series)
                Essays in Criticism (second series)
                The Study of Poetry

Morris: *Hopes and Fears for Art*
                "The Lesser Arts"
                "The Art of the People"
                "The Beauty of Life"

Meredith: *The Idea of Comedy...and the Comic Spirit*

Trollope: *An Autobiography*

Thackeray: *Punch's Prize Novelists*

Eliot:	"Silly Novels by Lady Novelists"
Buchanan:	"Fleshly School of English Poetry"
D. Rossetti:	"Stealthy School of English Criticism"

Pater:
The Renaissance
"Preface"
"The Poetry of Michelangelo"
"Leonardo da Vinci"
"Conclusion"
Appreciations

Wilde:
The Picture of Dorian Gray
"The Sphinx"
Salome
De Profundis

Hichens: *The Green Carnation*

G. Moore: *Confessions of a Young Man*

Gilbert: *Patience*

IV. The Victorian Novel

Dickens:
Pickwick Papers
David Copperfield
Great Expectations
Nicholas Nickleby

Thackeray: *Vanity Fair*

	Henry Esmond
E. Bronte:	*Wuthering Heights*
C. Bronte:	*Jane Eyre*
	The Professor
Eliot:	*Middlemarch*
	Adam Bede
	The Mill on the Floss
	Silas Marner
Meredith:	*The Egoist*
	The Ordeal of Richard Feverel
Hardy:	
	Jude the Obscure
	The Return of the Native
	The Mayor of Casterbridge
	Tess of the d'Urbervilles
Collins:	*The Woman in White*
	The Moonstone
Gissing:	*The Nether World*
	Isabel Clarendon
	New Grub Street
	The Odd Women
	The Crown of Life
G. Moore:	*Esther Waters*
	A Mummer's Wife

V. Victorian Lyric Poetry

Tennyson: "The Palace of Art"
                     "Ode on Death of Duke of Wellington"
                     "To Virgil"
                     "June Bracken and Heather"
                     "The Poet"

E. Browning: *Sonnets from the Portuguese*

R. Browning: Songs from *Pippa Passes*
                     "Cavalier Tunes"
                     "Home Thoughts from Abroad"
                     "De Gustibus"
                     "Love in a Life"
                     "Life in a Love"
                     "Memorabilia"
                     "One Word More"
                     "House"
                     "Wanting Is – What?"
                     "Now"

Emily Bronte: "Remembrance"
                     "The Old Stoic"
                     "Warning and Reply"
                     "No Coward Soul is Mine"

Arnold: "Memorial Verses"
                     "Philomela"
                     "The Scholar Gypsy"

D. Rossetti: *The House of Life*

C. Rossetti: "Song"
                         "After Death"
                         "A Birthday"
                         "An Apple Gathering"

Patmore: "Deliciae Sapientiae de Amore"
                         The Unknown Eros

Meredith: "Love in the Valley"

Swinburne: "Faustine"
                         "Laus Veneris"
                         "The Triumph of Time"
                         "A Leave Taking"
                         "A Match"
                         "Dolores"

Wilde: "Impressions"
                         "The Sphinx"

Stevenson: "To Alice Cunningham"
                         "Bed in Summer"
                         "Travel"
                         "The Land of Counterpane"
                         "The Land of Nod"
                         "Escape at Bedtime"
                         "Christmas At Sea"
                         "Requiem"

Dowson: "Non Sum Qualis...Sub Regno Cynarae"
                         "Amor Profanus"
                         "A Last Word"

Douglas:	"Impression de Nuit: London"
	"A Song"
	"The Dead Poet"

| Housman: | *A Shropshire Lad* |

VI. Victorian Narrative Poetry

Tennyson:	*The Idylls of the King*
	"The Coming of Arthur"
	"Merlin and Vivien"
	"The Last Tournament"
	"The Passing of Arthur"
	"The Lady of Shalott"
	"The Lotos Eaters"
	"Ulysses"
	"Tithonus"
	"The Charge of the Light Brigade"
	"The Revenge"
	"Rizpah"
	"Northern Farmer, New Style"
	"Northern Farmer, Old Style"

Browning:	"Porphyria's Lover"
	"Cristina"
	"Soliloquy of the Spanish Cloister"
	"The Pied Piper of Hamelin"
	"How They Brought the Good News"
	"The Bishop Orders His Tomb"
	"Love Among the Ruins"
	"Any Wife To Any Husband"
	"Two in the Campagna"

"A Grammarian's Funeral"
"The Statue and the Bust"
"Childe Roland to the Dark Tower Came"
"Fra Lippo Lippi"
"Andrea del Sarto"

Arnold: "The Forsaken Merman"
"Sohrab and Rustum"

Hardy: *The Dynasts*
"Heiress and Architect"

Patmore: *The Angel in the House*

Morris: *The Earthly Paradise*
"Rapunzel"
"Concerning Geffray Teste Noire"
"The Gillyflower of Gold"
"The Sailing of the Sword"
"The Wind"
"The Blue Closet"
"The Haystack in the Floods"
"Two Red Roses Across the Moon"
Sigurd the Volsung

C. Rossetti: "Goblin Market"

D. Rossetti: "The Blessed Damozel"
"My Sister's Sleep"
"Sister Helen"
"Eden Bower"
"The Ballad of Dead Ladies"
"Troy Town"

Wilde:	"The Harlot's House" "The Ballad of Reading Gaol"
Swinburne:	"Itylus" *Atalanta in Calydon* *Tristram of Lyonesse*
Kipling:	"The Ballad of East and West" "Tommy" "Gunga Din" "Mandalay" "Tomlinson" "The Law of the Jungle" "The White Man's Burden"

VII. Victorian Drama

Tennyson:	*Becket*
Browning:	*A Blot on the 'Scutcheon*
Robertson:	*Caste*
Jones:	*Michael and His Lost Angel*
Pinero:	*The Second Mrs. Tanqueray*
Taylor:	*Our American Cousin* *The Ticket-of-Leave Man*
Gilbert:	*Trial by Jury* *HMS Pinafore*

Pirates of Penzance
The Mikado
Utopia Limited

Wilde: *The Importance of Being Earnest*
Lady Windermere's Fan
A Woman of No Importance
An Ideal Husband

VIII. Victorian Parody and Nonsense

Carroll: *Alice's Adventures in Wonderland*
Through the Looking Glass
The Hunting of the Snark
"The Baker's Tale"

Lear: *The Book of Nonsense*
"The Jumblies"
"The Owl and the Pussy Cat"

Gilbert: *Bab Ballads*

Swinburne: "Nephelidia"

Calverley: *Fly Leaves*
"Companions"

As a final comment I should mention three other genres of some importance in the nineteenth century: autobiography, biography, and the personal letter. In our discussion of the prose writers we came across several autobiographies. Two of the most famous are those by Newman and Mill, but Ruskin's *Præterita* is of similar rank and so is

285

Carlyle's *Reminiscences*. None of the Victorians produced any biography as splendid as Boswell's *Life of Johnson* (1791). Yet some of the best of these books examined the lives of authors. A few are by Gaskell, Forster, Cross, Froude, and Trollope on Charlotte Bronte, Dickens, George Eliot, Carlyle, and Thackeray. Also of enduring worth are the letters written by Victorian authors. Many of them are warm and human and a pleasure to read.

A List of Authors and Titles

Matthew Arnold:

Preface to the *Poems*
On Translating Homer
Essays in Criticism
    "The Function of Criticism at the Present Time"
    "The Literary Influence of Academies"
    "The Study of Poetry"
Culture and Anarchy
    "Sweetness and Light"
    "Doing as One Likes"
    "Barbarians, Philistines, Populace"
    "Hebraism and Hellenism"
Literature and Dogma
God and the Bible
"Literature and Science"
"Civilization in the United States"

Samuel Butler:

Life and Habit
Evolution Old and New
Unconscious Memory

Luck or Cunning?
The Fair Haven
The Way of All Flesh
Erewhon
Erewhon Revisited

Thomas Carlyle:

"Characteristics"
"Biography"
Sartor Resartus
Historical Periodicity
The French Revolution
On Heroes and Hero Worship
Past and Present
"Shooting Niagara and After?"

Charles Darwin:

On the Origin of Species
The Descent of Man
Autobiography

Thomas Huxley:

"The Method of Scientific Investigation"
"On a Piece of Chalk"
"On the Physical Basis of Life"
"A Liberal Education and Where to Find It"
"Scientific Education"
"On University Education"
"Lectures on Evolution"
"Science and Culture"
"Agnosticism and Christianity"

Thomas Babington Macaulay:

"Milton"
"Southey's Colloquies"

"Francis Bacon"
"Lord Clive"
History of England

John Stuart Mill:

Three Essays on Religion
  "Nature"
On Liberty
Autobiography
The Subjection of Women

William Morris:

Hopes and Fears for Art
  "The Lesser Arts"
  "The Art of the People"
  "The Beauty of Life"
News from Nowhere

John Henry Newman:

Tracts for the Times
The Tamworth Reading Room
Apologia pro Vita Sua
The Idea of a University
  "Knowledge Its Own End"
  "Knowledge Viewed in Relation to Learning"
  "Knowledge Viewed in Relation to Professional Skill"
  "Knowledge Viewed in Relation to Religion"

Walter Horatio Pater:

The Renaissance
  "Preface"
  "Conclusion"
Appreciations

"The Child in the House"
Marius the Epicurean

John Ruskin:

Modern Painters
    "Of the Pathetic Fallacy"
Seven Lamps of Architecture
    "The Lamp of Sacrifice"
    "The Lamp of Truth"
    "The Lamp of Power"
    "The Lamp of Beauty"
    "The Lamp of Life"
    "The Lamp of Memory"
    "The Lamp of Obedience"
The Stones of Venice
    "The Nature of Gothic"
Unto this Last
    "The Roots of Honour"
    "The Veins of Wealth"
Sesame and Lilies
    "Of Kings Treasuries"
    "Of Queens' Gardens"
    "The Mystery of Life and Its Arts"
The Crown of Wild Olive
    "Traffic"
Time and Tide
Fors Clavigera

Herbert Spencer:

A System of Synthetic Philosophy
First Principles
Social Statics
The Developmental Hypothesis
Progress, Its Law and Cause

Leslie Stephen:

The Playground of Europe
Essays on Free Thinking and Plain Speaking
English Thought in the Eighteenth Century
Science and Ethics
The English Utilitarians
Hours in a Library
An Agnostic's Apology

Robert Louis Stevenson:

Virginibus et Puerisque
An Inland Voyage
Travels with a Donkey
Familiar Studies of Men and Books
The Silverado Squatters
Treasure Island
Dr. Jekyll and Mr. Hyde
Kidnapped
"Aes Triplex"
"Pulvis et Umbra"